LOST HOUSES OF BRITAIN

DAVID & CHARLES

Newton Abbot   London   North Pomfret (Vt)

LOST HOUSES OF BRITAIN

Anna Sproule

Sproule, Anna
  Lost houses of Britain.
  1. Country homes—Great Britain—History
  I. Title
  941   DA660

  ISBN 0-7153-8104-0

Typeset by ABM Typographics, Hull
and printed in Great Britain
by Butler & Tanner, Frome & London
For David & Charles (Publishers) Limited
Brunel House   Newton Abbot   Devon

Published in the United States of America
by David & Charles Inc
North Pomfret   Vermont 05053   USA

❧ Contents

Introduction

Didlington in south-west Norfolk is a village that has lost its focal point. Indeed, it is less a village than a loose collection of buildings, scattered over an East Anglian landscape of corn, woods and little rivers. The collection includes a church, a former schoolhouse and an ex-laundry of Victorian vintage. There are also two farms and a nursery garden with greenhouses to rival those at Kew. But the big house of Didlington—the building that held all the others together in terms of function—is missing. Today's big house has been ingeniously fashioned out of its predecessor's garage block. Its frontage is the old stable tower with its clock which, in gold figures on a black ground, shows that the time once was two minutes past seven. Beside it, the stabling still exists. Behind, to the south, a 40 acre lake glitters in the sun. And on the other side there is a grassy platform topped by a rectangular, house-shaped grove of wild birch and cherry. With ruler-straight precision, that grove marks the site of Didlington Hall, a brick mansion that was demolished in the early 1950s. During World War II, it had been a rest-home for army officers; in times of peace, it was the heart of its local community. The laundry was the estate laundry; the school taught the estate's children; the glasswork in today's nursery garden sheltered the big house's flowers and fruit. The 90ft Didlington ballroom is still remembered with affection for miles around: it had, so local residents recall, the best sprung dance floor in the whole area. As one resident remembered, 'the house *was* the village'.

Didlington reflected three hundred years of British architectural history. It had a seventeenth-century west wing, a Georgian south front, a north front erected the year after Waterloo, a water tower in Victorian Italian style and twentieth-century additions. Its contents, over the years, were equally varied. Horace Walpole mentioned that there were three Holbeins at Didlington: portraits of Henry VIII, of the Bishop of Rochester and of Lord Chancellor Berners. The nineteenth-century collections of Lord Amherst of Hackney (Didlington was then the Amherst country seat) included a Stradivarius, a harp that had belonged to Marie Antoinette and an embroidered table-cloth from the Summer Palace at Peking. And the fittings ranged from a marble canopy chimney-piece (said to have come from St Peter's, Rome) to an astonishing bath, now in a nearby town and still in use, with apparatus for making waves.

It is a strange feeling to look at a wood and visualise a drawing-room—

1 (*opposite*) Didlington Hall, Norfolk, photographed for a sale catalogue in 1911. Today, the house has gone. So have the twin trees, and the lawn is a vegetable plot. 2 (*above*) The seventeenth-century west front of Didlington; the avenue, now planted over, marks the line of the old carriage drive. Note the Victorian water-tower

a gold-and-white drawing-room, sited where the birch trees now grow— that had been familiar to such visitors as the future Edward VII and Viscount Montgomery. It is a feeling that can in essence be experienced anywhere in the country. Didlington is only one among the many distinguished houses whose disappearance has left a gap in their individual landscapes and a sense of deep loss amongst both those who knew the buildings and those who trace their sites and research their past. Large buildings or small, urban or rural, medieval or Victorian, they are the invisible ones: the lost houses of Britain.

There is, in fact, a strong fascination attached to the hunt for lost houses. Officially maintained ruins, with their notices and gravel paths, have a greater or lesser appeal; but it is the unofficial ones—the flight of steps that stands on its own in a wood, the gates that never open, the bomb-site with its vegetation and its evidence of forgotten tastes in interior decoration —that contrive to exercise a far stronger pull on the emotions. Few people, especially if they can remember a 'lost' building as it used to be, are immune, while surprising numbers, if asked, will produce directions to some private Didlington of their own. Nor is this interest a modern one, product of today's taste for nostalgia. It was felt, for example, over a hundred years ago by the incomparable country diarist Francis Kilvert, who in

9

August 1871 visited a manor house in Wiltshire at which he had been a regular guest in the 1860s. He found most of it in a state of utter dereliction. The great hall had gone; so had the main staircase, and the rest of the building was crumbling. His *Diary* account records:

> From the huge oak beam which runs across and supports the vast ruined kitchen chimney, we stripped off large pieces of the bark which had never been removed and which looked as fresh as when the beam was placed there, perhaps hundreds of years ago. The house seemed empty and deserted. Heaps of stone and rubbish lay round the yards. The orchards were tangled and over-grown, the garden run wild with weeds, rank and neglected. Pink stonecrop and some straggling Virginia Stock ran over the heaps of waste and rubbish stone. There was not a sound or sign of life or living thing about the ruinous deserted place. Nothing but silence and desolation. A shepherd lives in a part of the house which still stands but as the staircase has fallen he is obliged to go out of doors and across a rude scaffolding stage before he can reach his bedroom.

By a sad irony, several of the houses that Kilvert knew when they were still firmly in existence have now gone too; one, Llanthomas, is described in detail on page 193.

An appreciation of the picturesque qualities of a ruin—of ruins seen as an architectural happening rather than a nasty mess—has, of course, a long pedigree and, at the hands of real enthusiasts, has led to the creation of countless artificial ruins in the country-house landscapes of the eighteenth century. Indeed, it was a hankering for some ruins of his own that set the hugely wealthy and extravagant William Beckford, author and connoisseur, on the route that ended in the creation of Fonthill Abbey, most famous of all Wiltshire's lost houses and one of the most famous in Britain. (Beckford's Abbey, of which only a fraction is left, was started in 1796 and slowly became a great Gothic cathedral of a building, with cloisters, turrets, battlements and a main tower over 270ft high. The tower fell down in 1825, little over a decade after the building was completed.)

However, it was not the real or contrived ivy-and-battlements arrangement that Kilvert was celebrating in his note on the derelict manor house; nor, for the majority of observers, do Gothic follies have much more than a collector's interest. The lost-house hunter of yesterday or today is on the track of rewards other than those deriving from the merely picturesque: he is engaged in a voyage of personal discovery, the aim of which is to recreate in the imagination as much as possible of what has vanished. His pleasure is to a large degree related to the achievement of this aim, although some does stem from the extraordinary contrasts between past

10

and present realities that the ruins of a lost house afford. As indicated by Kilvert's shepherd, these can have their humorous side. Not long after Kilvert was writing, a similarly bizarre contrast could be observed in Lancashire, where a medieval great hall sheltered a dairy herd under its carved beams (see page 251). More often, the effect produced by disparities between past intentions and present fact is pathetic or, as in the case of bomb-sites, positively chilling. But an effect there will certainly be.

This only holds true, though, when some vestiges of a lost house remain. The inquirer ventures into far more difficult territory when the whole complex under investigation—house, stables, kitchen block, outbuildings and gates—has vanished, leaving not a sign of its former existence except, in urban areas, a clutch of street names. While such total annihilation of a dwelling place is not quite as common as might be imagined, it is still common enough; and, in the absence of visible stimuli to imagination and research, the details of missing buildings fade even from local memory with quite terrifying speed. This writer, for example, lived unknowingly for years within walking distance of the approximate site at Mortlake of the house owned by the sixteenth-century astrologer Dr John Dee. Its fame had not bridged the very small mileage involved. The exact site of the learned doctor's house, where he tried to raise spirits and where his offspring got into near-fatal mischief on the river bank, now seems to be a complete mystery, even though the building was still in existence early in the nineteenth century. Again, the streets and gardens of the writer's own area were dotted with enormous chestnut trees, clearly remnants of some large estate. Elderly local residents could remember the building that was the focus of the estate: 'There was a castle down the road,' they'd say, 'a castle right by the river'. It emerges, however, that the building was not 'right by the river'. It also emerges that, far from being a castle, medieval or Gothic Revival, Grove House in Chiswick had been a trim Palladian villa with an orangery and stabling for thirty horses. (In fact, it became one of the select band of houses that are not so much lost as translated; it was taken apart stone by stone and reassembled in the USA.)

True, local memory in a London suburb is not as long or as accurate as that in a rural area; nor yet has much general interest been shown in the former residences of Dr Dee and Earl Cowper. However, the same fogs and complications bedevil any inquirer into another lost house that, though a very minor one in terms of architecture, was of immense historical interest and has been mentioned by implication in every account of the area concerned. The area itself is this time a rural one, and at the other end of Britain from Thames-side suburbia; the house was the scene of the 'slaughter under trust' of Alasdair MacDonald, also called MacIain, twelfth chief of the MacDonalds of Glencoe.

The political assassination of the twelfth chief was the centre-piece and a principal aim of the Massacre of Glencoe, in which, on the orders of William III, a tenth of the glen's population was killed in the early morning of 13 February 1692. The dead included children and at least one woman; the survivors—those that did not die from exposure—stumbled through a driving blizzard to safety in the surrounding hills. The incident was judged peculiarly vile because it was a flagrant abuse of the hospitality on which much of Highland culture and, indeed, Highland survival depended: MacIain and his people had, with open hands, offered food and friendship to the troops billeted on them and, in return, had been butchered in their own houses. But where is, or was, the most important of those houses—the one in which MacIain himself became the second fatality of the massacre, shot in the back as he was dressing to bid his 'guests' goodbye?

Astonishingly, given the strength of rural traditions, given the mass of documentation surrounding the case and given the general lack of building ground in the area, no one appears to be sure. The contenders for the site are many and various: one is now a farm and caravan site at the glen's very entrance at Invercoe (it has a barn said to contain remnants of MacIain's house); another is some way up the glen near Clachaig, at one of the valley's widest and most habitable points; a third is right away from the main glen altogether, up a side valley called Gleann-leac-na-Muidhe. There are, in fact, two possibilities here, both of them summer farmhouses or 'shielings'. One has vanished entirely, while the knee-high remains of the other indicate that this is a lost house of the most modest category: 12yd long, 4½yd wide, plentifully overgrown with sedge and foxglove, its like can be found all over Scotland. In spite, however, of a plaque put to commemorate MacIain's supposed death on the spot, the feeling is now that the Gleann Muidhe theory will not do. Small though the still-visible building is, it is thought to have been too grand a subsidiary dwelling for the twelfth chief, who was not particularly well-off. Again, what was the chief doing at that time of year 500ft up the mountain in a summer farmhouse? Furthermore, Gleann Muidhe became one of the escape routes during the massacre from the violence below, a fact hardly compatible with the 'murder at the farmhouse' hypothesis. So the inquirer retreats back to the main valley, there to make the best sense he can of the reigning (and ancient) confusion. The most celebrated building in Glencoe is a lost house in the fullest meaning of the term.

3 The sixteenth-century east front of Beaudesert, created by Thomas Lord Paget

Few houses of interest go as thoroughly and completely missing as this one, even though the scene of MacIain's murder finds an unlikely parallel in the building that, even surpassing Fonthill, can lay claim to being the most important lost house in all Britain. As shown in the account on page 214, Henry VIII's magnificent palace of Nonsuch, in Surrey, not only vanished from view after less than two centuries in existence; it vanished so totally that it took accident, much dedicated research, and the efforts of five hundred volunteers to confirm its exact site. However, there are

13

countless other now-vanished buildings that, given time and lack of interest, may become as resistant to later inquiry as Dr Dee's house in Mortlake, if not Nonsuch itself.

It would be manifestly impossible to work out how many British houses of architectural or historical importance have disappeared since, say, the Tudor period. But some idea of the sheer size of the job can be gained from the bible of the modern lost-house hunter, the collection of essays entitled *The Destruction of the Country House 1875-1975* and published in 1974 in conjunction with the exhibition of the same name at the Victoria and Albert Museum. The book ends with Peter Reid's county-by-county checklist of major houses destroyed, partially destroyed, ruined or altered in England, Scotland and Wales over the previous century. The total runs to over 1,100, of which 318 are in Scotland, 46 in Wales and the rest in England. The worst area is the old (pre-reorganisation) county of Yorkshire, with nearly seventy losses. Nation-wide, the casualties range from such buildings as the Paget family's Beaudesert in Staffordshire (Elizabethan-built round a still older core, with later alterations and re-alterations) and the Jacobean Emral Hall in Clwyd (see page 136) to the great Victorian houses of last century's hereditary or self-made magnificos: Cheshire's Eaton Hall, reworked for the fabulously wealthy First Duke of Westminster, and partially demolished in 1961; Easton Lodge, the Essex home of Frances, Countess of Warwick (see page 128); and Dawpool in Cheshire, built in the 1880s for the shipping magnate Thomas Ismay, whose White Star Line was a major rival of Cunard. (White Star had achieved its eminence by concentrating on combining technology, comfort and extreme elegance; Ismay and his architect Norman Shaw seem to have brought the same approach to the house, which had fireproof ceilings and an extraordinary fireplace in Gothic style, topped with a minstrels' gallery. Oddly, one attraction it did not have was a flower garden: the building sat in the middle of a moor which, as *Country Life* noted, all but swept up to the doors.)

Of necessity, the Reid list represents no more than part of the picture. As explained in an article in *Country Life* in 1974 by Marcus Binney (one of the exhibition's organisers and also a contributor to the book), Mr Reid himself had already begun to wonder whether 2,000 losses might not turn out to be the right total. In addition, his efforts had been mainly concentrated on the buildings of greater significance: those that would have deserved the official 'listed' status of Grade I (outstanding), Grade II* (very important) and the best of Grade II (especially interesting). And, although Reid's list contains houses in areas that once were rural and are

14

4 Dawpool in 1911. The gardens consisted of little more than terraces and lawns of the type seen here

now urban, the exhibition's terms of reference naturally excluded such celebrated urban losses as that of Devonshire House in London.

Equally naturally, the lists represent only the tip of the iceberg as far as total losses—the losses sustained as far back as the inquirer cares to contemplate—are concerned. However, a faint idea of the size of the problem can be gained by looking at the earlier history of the sites of houses on the Reid list. It then becomes clear that many buildings were themselves replacements of even earlier lost houses. Near Perth, for example, there was a whole sequence of buildings called Dupplin Castle. The house that came down in the 1960s appeared in 1828, the year after fire had destroyed a mainly seventeenth-century Dupplin much praised in the eighteenth century by Daniel Defoe. It was, he wrote in his *Tour Thro' the Whole Island of Great Britain*,

15

a very beautiful Seat, and the Heads of the Families having been pretty much used to live at home, the House has been adorned at several times, according to the Genius, and particular Inclination of the Persons, who then lived there.... The House is now under a new Decoration, two new Wings being lately added for Offices as well as Ornament.

The old Building is Spacious, the Rooms are large, and the Cielings [*sic*] lofty, and which is more than all the Appearance of the Buildings, 'tis all magnificently finished, and furnished within; there are also Abundance of very fine Paintings, and some of great Value, especially Court Pieces, and Family Pieces.

The family in question was that of the earls of Kinnoull. But, as Defoe implies, this house in turn contained the remnants of a still earlier Dupplin, which dated from the fifteenth century. And this too had a predecessor: the first Dupplin of all, campaigning base of Sir William Wallace and a casualty of an armed quarrel between its owners and the people of Perth.

A more famous example of a 'nest' of lost houses is the Cassiobury group at Watford. The Cassiobury that vanished in 1922 was a Gothic semi-palace built for the Earl of Essex in about 1800, with state apartments, cloisters, battlements, towers, spires and no less than four libraries. The riches it had contained included paintings by Rubens, Van Dyck and Turner, curios such as a ribbon worn by Charles I at his execution, and Grinling Gibbons' carvings, badly eaten by worm, which had been retained from an older Cassiobury, pulled down to make way for the Gothic one. This older structure, also built by an Earl of Essex, was described shortly after its completion by another literary visitor, John Evelyn, who spent some comfortable days there discussing improvements with his host, examining the extensive Essex library and delighting in the garden's promise of 'an excellent collection of choicest fruit'. His *Diary* entry for 18 April 1680 lauds the Gibbons carvings, the chimney mantles of Irish marble ('not much inferior to Italian') and the library, but deprecates both the building's site and the circumstances leading to its choice:

> The soil is stony, churlish, and uneven, nor is the water near enough to the house, though a very swift and clear stream run within a flight-shot from it in the valley, which may fitly be called Coldbrook, it being indeed excessive cold, yet producing fair trouts. It is pity the house was not situated to more advantage; but it seems it was built just where the old one was, which I believe he only meant to repair; this leads men into irremediable errors, and it saves but a little.

Like many others before and since, Arthur Capel, first of the Capel earls of Essex, had been bitten by the building bug. The house he only meant to repair was a relatively new building, completed in the Elizabethan period; by the time Arthur had finished with it, however, only a wing of this earlier structure was still intact. Sadly, his last sight of the house he had been at such pains to create was taken in the oppressive company of a party sent to arrest him for complicity in the Rye House Plot. He was imprisoned in the Tower where, on 30 July 1683, he was found with his throat cut. He had committed suicide.

Other 'nests' of lost houses, built either on the same site or in the same area, are not hard to find, and some, like Dupplin, are surprisingly large. There are, in all, no less than five lost Fonthills: Beckford's Abbey was Fonthill Number III, while Numbers IV and V (which co-existed for many years) were a second, Scottish Baronial, abbey and an early twentieth-century house that ingeniously incorporated the front of a seventeenth-century manor. Wimbledon was the home of five more houses of importance, the first of which—the Wimbledon House built by Sir Thomas Cecil in 1588—was thought by contemporaries to be in the same league as Nonsuch. It was demolished in 1717 to make way for another building; this, started but not completed by a gentleman who had problems with the South Sea Company, was pulled down by the Duchess of Marlborough, who proceeded to build two more. The first, not to her liking, she demolished herself, while the second burnt down in 1785. The last of the group was started in 1797 and disappeared in 1949. And, in what is now the Metropolitan Borough of Bury, there stood at various times the members of a whole sextet, the last of which is still in existence.

We are so preoccupied today with economic difficulties—and, where great houses are concerned, with the crushing effect that lack of money has on their existence—that it comes as something of a shock to realise that people have been destroying mansions ever since there were mansions to destroy. Our century may be guiltier than most; significantly, Binney's *Country Life* article pointed out that over half the losses listed in *Destruction* had taken place, not merely since 1900, but after World War II. But, obviously, it was not the peculiar problems of modern society that destroyed all the many thousands of houses that vanished before the beginning of the century. And, great and small, what an array they make: Nonsuch and the first Theobalds, where James I tried to raise silkworms; Whitehall Palace, burnt—except for two gates and the banqueting house—to ashes in 1698; the first Inveraray Castle, forgotten predecessor of the well-known present building; the semi-legendary Canons (see page 86); the mysterious Gowrie House (page 148) and Elsyng, beguilingly connected with top-flight imposters (page 133); Holdenby House, a great mansion in Northampton-

17

shire built by Queen Elizabeth's Lord Chancellor, Sir Christopher Hatton (its construction nearly ruined him); the first Copthall in Essex, another mansion created by another of Elizabeth's favourites, Thomas Heneage; Kew House, also called the Queen's Lodge, where Queen Charlotte and her daughters lived while the insane George III was immured in the Dutch House across the way; Streatham Park, home of Dr Johnson's friends, the Thrales, and Bachegraig in North Wales, owned by Mrs Thrale and visited by Johnson in 1774 . . .. All these, and many more, vanished before the great social changes of the present century began. All, furthermore, disappeared well before death duties were introduced in 1894. And most of them went before the first, temporary, appearance of income tax in 1797.

What was it that drove them all out of existence? Indeed, what is it that, at any period, turns a house of interest or importance from a cared-for, functioning entity into a tattered shell or heap of rubble? The answer, present circumstances notwithstanding, is not as simple as mere poverty on an individual or national scale. Considering the picture as a whole, it is in fact possible to distinguish five separate forces that push houses out of existence, all of which, in one form or another, are as lively in the current century as they have been in the past. They can be summarised as: accident, political disturbance, lack of money, availability of money (with a sub-section headed 'civic improvements') and idiosyncracy on the part of the owner.

Death from accidental causes is one of the most common ends for a great house. It is also the cruellest, for it destroys a building that can still be at the peak of its beauty, usefulness and economic value. As the account of Hamilton Palace shows (page 165), accidents can be of a slow, creeping variety, but the commonest accident of all is the complete opposite: fire. The history of architecture is lit throughout its length with the flames of blazing buildings: Whitehall, set alight by a servant drying clothes; the first Montagu House (see page 210), a victim of closely similar circumstances; the beautiful Penicuik House in Midlothian, Palladian creation of the Clerks, gutted in 1899; Alloa, great house of the earls of Mar, destroyed in a single August night in 1800 (see page 29). 'No engine', local historian James Lothian wrote later in connection with Alloa's end, 'could be procured for some hours after the discovery of the fire, and the rivulet near the house happened unfortunately to be dried up. No assistance being thus within reach, the flames continued to rage with incredible violence, till, by two o'clock in the morning, the roofs had fallen in.' However, the presence of water was by no means a deciding factor in these battles for a house's life: supplies from the Thames did not douse

5 The remains of Edderachalda, victim of fire, also known as Calda House, with Loch Assynt in the background

the Whitehall conflagration, while a much more obscure lost house—the eighteenth-century Edderachalda in Sutherland—stood on the very brink of Loch Assynt. (It was whispered, however, that Edderachalda was a victim, not of accident, but of arson; criminal activities are another force inimical to houses' survival, though one difficult to quantify.)

Woefully inadequate though the fire-fighting equipment of the past was, it should not be thought that modern technology has succeeded in banishing the threat of fire altogether. On the contrary, Reid's list is scattered with houses 'destroyed by fire', and many of these losses occurred after World War II. Among them was Foots Cray Place in Kent, an important copy of Palladio's Villa Almerico in Vicenza, and the even more important Coleshill House in Berkshire, dazzlingly original when it was built. It was designed ten years before the Restoration by Roger Pratt who was later responsible for Clarendon House, Piccadilly (see page 94) and, after the Fire of London, was knighted for his work in the rebuilding operations. Pratt's patron in Berkshire was his cousin, Sir George Pratt, whose own efforts at building had not been very successful; at least, Roger and his friend Inigo Jones persuaded him to pull down his own partly-built Coleshill and to start again. (The site of George's building was later put to use as a cucumber patch.) In Nathaniel Lloyd's *History of the English*

19

6 & 7 Two more victims of fire: (*top*) Foots Cray Place, shown here in 1783; and (*above*) Coleshill House, in an architectural drawing by G. Vertue, 1735

House, Roger Pratt's Coleshill is described as 'the most remarkable building of its period'. Mark Girouard, in his *Life in the English Country House*, indicates some of its most remarkable points: the parlour and the great dining chamber above it had been moved into an unusual position, exactly in the centre of the house; while the servants—possibly for the first time in the history of the English country house—had found their eating quarters moved from the traditional great hall to a servant's hall of their own, in the basement. John Harris in *The Destruction of the Country House* summed up the loss of the building in 1952 as calamitous.

Compared with the numbers of great houses that perish by accident, those that are brought low as a result of political upheaval must now be small. While the tradition of destroying buildings to make a political point is still, for example, being upheld by Welsh extremists, the last major threat of political origin was, of course, the bombs of World War II (see page 80). Beyond this, though, stretches a line of fires, civil uprisings and full-scale wars that accounted for such major casualties as Nottingham Castle (see page 100) and Corfe Castle, one of many houses besieged and wrecked by the forces of Parliament during the Civil War. And there are other, subtler, ways than mere violence of destroying a political opponent's house: the cowshed referred to earlier—the second of the Stand Halls—may have lost much of its fabric and all of its prestige when, following the Battle of Bosworth, the first Earl of Derby turned the home of a defeated Yorkist into a barn.

Despite the intensity of the damage they cause, national or local convulsions of a political nature are normally relatively brief. By contrast, the general state of not having enough money is continuous and timeless. We know all about it today; Barbara Villiers, Duchess of Cleveland and wrecker of Nonsuch, knew all about it in the seventeenth century. So did the various residents of Roehampton who, through some canny sales, contributed to a state of affairs described in 1876 by James Thorne in his *Handbook to the Environs of London*: 'Many of the good old houses remain, but several have been demolished to make way for modern villas, and more seem doomed to be ere long the prey of the builder.' And so does the householder of any period when he faces the ravages caused by *Merulius lacrymans*, the perpetrator of dry rot. *M. lacrymans* and its ghastly fellow-agents of a building's physical decay are in a class of their own as house-wreckers. They almost group themselves under the 'accident' heading, but not quite, for the householder does have a choice about his ultimate course of action. As great numbers of demolitions bear witness, the cost of fighting back quickly passes the limit of the bearable.

21

8—11 (*above and opposite*) Study in dereliction: Bathford House, in the old county of Somerset. Bathford became the home in the 1750s of an immigrant from Ireland, Andrew Sproule, whose daughters were the toast of nearby Bath. The Sproules moved away in about 1800. Bathford House survived over a century longer before succumbing to a chimney fire on 23 November 1913. The site remained abandoned until the early 1920s when the stables were converted into a new Bathford House. The only fragment of the earlier building now remaining is an arched doorway in a stone wall

Dearth of money is, of course, a real killer where houses are concerned, and the different forms it takes are notorious. Family fortunes stagger under the burden of bad management, bad luck, or heavy taxation: the family seat is a speedy casualty. A family or organisation whose fortunes are on a firm footing cannot confront the nightmare task of bringing an enormous building such as Panmure (see page 115) up to contemporary standards of heating, lighting, decoration and sanitation. The size of a great house is in itself a drawback: a fact that, where a sequence or 'nest' of houses is concerned, sometimes leads to the odd result that the more ancient sections of a building complex survive their grander and more unwieldy successors. (An eighteenth-century House I, for instance, may become the stables or laundry or servants' quarters of the Victorian House II; on the demolition of the latter, the owner reconverts the once-despised earlier building and moves back into it. At Panmure itself, a slightly different sequence of events took place. Some of the original seventeenth-century buildings became a garage block in the 1920s; this, one of the few remains on the site, is now used as a social club.)

22

The dismay caused by the prospect of owning a huge house is, to a large degree, a twentieth-century emotion; but, again, not quite. Between the 1840s and 1901—a period not noted for thinking small in matters of stately housing—there stood empty in Devon a mansion with the official name of Silverton Park and the unofficial one of Egremont's Folly. It was an extraordinary building, all columns—something like a small Parthenon perched on top of a bigger one. Its creator, the fourth Earl of Egremont, died in 1845, by which time his Folly had cost him a quarter of a million pounds. It had not been finished, but a purchaser would still have acquired a house that boasted 187 rooms, 230 marble mantlepieces, a marble bathroom, and even a marble bath carved out of a single block. (The doorknobs of the main rooms were of an even more luxurious material, amber; understandably, some of these vanished while the house was unoccupied.) And yet, for all its exterior grandeur and interior luxury, there were no buyers. It was too expensive to finish, let alone to maintain. In the end, the fittings were all sold off—the mantlepieces fetched £50 each—and in November 1901 the building was blown up before a fascinated crowd of spectators.

Silverton Park was not the only casualty on the site. The late earl had started operations by building right round an older mansion called Combesatchfield, thus rendering this earlier structure victim to the opposite of the 'money-dearth' condition: the condition of 'money-surplus'. Combesatchfield went the way of the Tudor Wanstead House (see page 261) and many others; it was improved out of existence by an owner with money to spare, pretensions to increased grandeur and a hankering to be in the modern fashion. In an article on the first Copthall in a collection of architectural essays called *The Country Seat* (1970), John Newman commented: 'The destruction of old buildings wrought in the eighteenth century has never been assessed. It would be instructive and sobering to do so.' The rebuilders of the Age of Reason were not the only guilty ones. The first Earl of Essex, without at first intending to, destroyed all but a part of Cassiobury I. The Mellishes of Blyth and the Pulestons of Emral (see pages 54 and 136) both got rid of old buildings before creating handsome new ones. And the architects and their clients of the nineteenth century naturally did the same. It was a wonder, for instance, that the second of the two Gidea Halls at Romford survived to make an entry for 1930 in Reid's list, for Thorne, expressing Victorian taste, condemned it in 1876 as a 'bald commonplace rectangular building'. (By today's standards, this beautifully proportioned brick house of the 1730s was nothing of the kind.) Victorian peers and

Victorian commoners threw themselves into the pursuit of disguising or abolishing their 'commonplace' dwellings if they could afford to do so, Her Majesty giving a lead in the game (see page 233).

The business of new lamps for old continues, of course, but in its present manifestation it is more indicative of the money-dearth state than of its opposite. The owner of Wanstead demolished a manor house and built a semi-palace; the tendency has now become to use a great house's site for something labour-saving, economical to run and small. It is in connection with a different type of 'improvement'—the civic or commercial variety—that the twentieth century has made its mark. The need for new roads, new commercial premises and new official buildings seems constant. It should be noted that a decided gain has sometimes been involved as well as a loss. The present Somerset House may not be as fascinating as its predecessor, but it is still magnificent. So is the British Museum, built on the site of Montagu Houses I and II. Whatever the attractions of Mirefleur (see page 206), they are surely surpassed by those of its successor on the site, the old Royal Observatory, one of the loveliest buildings in London. The same, alas, cannot be said of Northumberland Avenue.

The last of the forces that work for a building's destruction appears the least important: owner's idiosyncracy, owner's whim. It is, none the less, a force to be reckoned with; all the more so since it is so frighteningly independent of practical considerations such as money and lifestyle. The writer knows of one Jacobean house that was demolished by an owner as an act of pure revenge on his past: his childhood there had been miserably unhappy. One of the Pulestons, desolated by the death of his wife, abandoned Emral Hall to the fate that would have certainly overtaken it if it had not been for the heroic efforts of his daughter-in-law. Again, Thorne tells how Baroness Howe, occupant of the late Alexander Pope's villa at Twickenham, became tired of receiving visitors who wanted to see where the great man had lived. In 1807, she tore the villa down and destroyed his much-loved garden. Such speedy indulgence in a destructive whim is now controlled by the laws that govern the demolition of houses of historical or architectural importance. Baroness Howe, if she had lived today, would in all likelihood have had to go through the procedure of applying for consent to pull down a listed building; of showing reasonable grounds for demolition (the real reason would not have been acceptable); of appealing if consent were refused; and then facing the publicity of an inquiry into the issue. There are, however, ways round and under this network of regulations, the most drastic of which is to demolish without consent. (At the time of writing, the average penalty imposed in a magistrate's court for an illegal demolition is £300 to £400; in a Crown Court, the average is £3,000 to £4,000. Imprisonment can in theory be involved, but appears to be unheard of in practical terms.) It is a tragic fact that, while the interest of an owner may not succeed in saving a house, an owner's antipathy may still do much to destroy it.

When a house goes, what is it exactly that posterity loses? First and most obvious, there is the building itself, with—in many, if not all, cases— its garden. Sometimes, however, portions of the fabric are preserved elsewhere (see page 269). In addition, houses demolished in recent times are to some degree privileged, for the regulations mentioned above contain the stipulation that, when consent to demolish or partly demolish a listed building is given, the Royal Commission on Historical Monuments has the right to record the building before it goes. This is usually done photographically. Furthermore, the National Monuments Record, which is now attached to the Royal Commission, contains material in its collections that dates back far beyond the Record's establishment during World War II. Other major picture collections exist, one of which is to be found in the massive volumes of the magazine *Country Life*, which ever since 1897 has been recording in words, photographs and plans the appearance of Britain's great houses. So, on many occasions, a memory of how a building looked has been preserved. But there are of necessity gaps, and these are most apparent in the cases of very old buildings that were also of relatively minor importance. This writer, for example, knows of only one picture of Dr Dee's house, published in 1900; the picture collection in which the original existed has itself vanished without trace.

The next loss suffered when a great house goes is that of its contents, and especially the sum of its contents. When the house is destroyed by accident or act of war, the contents may themselves be destroyed to a greater or lesser extent; otherwise, the tragedy stems from the break-up of collections that may have taken generations to accumulate and that show at every turn the peaks of creativity and taste attained by those generations. Mentmore Towers still stands, but the name is enough to give a chill to all those who deplored the auction of its £6 million worth of contents. The demolition of Cassiobury III was preceded by a comparable dispersal of beauty in 1922. So was that of Hamilton Palace; the Hamilton sale was the second to have taken place within half a century. Whenever such sheddings-off occur in a house's history, they give rise to an additional tragedy by divorcing the collections, the furniture and the books from the settings they once graced. The Hamilton case is only one example out

12 Weald Hall, demolished 1950. The site is in Essex County Council's Weald Country Park

of many; another is the departure of the Deepdene statues from the Deepdene sculpture rooms and conservatories (see page 104). And a uniquely bizarre addition to country-house decor vanished when Weald Hall, Essex, lost the antique guillotine that stood in the corner of its Georgian great hall. Though the opposite of a work of art, this gruesome object had, by tradition, had the distinction of claiming Marie Antoinette among its victims; hence, presumably, its place in Weald's collection of china, tapestry and furniture at the end of the nineteenth century.

If circumstances favour them, students of architecture can continue to appreciate the physical details of houses that are no longer in existence. The connoisseur can scan the sale catalogues of a Hamilton or Beaudesert and perhaps trace the objects there shown to their new homes. But a house is more than a mere building, however distinguished its appearance and contents may be. It is a place where people lived, influenced their surroundings, allowed their surroundings to influence them. It is a place where things happened and, in happening, set up chains of events that affected a house's inhabitants, appearance and future. Without this complex relationship between people, events and a place, there would indeed be no such thing as a house, only a structure. The relationship is,

27

of course, fully appreciated by the writer of even the slimmest guide to a building that still exists. But, once the building itself goes, the guidebook becomes a collector's item and its contents, unless they concern events or occupants of immense fame, begin to vanish from current knowledge.

One of the present writer's informants, describing a lost house's statuary, indicated that it was all, in some symbolic way, meant to represent the history of the family that had once owned it. He himself, however, did not possess the key to the riddle; the last person who had was a long-dead peeress. 'Nobody', he added, 'is interested in these things, because the house is no longer there.' And that is the heart of the matter. 'These things'—the minor and major points of decoration, their underlying meaning for a group of people, the history those people were hoping to commemorate—lose much of their claim on our memory once the entity that held them all together disappears. And with them goes the intangible thing we usually call a house's atmosphere: the thing that, in connection with an existing house, we remember long after we have forgotten the number of its chimneys and the appearance of its gables.

The matter of atmosphere is, obviously, a highly subjective one: so subjective that even the most sensitive and skilful observer of a house in its palmy days cannot help recording his own reaction to reality rather than the reality itself. However, there are other ways by which one may begin to rediscover this essence, otherwise irredeemably vanished, of a lost house. A knowledge of what took place there will be of use; so will an acquaintance with the personalities of the owners, occupiers and visitors; so, in retrospect, will an understanding of the circumstances leading to the house's disappearance.

This book aims to recreate something of the appearance and essence of fifty houses that have been erased from the map of Britain over the past three centuries. Some, like Canons, Hamilton and Nonsuch, are already well known; others, such as the astonishing Brandenburgh House in Hammersmith, have not attracted the general attention they deserve. Several have literary connections of the highest order; others are the focus of legends that, while not, perhaps, having much to do with truth, throw an illuminating light on the way in which the attitudes and activities of the occupants were perceived by their contemporaries. Some represent important landmarks in Britain's architectural history; others again, while of little interest to the architect, have histories attached that turn the most casual inquirer into a passionately committed historian. Taken together, they represent a fragment of our invisible heritage that still excites the imagination.

❋ Alloa House

Overlooking a housing estate in Alloa stands a tall, imposingly solid building, dating from about 1497 and now much loved by pigeons. Famous locally as Alloa Tower, it is the last surviving remnant of a group of great houses whose creation spanned every century from the fifteenth to the nineteenth. Alloa Tower, Alloa House I, Alloa House II and Alloa House II (revised version) were by no means the greatest houses in Scotland, nor yet in Britain as a whole; but, between them, they represent an accurate version in miniature of the total British picture of the change, development and destruction of buildings.

Alloa Tower and Alloa House I were, in fact, for centuries one and the same entity; the stronghold-turned-mansion of the Erskines, earls of Mar and once the official guardians of the heirs to the Scottish throne. Under the care of the first Earl, John (also known as the sixth Earl; Mar genealogy is complex), James VI of Scotland and I of England spent part of his childhood there, and founded a friendship with the next earl, only eight years his senior. The king chose his childhood friend as guardian for his own son, so the short-lived Prince Henry knew Alloa too; so did his brother, who became King Charles I. When they moved away, they left the detritus of babyhood behind them: a baby's chair, a small golf club, a solidly built cradle in which the infant James had been rocked to sleep.

In the mansion's early days, the duty of the Erskines to their masters meant that the royal nursery had to be a strong place indeed. (The more usual childhood home of James and Henry was the massive pile of Stirling Castle.) But the earls could be military aggressors on their own account if it so suited them. The first, who had acted as host at Alloa to Mary Queen of Scots in 1566, was one of the leaders in the rising that resulted in her losing the throne. The second, James's childhood friend, was a member of the gang of political kidnappers who organised the 'raid of Ruthven' in 1582 and abstracted the young king from the influence of a rival faction. The earl of the Civil War period was more delicate about expressing his politics, but he did allow the Marquis of Montrose, Charles I's lieutenant-general in Scotland, to use the Mar fortress of Kildrummie, and, on the day that Montrose's troops cut a swathe through Alloa town, he entertained the marquis to dinner in style at Alloa Tower. And the sixth Earl of Mar achieved enduring fame by leading and losing the Jacobite rebellion of 1715.

13 The great house of Alloa, before 1800. All that now remains is the Tower of Alloa itself, here shown dominating the rest of the building

All this time, the Erskines' home had been steadily growing. Going by evidence in the tower itself, alterations were made in both the sixteenth and seventeenth centuries. A further indication of building works is provided by Daniel Defoe, who in the 1720s published his three-volume description of Britain based on his own extensive journeyings. At Alloa, he much admired the Erskines' house. 'This fine Seat', he added significantly, 'was formerly call'd the Castle of *Alloway*, but is now so beautify'd, the Buildings, and especially the Gardens, so compleat and compleatly modern, that no Appearance of a Castle can be said to remain.' A great many Scottish houses had been 'beautify'd' during the second half of the seventeenth century. Fashions had changed; security could at last be subordinated to convenience (events such as the 1715 rising were not envisaged); and the great Scottish lords were coming under the influence of the court they frequented in London. A further influence making itself felt was Louis XIV's France and it was this, in particular, that informed the creation of the new Alloa gardens. These were the special work of the sixth earl who, in the days when he was still a member of the British government, employed the Sun King's landscape gardener to design for him something in the order of a modest Versailles. The results were described thus by a visitor in 1722:

The seat of the Earl of Marr, with fine gardins lying betwixt the house and Forth, are very much commended throu the kingdom, and by all strangers that see them, for their situation, fine walks, and regularitie. On the east side

30

of the house lyes a large wood throu which are cut several fine *vistues*. On the N.E., upon very handsome terrace walks, cut out of a rising ground within the wood, is designed a fine summer-house.

By this time, however, the earl himself was in exile, and he was never to see his 'fine vistues' again.

John Erskine, sixth (or eleventh) Earl of Mar, was thirty-nine in 1714 when Queen Anne died and George I, first representative of the House of Hanover, came to the throne. Mar, Secretary of State for Scotland, had indicated that he was fully prepared to be as loyal to the newcomer as he had been to the late queen. But George, acting on the principle that any friend of the late Establishment was no friend of his, sacked him from office. Even so, Mar hesitated for some while before declaring for the Jacobite cause. But, in 1715, he left the British court, slipped back to Scotland in disguise and, in September, proclaimed James Edward Stuart King James VIII. (In Scotland, James VII was the 'Old Pretender's' father, more usually known as James II.) The impetus of the rebellion gathered pace, with Mar as its commander-in-chief, and in November the earl found himself facing the forces of the Duke of Argyll at Sheriffmuir near Dunblane.

In military terms, the Battle of Sheriffmuir was not so much a disaster as a complete shambles, for, up to a point, both sides won. Both Mar's and Argyll's right wings played havoc with their immediate opponents and failed to see what was happening on their left. The confusion was later summed up by a local rhymester:

> There's some say that we wan,
> And some say that they wan,
> And some say that nane wan at a', man;
> But of one thing I'm sure
> That at Sheriffmuir,
> A battle there was, which I saw, man.

Mar, however, made the crucial mistake of failing to press home what advantage he had gained. He fell back to Perth, leaving Argyll in possession of the battlefield, and wrote a dismal report to his king; most of his Highlanders, he said, had now decided to go home. James Edward arrived in Scotland and Mar struggled on for a while. But the rising was doomed and, the following February, the earl and his master quietly boarded a ship for France. Five years later, the Hanoverian dynasty forgave Mar to the extent of granting him an annual pension, and he left the Jacobites soon afterwards. But he was never allowed to return home, and he died at Aix-la-Chapelle in 1732.

As Defoe's account shows, the fall of the sixth earl did not lead to the decay of his Alloa home. The estate was seized by the government but was then bought back by Mar's brother, Lord Grange, who in 1732 edified the townspeople by organising a magnificent funeral for his wife. (It was not realized at the time that Lady Grange was still alive; she was a half-crazed alcoholic, and her husband had her kidnapped and confined first in the Outer Hebrides, then on St Kilda and then in Skye. Her real death took place in 1749.)

Late in the century, further alterations to Alloa House were made, but its end was by now drawing near, and the agent of its final destruction was to be, not war, but something far more powerful and common. In the late evening of 28 August 1800, a servant reportedly knelt down by a bed with a lighted candle, hunting for something under the bedstead. The covers caught fire, and the fire spread. It raged through the house and, because the

14 One of the inmates of the Erskines' royal nursery: James VI of Scotland, here seen at the age of eight. Portrait attributed to R. Lockey

Brathy Burn nearby had dried up, water was in short supply. By two in the morning, the roofs had gone; by dawn, only the old Tower itself still stood. The rest was a charred, smoking waste. No one died and many of the house's contents were saved, including the cumbersome royal cradle. But the losses included a unique picture of a former guest, Mary Queen of Scots. Given away by the queen before her execution, it was thought to be the only contemporary portrait of Mary then left in Scotland: 'the features', wrote an eighteenth-century observer, Sir John Stoddart, 'were probably drawn with accuracy, but what little character these possessed was unpleasant.'

Alloa House I had gone, leaving only its fortress section behind. In 1834, however, Alloa House II appeared, some way from the Tower. This, built by another soldierly Erskine (he had been wounded at Waterloo), was a mansion pure and simple: a rather austere one, though, with little ornament but a parapet round the roof. As the century went on, however, few were privileged to see it from close quarters, for the Earl of Mar and Kellie—the titles came together in 1835—turned into the town's best-known recluse and finally shut himself away from everybody but his factor and his doctor. Visitors were firmly discouraged from approaching the house of mystery, although some unauthorised ones found it a powerful attraction; it was a paradise for small boys daring enough to penetrate the grounds. One of them, when caught by the earl, fell back on the terrified and hopeless excuse that he was looking for his father's donkey. But Mar does not appear to have minded these juvenile invasions too much.

On the death of the recluse earl in 1866 the two titles became temporarily separated, and it was the Earl of Kellie, a cousin, who took over at Alloa. Almost at once, he brought his property back to the notice of the town by having it extended and refashioned. The old mansion changed its appearance dramatically: it sprouted a sizeable (and taller) wing on each side, and the recluse's stables were transformed into kitchens. The old Tower was repaired and, in the long-established Erskine tradition, gardens received special attention. Kellie relied almost completely on local expertise and, as James Archibald, an Alloa historian, noted later, 'when all was done he [the Earl] declared he could not have been better advised and served supposing he had called some city man'.

The product of these labours—a dignified three-storey building that was still ornamented by a balustraded parapet running round the roof—was not as enormous as some of the mansions constructed during the Victorian period. But, with its ninety rooms, it was still big enough, and it was its size that ultimately led to its undoing. Within less than a century of its creation, it appeared dauntingly large and dauntingly unmodernised. When the present Earl of Mar and Kellie succeeded to the titles in 1955, he moved himself and his young family out of the hotel-sized structure he had inherited and set about looking for a new use for it. He approached various government departments; they ended by turning it down. He approached a public school with the same result. Finally, his only option was to sell Alloa House II and its fifty surrounding acres to the then Alloa Town Council. The house was demolished in 1965 and the housing estate, known as the Mar Policies, that laps round the old Tower was built shortly afterwards.

It is a story that, in its essentials, has been repeated time and time again both north and south of the Border.

On a snowy day in the spring of 1626, a gory little episode in the furtherance of science took place at the bottom of Highgate Hill. Under the eyes of two distinguished visitors to the area, a cottager's wife caught one of the hens in her yard, killed it and pulled out its innards. Then the luckless fowl was stuffed with snow. One of the two men tramping round in the mess of blood, feathers and slush was a physician called Witherborne. The other was the philosopher Francis Bacon, Viscount St Albans, formerly Lord Chancellor and now, following his confession that he had taken bribes, a man whose career in office was finished. His career as a thinker, however, had proceeded undimmed.

The stuffing of the hen had been entirely his idea. Noticing the snow on the ground as he drove towards Highgate, his speculative mind formed the question: 'Can snow, like salt, be used for preserving meat?' He and his friend stopped their coach, completed the transaction with the henwife and carried out the experiment, Bacon himself helping to pile snow into the dead hen.

This early test of the theory of deep-freezing succeeded, Bacon recalled afterwards, 'excellently well'. But, as things turned out, his opinion was

16 A school of the 1820s—and once, according to the *Survey of London*, part of Arundel House, Highgate. From the Potter Collection at the British Museum.

premature, since he did not have the chance to see how long the hen really could be preserved. By the time the stuffing operation was over, he was thoroughly chilled and felt too unwell to complete the journey back to his lodgings in the Temple. However, there was a haven near at hand: the Highgate house of his friend, the second Earl of Arundel. The sick man stopped at Arundel House and was surrounded with attentions although the Earl, in disgrace himself at the time, was temporarily under house arrest on his estate in Sussex. A bed was speedily warmed, Bacon was made comfortable and a member of the household took his pen to help the philosopher to explain his arrival to his absent host.

From the sound of it, the amanuensis was probably the Earl's house-keeper himself, since Bacon went out of his way to acknowledge the kindness the man had shown to him:

> Your house-keeper is very careful and diligent about me, which I assure myself your Lordship will not only pardon towards him, but think the better of him for it. For indeed your Lordship's house was happy to me; and I kiss your noble hands for the welcome I am sure you give me to it, etc.

This is possibly the most poignant bread-and-butter letter ever written. Arundel House may indeed have been 'happy' to Bacon but for all that, it was to be the scene of his fast-approaching death. His chill quickly turned into bronchitis and the fault, unhappily, lay at the door of those same people who had rushed round on his arrival and done all they could to make him comfortable. Aubrey, who concludes his *Brief Life* of Bacon with an account of the experiment with the fowl, explains that they had 'putt him into a good bed warmed with a Panne, but it was a damp bed that had not been layn-in about a yeare before, which gave him such a colde that in 2 or 3 dayes as I remember Mr. Hobbes told me, he dyed of Suffocation.' In fact, Bacon lasted slightly longer than that but, early on Easter morning (9 April), the damp bed claimed its victim.

Bacon was not the only distinguished visitor Arundel House had received. He had, in fact, been there before during his heyday, accompanied by the Lords Justices and Sir Julius Caesar, Master of the Rolls. In addition, King James I had used the place as a hunting-lodge. During the time of a previous occupant, Sir William Cornwallis, it was probably visited by Queen Elizabeth as well. After Bacon's death, however, its connections with the leading figures in the kingdom were soon to come to an end. Arundel got rid of his Highgate estate in 1632. The house changed hands several times, was divided into two, changed hands again and finally vanished from public attention. It vanished so completely that

17 Francis Bacon, Viscount St Albans. Portrait by J. Vanderbank

its site became almost a thing of legend: during the nineteenth century, the main theory was that it had been on The Bank, on the north-east side of Highgate High Street. According, however, to the London County Council's *Survey of London*, in all likelihood it consisted of a row of buildings that stood next to, and partly on the site of, the magnificent William and Mary mansion in South Grove called the Old Hall.

After its division in the 1670s, one part of the old Arundel House was swept away when, twenty years later, it was rebuilt as the new mansion's main block. The house immediately to the east, however, survived for much longer and, in the illustration, is shown in one of its later guises as the nineteenth-century Grignon & Hull's Academy. Fragments of Bacon's place of doubtful refuge still survive in the Hall, particularly in its one-storey east wing, but the rest of the buildings have now gone. By the time the district was investigated for the *Survey of London* in the 1930s, the area had become a tennis court, and today new houses are neatly arranged on the Arundel House site. The only real reminder of the man who was killed there by kindness is a narrow thoroughfare leading away down the hill: it is called Bacon's Lane.

In the grounds of a youth service training centre in Buckinghamshire is a wistful memorial to past affections: a burial plot for dogs. During their lifetimes, the animals whose remains lie there—Skye and Yorkshire terriers, spaniels, a pug much admired for his intelligence—were beneficiaries of enormous wealth, for they belonged to a branch of the great Rothschild family. Their owners were Sir Anthony de Rothschild, his wife Louisa (*née* Montefiore) and his two young daughters Constance and Annie, while the house around which they trotted was Aston Clinton, one of the six magnificent establishments that gave the area its unofficial title of Rothschild country.

Together with a small patch of land at Mentmore to the north, Aston Clinton represented the family's bridgehead in the district that its members soon came to dominate. But the house's importance went further than this. It also represented a key stage in the process that would turn the British-based branch of the Rothschild family from ultra-rich exotics, suspect on account of their religion and origins, into members of the British ruling class, accepted by royalty and Buckinghamshire voters alike. (Starting in 1865, a Rothschild was to be put into Parliament by the Aylesbury electorate for over half a century.)

At a time when class status was still closely linked with the ownership of land, Aston Clinton and the other Rothschild houses in the country helped their owners to integrate with British society as few other things could have done. This was, of course, a process that, both in the nineteenth century and earlier, many owners of 'new' wealth had exploited to the full. But the Rothschilds, whose enormous resources were backed by taste, generosity and enthusiasm of a very high order, achieved results on all fronts that were unique.

The process was first put in train by Sir Anthony's parents. In 1835, his father bought a house in then rural Acton, Gunnersbury House, while his mother, worrying over the unhealthy effect long hours in the city could have on her sons, begged them to spare time for a little regular hunting. In her *Reminiscences*, Constance pointed out that the old lady was a 'far-seeing and clever women', and her advice was indeed extremely sound.

To give added force to her encouragement, the matriarch even presented her sons with a base from which they could make their sporting forays: '. . . a few fields in the village of Mentmore, in the very centre of the best

18 Aston Clinton House, under one of its later aliases, the Green Park Hotel

hunting ground in Buckinghamshire.' The scheme was a brilliant success, and the youngest of her sons, Mayer, took it a stage further by setting up house on the property. As the first of the Rothschild houses in the area, this establishment was modest indeed—it was later put to use as a laundry —and in 1850, after Mayer's marriage, plans were set under way for what would be Mentmore Towers. But, in 1851, the second eldest of his brothers stole a march on him by buying an existing gentleman's residence: Aston Clinton House. Like Mayer, Anthony then immersed himself in building works and, in 1853, the family moved in. Their home for six months of every year was described admiringly by a contemporary guidebook:

> This beautiful structure is situated under the base of the Chiltern Hills, and is a large square pile with four fronts—the principal one being of Grecian Doric design. On the north west side is a handsome conservatory with a dome of curvi-lineal form, which, with the sides, is filled with plate glass. A long corridor leads to the principal apartments, which are fine and spacious, and contain a rare and valuable collection of articles of *vertu*. A considerable quantity of rich tapestry adorns the walls. The park of about 200 acres is well wooded.

In this elegant setting—which, grand though it was, came to be considered modest compared with other Rothschild houses—life was led according to the established pattern of every English country house: Sir Anthony shot and hunted, his wife received a long string of guests and the girls did their lessons. But an unmistakable Rothschild flavour was always present. Prominent among the girls' lessons, for example, was

39

Hebrew. Sir Anthony's pheasant shoots were on a grand scale, and the bag was complimented on by no less a person than Disraeli (the quantity, he said, was matched by the quality). And the guests included royalty (the heirs to both the British and Russian thrones), politicians (Dizzy himself and Gladstone) and poets (Browning, Tennyson and Arnold).

In and around the social life led by their elders, the two girls followed interests that, while broadly similar, were not identical. Annie was the one that loved hunting, and she was also the household's dog-handler *par excellence*: she lavished care on them, drew their portraits and, if one was shut out at night, braved the terrors of the darkened, tapestry-hung rooms and let the wanderer in after everyone had gone to bed. Constance's preoccupations, in contrast, were educational; she relentlessly passed knowledge on to her sister and, by the age of eleven, was widening her scope to take in the little 'plaiting schools' run by old women in the village. (Straw plaiting was the area's main cottage industry.) The experiment was abruptly stopped by Louisa de Rothschild, who found her daughters lording it over a fetid room full of sad little plaiting-girls. But Constance persevered: she persuaded the local rector to lend her the boys' school building on Saturdays, and the lessons in reading and writing went on.

Finally, Louisa suggested a compromise. The girls' school would continue, but it was to be a proper one, built and donated to the village by Sir Anthony. 'Never', Constance recorded, 'has the building of any edifice been so carefully and affectionately watched as this was by our young selves. I even tested the growth of the walls by going each day to jump over them, until my efforts were out-distanced by the masons' work.' Her father later enlarged the building and, when Constance asked for a village *infants'* school for a birthday present, built that too. 'Matthew Arnold', the young educationist went on, 'was our first Inspector, and became one of our greatest friends.'

As children, the girls of Aston Clinton House integrated themselves almost too heartily into the life of the village. Grown up, they brought an equal determination to the continuing business of integrating the Rothschild family into British upper-class life. This time, Annie set the pace: against a background of family dismay and social amazement, she married the Honourable Eliot Yorke, at the same time retaining her faith. Later, Constance also married outside the Jewish community, and exchanged her exotic surname for the more homely one of Flower (to which the title of Battersea was later added).

By the time of this wedding, Sir Anthony was dead and Aston

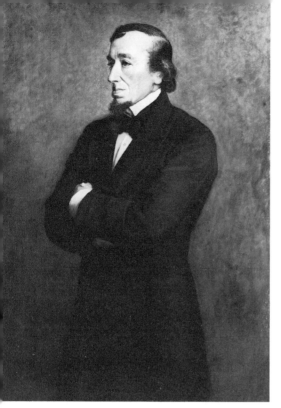

19 (*Left*) Benjamin Disraeli, statesman and sportsman. Portrait by John Everett Millais and 20 (*right*) Aston Clinton's owner: Sir Anthony de Rothschild

Clinton was thereafter mainly a woman's house. The Dowager Lady de Rothschild made it her principal home until her own death in 1910; afterwards, the two sisters kept it on out of sentimental attachment. But, between the wars, its career as a home ended. In 1935, after a period of use by a local sports club, it had become the Howard Park Private Hotel. By the onset of World War II, another name change had taken place, and Sir Anthony's house had been renamed the Green Park Hotel. The property ended by being bought by Buckinghamshire County Council; the 'large square pile with four fronts' was demolished, and in 1964 the Green Park Youth Service Training Centre was established on the site.

However, some fragments from the Rothschild period survive, notably the stable block; at the time of writing, a major conversion project is on hand to turn this into a conference hall, a cafeteria and offices for voluntary youth organisations. According to the centre's programme, the offices will provide 'pooled resources of the more expensive type of office equipment, which many individual organisations need but cannot afford to rent or purchase'. Constance, always practical in her enthusiasms, would have approved.

41

When, near Tremeirchion in North Wales, the mansion of Bachegraig suddenly appeared in the sixteenth century, the locals said it had been built by the devil. Less innocent observers also stretched their eyes, for the house was like nothing that had ever been seen in the area before. With its cupola, stained-glass windows, brick-built walls and totally astonishing outline, it did not belong in Wales at all; its proper home was somewhere like Amsterdam, where the new weighing house had been built in the same pattern.

The creator of this bizarre link between the Low Countries and a wooded Welsh valley was a merchant called Sir Richard Clough. Sir Richard's business activities were international: he had a strong connection with Antwerp, where he acted as agent for Sir Thomas Gresham, the builder of London's Royal Exchange. But he also hoped to stimulate trade in the less commercially active Vale of Clwyd, and Bachegraig was the result. 'Tradition', explained the eighteenth-century guide by Francis Grose,

> says that out of regard to his native country, Sir Richard being born in this neighbourhood, he intended to have introduced trade and manufactures into it, and that he meant this building and its offices for a magazine of merchandize for this part of the kingdom; and moreover had formed a scheme of cutting a canal hither from Rutland [Rhuddlan] or of making the river Clwd [*sic*] navigable up to this place.

Bachegraig went up in about 1567, and went up quickly. Sir Richard was probably away most of the time but, according to the people of the district, another party was not. 'This house', Grose went on, 'is vulgarly reported to have been built by the devil in one night, on account of the small time spent in its erection, compared with that usually taken in like structures.' Indeed, the 'devil as builder' story collected all manner of Faustian overtones, but the explanation, Grose pointed out, was quite simply that Clough had enough money to employ more and better workmen than might have been expected in this out-of-the-way spot.

The workmen may or may not have been mainly Welsh, but there was no question as to where the design of the house originated. Many of its materials, too, came from the same source; the stones, a contemporary poet claimed, came from Antwerp, and the little red bricks—'small but very hard and fine', Grose reported—were also of Low Countries origin.

They were used for building both the house and the range of outbuildings that stood round it. The whole arrangement enclosed a square court, in the middle of which was a well.

As shown in the engraving, the outbuildings indicate the remarkable scale of the mansion itself. The cupola included (which Clough used as an observatory), it had seven storeys in all. While the hall and parlour on the main floor were grand enough, the slope of the roof higher up appears to have made the other rooms awkward to live in. Dr Johnson, who visited Bachegraig in 1774, did not think much of the arrangement or, indeed, the state of the house. The entry for 30 July in his *Journey into North Wales* runs as follows:

> We went to Bachygraig, where we found an old house built 1567, in an uncommon and incommodious form. My Mistress chattered about tiring, but I prevailed on her to go to the top. The floors have been stolen; the windows are stopped. The house was less than I seemed to expect . . .. The woods have many trees, generally young, but some which seem to decay. They have been lopped. The house never had a garden. The addition of another story [*sic*] would make a useful home, but it cannot be great. Some buildings which Clough the founder intended for warehouses would make storechambers and servants' rooms. The ground seems to be good. I wish it well.

21 Bachegraig, with Sir Richard Clough's initials prominently displayed.

22 Samuel Johnson. Portrait by Joshua Reynolds

Johnson's visit had come about through the agency of his friends, the
Thrales. Mrs Thrale—Johnson's chattering 'Mistress'—was a descendant
of Sir Richard Clough. The house had become the home of her family, the
Salusburys, and, on her mother's death in 1773, it had come to her. On
their journey to Wales the following year, she, her husband and Johnson
all went to see how things stood there. As Johnson's account indicates,
they found that Bachegraig was somewhat the worse for wear.

Over the next quarter-century, the house and estate went even further downhill. The lopping, too, continued with a vengeance, and Mrs Thrale was particularly incensed over the desecration of the Bachegraig woods. But the process was briefly halted at the very end of the eighteenth century, after Mrs Thrale had married again. Her new husband, the Italian musician Gabriel Piozzi, had built a Welsh home of their own at top of the hill. Called Brynbella, it brought another foreign style, this time Mediterranean, to the Clwyd countryside. Now they turned their attention to restoring the older building in the valley. The house was renovated from top to bottom and respectable tenants installed, among them the local curate (for good measure, the Piozzis also restored Tremeirchion Church).

But this upturn in Bachegraig's fortunes was only temporary. In 1818 Mrs Piozzi was again lamenting its general state and its lack of sur- rounding woods; in 1821, she died and her adopted son, John Salusbury Piozzi Salusbury, pulled down the old Clough mansion soon afterwards. Some of the other buildings round the courtyard were turned into a farmhouse which exists today, so the 'small but very hard' red bricks that Clough imported can still be admired. But the amazing quality of this contribution to Welsh architecture can now be judged only from con- temporary descriptions, prints and the awe-struck reactions of residents in the Vale of Clwyd.

❧Berkeley House and Devonshire House

Shortly after the restoration of the British monarchy in 1660, three palatial buildings appeared on what is now Piccadilly. Working westwards, they were Burlington House, Clarendon House and Berkeley House. Burlington House is still with us in a much altered state, but the other two are not. Indeed, Clarendon House (see page 94) came down only two decades after it had been built. Berkeley House, too, was relatively short-lived; it was destroyed by fire in 1733. But, before going up in flames, it had passed from the Berkeleys to the dukes of Devonshire, and its successor on the site, Devonshire House, existed until well within living memory, carrying with it further and more distant memories of political intrigues, of a scandalously complicated household, of heights of endeavour in the fields of art and literature and of Victorian society life at its most magnificent and prodigal.

The curious thing is that it was the less famous of the two, Berkeley House, that had the more superb appearance. The face that Devonshire House showed to the world was, even to those who penetrated behind its high sheltering wall, unassuming and notoriously homely. It also stood in

23 'Not very convenient': Berkeley House, with Britannia sheltering under the pediment. From the Crace Collection at the British Museum

24 Plain without, magnificent within: the new Devonshire House, shown here at the beginning of the nineteenth century

smaller grounds than its predecessor, for in the 1680s the widowed Lady Berkeley had improved her finances by slicing off two pieces of her garden and letting them for building; the results were Berkeley Street and Stratton Street, the eastern and western boundaries of the grounds of Devonshire House.

Berkeley House was built at a cost of £30,000 in 1665 for Lord Berkeley of Stratton, a staunch supporter of Charles I during the Civil War. John Evelyn, to whose interests and social activities we owe so much information about lost houses, visited it in 1666 and went back there again six years later. The effect it made on him cannot have been the one Lord Berkeley might have hoped for: 'It is very well built', Evelyn commented in his *Diary*, 'and has many noble rooms, but they are not very convenient, consisting but of one *Corps de Logis*; they are all rooms of state, without closets. The staircase is of cedar, the furniture is princely: the kitchen and stables are ill-placed, and the corridor worse, having no report to the wings they join to.' And this impression of second-rate splendour went right through the building. 'The porticos', Evelyn went on coldly, 'are in imitation of a house described by Palladio; but it happens to be the worst in his book, though my good friend, Mr. Hugh May, his Lordship's architect, effected it.' Having seen through his Lordship's pretensions, however, Evelyn judged the forecourt noble, which indeed it was, and the gardens 'incomparable'. He particularly liked the fishpond; he also made

47

a particular note that he had helped to plan the holly hedges on the terrace. (As indicated on page 242, Evelyn had a passion for holly hedges.)

The full point of Evelyn's strictures on the kitchens is made clear by an account published at the beginning of the eighteenth century, when the dukes of Devonshire had already taken over. This fine brick and stone house, with its pediment framing a statue of Britannia, had its kitchen and laundries situated 'at some distance' on the east side of the main building, with one of the curving wings connecting the two. Although this seems the ultimate in inconvenience today, Lord Berkeley and Mr May were, between them, being ultra-modern; the idea of siting the kitchen and its smells away from the main body of a house was then scarcely heard of, although later it became very popular. Evelyn was evidently a conservative.

By 1684, however, he had changed his mind about Berkeley House, mainly because it had come under threat from its owner. Lady Berkeley had called him in to advise on how the edges of the grounds could best be trimmed. 'I could not but deplore', her adviser wrote afterwards, 'that sweet place (by far the most noble gardens, courts, and accommodations, stately porticos, &c. any where about the town) should be so much straightened and turned into tenements.' But he added that the demolition of Clarendon House next door gave Lady Berkeley some excuse for being tempted by the going rate for land in the area: almost £1,000 a year in ground-rents. Later, Lady Berkeley let the house itself to the then queen's sister, Princess Anne, who lived there with her husband, George of Denmark, from 1692 to 1695. When, following her sister's death, Anne moved to St James's Palace, the Berkeleys soon sold their house and garden on Portugal Street, as that part of Piccadilly was then called. William Cavendish, first Duke of Devonshire, took possession and within months was entertaining the sovereign who, for outstanding services rendered during the revolution that had put William of Orange on the throne, had recently awarded him his dukedom.

The first Duke of Devonshire was a remarkable man. He distinguished himself as a duellist, a ladies' man, a builder (he remodelled Chatsworth) and, on one occasion, as a doughty character who might have stepped straight out of a far earlier period—when James II sent troops to Chatsworth to arrest him for the non-payment of a fine, he collared the lot and imprisoned them. As a prominent member of the Whigs, he was also, of course, a politician and statesman. He became Lord High Steward and, like his son (who succeeded him in 1707), he was a Lord Justice of England during the sovereign's absence. The third and fourth dukes imitated their example; the fourth, indeed, took the family political tradition to its ultimate by serving, if for a very short while, as prime minister.

At the same time as this parade of dukes was making its way through the council chambers of the eighteenth century, the family was also evolving for itself a style that was oddly at variance with the Devonshires' wealth and power, but that had an important bearing on the future of the building they owned in Piccadilly. Horace Walpole once commented that, in spite of their estates and high standing, they deliberately clothed their pride with the manners of the ordinary English gentry. This image of prestige hidden under a plain exterior exactly matches the reality of the house, the new Devonshire House, that was built when Berkeley House met its end.

The end came in the time of the third Duke, in 1733, when workmen repairing Berkeley House accidentally set light to it. The fire was spectacular and disastrous enough to draw a large crowd, among whom was the Prince of Wales. While much of the 'princely' furniture was saved, the damage was reckoned to stand at even more than the building's original cost. As a coda to the catastrophe, the statue of Britannia, which had survived the flames, was dropped a few days later and smashed to pieces.

Instead of erecting something more elaborate than the now-ruined mansion of the Berkeleys, the no-frills third duke paid architect and landscape gardener William Kent £1,000 to plan an extremely no-frills building. When, at a cost of £20,000, it went up four years after the fire, much of its simplicity was hidden away behind a wall that was a legacy from Berkeley House. But this concealment did not stop criticisms being levelled at it. A degree of ducal splendour was what the public expected of dukes and, with his building operations at Chatsworth, the first Duke of Devonshire had lived up nobly to the code of his class. The new Devonshire House, in contrast, was felt to look like a storage depot. However, the criticism faded as soon as the building was associated with some intriguing history. It might be plain, but it was also the home of the fifth duke and his head-turning duchess, Georgiana. It might look like a warehouse, but it was also one of the great Whig strongholds of the day, a social and political centre frequented by the future George IV, the playwright Richard Sheridan, and Charles James Fox, on whose behalf the duchess plunged into an electoral campaign that involved kissing 'don't-knows' to win their votes. (Fox won. Among other memories of the canvassing that the duchess treasured was that of an old Irishman who asked to light his pipe at the sparkle of her eyes.) In addition, the house behind its sheltering wall was home to a *ménage à trois* of remarkably long standing and to the legitimate and natural children that it produced.

The three members of the triangle were the duke, his duchess and Lady Elizabeth Foster, whom Georgiana had first brought into the Devonshire House circle as a governess for the duke's first child—a by-blow resulting from a pre-marital affair with a milliner. The duke embarked with Elizabeth on what turned out to be the great involvement of his life, and in the meantime played his part in ensuring that his wife produced him an heir. Georgiana had two daughters; Elizabeth, forced by circumstances to seek secrecy abroad, had a daughter and a son. Georgiana then produced the long-awaited heir, followed by a daughter fathered by Charles Grey, who later became prime minister. With the exception of this last child, whose conception put the duchess in deep disgrace and who was adopted by the Grey family, all of them passed through the Devonshire House schoolroom, watched over benignly by their various parents. (For appearances, Elizabeth's two children, 'children of the mist', were presented as a refugee from France and as an adopted son.) Their number was swelled still further when Elizabeth's legitimate children by an oafish husband she had married in her teens were finally free to join her.

After Georgiana died, Elizabeth married the duke the two women had shared so amicably. But the duke himself died in 1811 and, from then on, Devonshire House lacked a reigning duchess for over two-thirds of a century. Georgiana's son never married, and the marriage of the seventh duke, a cousin, was cut short while he was still Earl of Burlington by the death of his young wife. Their son, Spencer Compton, left his marrying till late in life, but his wife, when he finally took one at the age of fifty-nine, made up for lost time by setting her title on everyone's lips as a leader of society. She was stout, bitchy and had a degree of sexual notoriety. Nicknamed the Double Duchess on account of her first marriage to the Duke of Manchester, she had been involved with Devonshire for years before her first husband's death. Under her guidance, however, Devonshire House became as great a stronghold of the Conservatives—her husband had broken with the family political tradition—as it had been of the Whigs under Georgiana. As Henry Leach, a contemporary biographer of her husband, commented:

> Devonshire House soon became the temple of Conservative society, and her grace conducted all its imposing rites with an inimitable skill and impressiveness. It was the most living contemporary *salon*. All the best entertaining of the party was here performed. The great party dinner in Piccadilly on the night before each parliamentary session opened was regarded as its chiefest function.

25 Reception in the grand saloon of Devonshire House, *c*.1840

But the peak of the Duchess's career as a hostess was probably not a political event but a purely social one: the fancy dress ball she gave in honour of Queen Victoria's Diamond Jubilee in 1897. The Queen, of course, was not present, but the Prince and Princess of Wales were, dressed as a Knight of Malta and Marguérite de Valois. (The Duchess of York, the future Queen Mary, also arrived as Marguérite.) Society members had put frenzied efforts into preparing their costumes: many had found their unaccustomed way to the print room of the British Museum, and two had even rushed off to Paris for completely new outfits days before the ball. And the Double Duchess's staff had been sweating similarly: 'Devonshire House', Leach said,

> had undergone a wonderful adaptation. It was a palace of flowers and light. The perfume of a million posies gathered in the Chatsworth gardens floated through the evening air. Crystal ceilings and mirrored walls dazzled as they seemed to make the light waves quiver. The guests walking to the supper

26 William Cavendish, fifth Duke of Devonshire. Portrait after Joshua Reynolds

room passed down a staircase specially constructed, and the midnight feast was held in, as it seemed, a noble hall hung with costly tapestry and with glittering chandeliers pendant.

By the next day, however, everything had gone. The effect, Leach went on, 'was made for this night alone, and on the morrow it faded like the thin vision of a dream castle, leaving but the green grass of the velvet lawns where it had stood'.

Phantasmagoric though these delights may have been, others on view to visitors to Devonshire House were far more solid. There was the magnificent main staircase, made of alabaster and marble, with crystal rails, that rose so gently that walking up it was said to be no more trouble than walking down most others. (The sardonyx tiger's head at its foot was reputed once to have been part of the chair of the Emperor Augustus.) There were the contents of the picture galleries on the first floor: Rembrandt, Titian, Tintoretto, Rubens, Van Dyck and Reynolds. There was also the library, where a £2,000 purchase of the sixth duke (the bachelor) held pride of place: it was a collection of English plays made by the actor-manager John Philip Kemble, and included several first editions of Shakespeare.

At the time the duchess gave her ball, it would have seemed inconceivable that there should not be Devonshires and a Devonshire House in Piccadilly. The duke, however, had already had forebodings. When death duties were introduced shortly before the Jubilee, he sombrely remarked that his successors would find it impossible to maintain Chatsworth and Devonshire House. His immediate successor, his nephew Victor, became ninth duke and owner of both houses in 1908. Six years afterwards, World War I broke out and the mansion on Piccadilly became host, not to society at play, but to the Red Cross. In 1918, the duke decided to sell, and Devonshire House changed hands for £1 million. The ducal pair, meanwhile, planned to move to a smaller home in Carlton Gardens, and the duchess was reported to be wondering how the family pictures would look there.

Plans for use of the site varied—one of them featured an entertainment centre—and it was only at the end of 1924 that the house started to come down. Offices and flats were built on the ground where the Jubilee Ball had taken place. As with its predecessor, Berkeley House, the mansion's end caused a considerable stir. No Prince of Wales visited the scene this time, but the duke and duchess did; it is a measure of the house's curious pull on the imagination that the spectacle they watched is probably the most famous demolition to have taken place this century.

Blyth Hall

Just outside the range of living memory, congregations at Blyth Priory Church in Nottinghamshire were warned in a highly idiosyncratic manner of the fact that the squire and his party were about to make the few yards' journey to worship from Blyth Hall next door. The hall procession was headed, not by the hall's owner, but by one of his servants armed with a 'pig' or stone hot-water bottle. This chunky object was installed in a special gallery, the servant withdrew and the hall residents took their places on upholstered pews, their personal handwarmer within reach. Slightly later, a further aid to comfort was added in the form of a private lavatory.

Blyth Hall and Blyth Church had always been joined in a more than usually tight relationship, with the hall tending to regard the priory as something like a house extension. The relationship dated back to the seventeenth century, when a rich merchant family called Mellish bought the land on which the living quarters of the former priory had stood. They pulled down the old buildings and cleared further space for themselves by lopping off a part of the church itself. By 1684, a new house—a brick-and-stone mansion believed to have been designed by William Talman—had grown up where the old building had been. The archway of the truncated church building was meanwhile filled in with a blank wall, and the resulting deep alcove was used at one time as a huge birdcage.

Vandals though they may have been where churches were concerned, the Mellishes none the less produced a building that earned the praise of their contemporaries. Celia Fiennes, who visited Blyth during her horseback journey round the country in the last part of the seventeenth century, was delighted by the house: by its solid, four-square appearance, its neat gardens with gravel and grass walks, its commanding situation and its fruit trees. A Mellish of the mid-eighteenth century improved the property still further; he built roads, planted more trees, drained his estate into a new river four miles long and made the house even more handsome than it had been before.

'The most elegant apartment', wrote a visiting Mr Laird in the early nineteenth century,

is a magnificent drawingroom, forty feet long, twenty-two broad, and eighteen in height, with a circular bow window of twenty-one feet span, so as to form a very agreeable proportion. The chimneypiece is extremely elegant, consisting of Ionic pillars formed of Egyptian granite, fluted with stripes of white marble, and supporting the frieze in which is a tablet with an ancient sacrifice in bas relief. The furniture is appropriately rich, with the beauty of the apartment; and the chairs and carpet are of crimson velvet, embroidered with yellow silk. The view from this apartment, and from many of the others is extremely grand, looking over a fine piece of water, winding through the lawn for a mile and half, and of the breadth of from fifty to seventy yards.

Compared with, for instance, the Pulestons of Emral Hall (page 136), the Mellishes remained in the house they had created for a very short while. But, during the 171 years they were in possession, they still contrived to present a perfect picture, almost a caricature, of a landed family in all its aspects. The first Mellish of all bought, obviously with an eye to the future. The second, Edward, who had made his fortune trading in Portugal, built. William Mellish, MP for East Retford in the mid-eighteenth century, improved, so as to fit both house and estate more perfectly to his well-established station in life. His son Charles, not needing to justify himself by works, lived a pleasant existence of leisure and letters. And Charles's son, Henry Francis, was that absolute bogey-figure of the landed gentry: the heir who Gambled It All Away. He did not, in

27 Blyth's most notable visitor: the future Prince Regent, here shown aged thirty. Miniature by R. Cosway

fact, lose everything; the nearby Hodsock Priory, also a Mellish possession, remained in the family. But it was scarcely for the want of trying.

Even in a period of quite astonishing gambling, Colonel Henry Mellish was a gambler of extraordinary calibre. (He was also an excellent fighting man, but his effect on his comrades-at-arms was such that the army, with regret, kept having to dispense with his services.) His field of action embraced both the tables and the Turf, and his gambling cronies included the future Prince Regent and the prince's brothers. The bets he made were legendary: on one occasion, when the prince visited him at Blyth, he is believed to have coolly staked £40,000 on one throw of the dice. He lost.

But what really marked Henry Mellish out as a prodigy among gamesters was the element of pure fantasy that he injected into his obsession. This, too, reached one of its most famous peaks at Blyth Hall, where in 1805 he wagered his home and estate, not on the turn of a card, but on the inherent stickiness of butter. He bet a guest that he could fillip a pat of butter up to the 18ft high ceiling and make it stick. And he lost again. Somehow, however, he won the place back. He must have done, for it was not until the following year that his luck finally gave out and his family moved to Hodsock. Blyth was sold to a Sheffield ironmaster called Joshua Walker, while Mellish himself went off to the Peninsular Wars. He died eleven years later, aged thirty-seven.

After this harum-scarum interlude, Blyth Hall returned to its normal role of a country gentleman's sedate residence. The Walkers remained in

28 Blyth Hall in 1929, with the priory church on the right

possession for a long while and established themselves in the area. Disraeli visited and planted a tree in the grounds; other visitors came and went, blessing their hosts for the arrangements made for their church-going comfort.

The photograph shows the Hall in the last years of its time in the sun, with pampas grass waving on the terrace and glass in the windows. By 1938, an essay in the *Transactions* of the Thoroton Society of Nottingham-shire noted that the building was now represented by a 'shell'. In spite of this, however, it still took over thirty years finally to disappear. In the succinct summary of the Royal Commission's *Interim Report, 1976*, it was 'vandalised by troops during the war, and abandoned thereafter'. But, roofless, it continued to stand until the early 1970s.

Within days of the announcement in 1972 that the grounds would be sold as eighteen building plots, thirteen were snapped up. The house had gone, but the situation that had so pleased the Mellishes, Celia Fiennes and many others remained as desirable as ever.

❧ Boleyn Castle

Of Henry VIII's wives, Anne Boleyn is perhaps the best known, not least for her violent end and the flicker of the abnormal as testified by her rudimentary sixth finger. It is therefore scarcely surprising that, as a real or imagined occupant of English houses, she should rank with her daughter Elizabeth as an object of attention. In some cases—Hever Castle and the first Blickling Hall are examples—the link is well-established: Anne was born at Blickling and spent much of her childhood at Hever. Elsewhere, however, legend takes over from fact and leads inquirers down a variety of dead-ends.

Did Henry VIII's second queen, for instance, really live at Green Street's Boleyn Castle, in what is now the London Borough of Newham? The verdict is the damping one of 'anything but proven'. But, even so, story-tellers have been having fun with the supposition for centuries. The Tudor mansion—set in what, by the twentieth century, had become the highly incongruous surroundings of urban East Ham—is supposed to have been the scene of Henry's courting. The octagonal structure in the grounds (known, of course, as Anne Boleyn's Tower) was allegedly built to please its namesake. And this same building was, according to tradition, used to confine the queen for a short while before her execution.

Towers are obvious locations for tales of imprisonment, and it also

29 Green Street House, otherwise known as Boleyn Castle. The Tower is on the left, half-hidden by a cedar

30 Boleyn Castle in the nineteenth century, before the cedars had grown; from Katherine Fry's book, *A History of the Parishes of East and West Ham*

sounds as if the myth-makers had confused the Boleyn Tower with another, real, Tudor love-nest and sometime prison across the river in Greenwich (see page 206). The link between the two areas would appear to be an East Ham resident called Richard Breame, who owned a house in Greenwich as well. Breame, at least, is not a myth; he was one of Henry VIII's servants. He may have built Boleyn Castle (which was originally called Green Street House), and he certainly owned the land on which it was situated. Most of the castle's later owners, tenants or occupiers are equally genuine: they include a line of baronets called Garrard; a Mrs Whiteside who had vandalistic tendencies; a corn merchant called Morley; the staff and pupils of St Edward's Catholic Reformatory School for boys; and West Ham United Football Club.

Intriguing contrasts though these represent, the most intriguing of all grew to be the one noted earlier. A map of the area given in a history of London architecture published in 1911 shows an apparent desert contained by two railways and bisected by the Northern Outfall Sewer. In the middle of the desert stood Boleyn Castle. Trains rumbled by to the

59

31 Boleyn Castle, from Green Street, East Ham

north; trams clanked past the front door. These were the unlikely surroundings of a building that would soon be classed as unique; that would, indeed, be judged by the chairman of the Society for the Protection of Ancient Buildings as worthy on some counts of being compared with Hampton Court.

The house first appeared on the SPAB's files in 1944, shortly before it was damaged by a bomb. In the same year, its distinctions were recognised by inclusion on the Commissioner of Works' list of ancient monuments. Given the effects of the war on London, it was lucky to have survived so long, but the real miracle was that so much of it had survived in a more or less untouched state. Its great hall was still there (now in the twentieth-century guise of a billiard room); so was the main staircase, whose turned balusters were a classic example of the earliest English efforts in this direction. Inside, much of the panelling belonged to the sixteenth or early seventeenth century; outside, much of the brickwork (especially in the tower) dated from the house's first appearance in about the 1540s. There had, inevitably, been alterations and additions—a kitchen block, a new

60

eighteenth-century wing and eighteenth-century windows in the tower. And there had been one minor and one major set of depredations. In the eighteenth century, Mrs Whiteside is believed to have cast a thoughtful eye on the gold-embossed leather hangings that decorated one of the tower's rooms. The story is that she pulled them down, burned them, sifted the gold from the ashes, and sold it. Further pulling down, on a larger scale, took place when the building became a reformatory: the church authorities took down the castle's main gateway on to Green Street and built along the frontage. But, apart from this, East Ham's equivalent to Hampton Court managed to escape serious damage from the time when it was surrounded by fields (in Mr Morley's period, one of these was charmingly known as the 'Hoppit') to the present century.

The railway, now the District Line, and the Northern Outfall Sewer still exist today. But Boleyn Castle does not. Its troubles appear to date from around the 1920s when the Royal Commission on Historical Monuments described the condition of the house (though not of the famous tower) as 'poor'. After the war, it was the tower's turn to be in difficulties: in 1951, the *Daily Telegraph* reported that the Ministry of Works had given permission for it to be demolished, the deciding factors being the extent of the dilapidations and the cost of putting them right. In 1953, the *Evening Standard* ran the headline, 'Is castle doomed? Cracks in walls'. In 1955, most of the complex came down; the northernmost part of the house became a factory, but this too vanished in the 1970s. The ground occupied for almost four centuries by Green Street's most notable landmark is now the site of a school and an engineering works.

❧Brandenburgh House

Outside the royal palaces, there can be few British homes that have sheltered such a string of celebrated, controversial or otherwise extraordinary characters as Brandenburgh House, Hammersmith. From the time of the building's construction in the 1620s to its demolition in 1822, it enjoyed little more than half a century of nonentity, most of it in the hands of a blameless family of dyers called Lannoy. For the rest of the time, it was occupied by, among others, General Fairfax, commander-in-chief of the New Model Army; the mistress of his sometime opponent, Prince Rupert of the Rhine; a bulging Georgian politician of swaying loyalties and quite prodigious conceit; a peeress whose morals were such that her daughters refused to call on her; and a queen facing divorce. There is something almost supernatural about the way the members of this colourful mob followed each other across the Brandenburgh stage. Just what was there that attracted them all to this rather ordinary villa beside the Thames? Its position—out of London, yet connected to it by road and river—was convenient, but so was that of a thousand other houses. In the words of an eighteenth-century writer, its owners enjoyed the benefit of a 'sweet and wholesome air', but they would also have cursed at the periodic flooding. When first built, the house was grand enough, and a fortune was later spent on its renovation; yet, as pictures of the exterior show, it obstinately remained a commonplace, four-square box, whose unpretentious exterior was in marked contrast to the array of strong human personalities that expressed themselves within. Brandenburgh House was a phenomenon.

Its creator was a seventeenth-century businessman called Nicholas Crispe. He had business interests in several areas: he made a fortune out of his monopoly of the Guinea Coast trade in gold and slaves (and complained bitterly when unauthorised slavers broke in on his operations); he imported indigo and exotic timbers; and he was credited with having made a revolutionary, though now unknown, change in the process of manufacturing bricks. Originally he came from Gloucestershire but, when still in his twenties, he settled himself just within the boundary of Fulham and spent almost £25,000 on building himself a fine family house by the river. A description published by the antiquarian John Bowack seventy years later showed that Crispe's interest in bricks and what could be done with them dated back at least to this period. Indeed, the 'Great House'

32 (*left*) Thomas Fairfax, two years before his visit to Brandenburgh. Medal by T. Simon and
33 (*right*) Prince Rupert of the Rhine: did he buy Brandenburgh for Margaret? Portrait after
Peter Lely

was to be a handsome advertisement for his business affairs. It was
'very lofty, regular, and magnificent, after the modern manner, built with
brick, cornered with stone, and has a handsome cupola at the top. It
contains several large handsome rooms, very spacious, and finely finished.
The foundations and walls are very substantial, and the vaults underneath
arched in an extraordinary manner.'

Crispe's rising fortunes—he was made a knight in 1640—matched the
splendour of his home until the outbreak of the Civil War. A strong
supporter of the Royalist side, he gave financial backing to the king, was
found out, escaped and ended up in France, where he went on working
for the Royalist cause. Meanwhile, the forces of Parliament ran riot
through his possessions: his stores of indigo, redwood and bullion were
confiscated, his rents sequestered and his house at Hammersmith plundered, then used as an army hospital. In spite of these depredations, Lady
Crispe appears to have gone on living in her home and, when the Parliamentary army stationed itself in the area in 1647, found herself playing
involuntary hostess to Thomas Fairfax, who made the house his head-
quarters. This uncomfortable interlude was scarcely over when an even
more embarrassing incident occurred. A French cook approached Fairfax,
who had by then moved to Turnham Green, with an invitation to return
to Lady Crispe's house for dinner. He then approached Lady Crispe

34 (*left*) The 'little actress called Hughs'. Portrait after Peter Lely and 35 (*right*) George Bubb Dodington, as seen by a contemporary. From the Townshend Album at the National Portrait Gallery

herself, with the message that Sir Nicholas had authorised the invitation. The cook set to work. The party, which included a number of army officers, sat down to the meal; and then, apparently, the guests were struck by a mystery illness. It was probably food-poisoning (the cook had made a great show of his skill at working on a limited budget), but suspicions ran otherwise and the cook vanished from history into prison. The party recovered.

At the Restoration, Sir Nicholas retrieved some of his lost wealth and picked up his life at Hammersmith where it had left off. Further recognition of his services came when Charles II gave him a baronetcy. But he died shortly afterwards, in 1666, leaving a mass of complex instructions on how his body should be disposed. One of them gave rise to a macabre little annual ceremony in Hammersmith Chapel, to the building of which he had donated the bricks. The baronet's heart, preserved in an urn near his former pew, was every year taken out on the anniversary of its entombment and 'refreshed' with a glass of wine. Startlingly, this practice continued until the beginning of the nineteenth century, by which time the organ was in such a decayed state that it was entombed in its urn for ever.

The Great House, as it continued to be called, remained in the hands of the Crispe family until the early 1680s, when they sold it to a woman called Margaret Hughes, mistress of Prince Rupert, the former general of Charles I's army, and mother of one of the Prince's natural children. Margaret—'a lady', Bowack wrote, 'much esteemed at Court about that time, for her air and beauty'—had come to the notice of the public and her lover in a way that has since become traditional but was then almost unheard of. At a time when female stage parts were still usually played by boys, she was one of the first English actresses. Her impact on the Prince, most of whose life had been a combination of military, scientific and artistic activities, was described with gusto in the near contemporary *Mémoires de la vie du Comte de Grammont*:

> Prince Rupert found charms in the face of another little actress, called Hughs [*sic*], who brought to reason everything that was wildest in his nature. Farewell to alembics, crucibles, furnaces and all the dark apparatus of the smith; farewell to the mathematician's paraphanalia; farewell to his speculations. The pert hussy wished to be courted in the usual manner: rejecting money (so as to sell her favours more dearly later), she made this poor Prince behave so unlike himself that the change scarcely appeared likely.

Rupert died in 1682, at the age of sixty-three. Accounts differ as to the date his mistress came into possession of the Hammersmith house and the one most often quoted—that given by Daniel Lysons—has Rupert buying it for her in the year after his death. There is the possibility, however, that the second Crispe baronet sold it in 1681, in which case Margaret's ageing lover was starting to make the arrangements for her that he continued in his will (which left all his property in trust for the actress and their daughter). Margaret herself went on living there for about ten years, then set it on its career of respectable obscurity by selling it to the rich merchant family of Lannoy.

This calm period, marked only by Lannoy births, deaths and marriages, came to an end in 1749, when a new owner moved into the Great House: George Dodington MP, also known as George Bubb Dodington, also known as 'Sillybub'. Bubb was, in fact, his original surname; he changed it when his extremely rich uncle died, with the stipulation that George, his heir, should change his name to the uncle's own. Much to the heir's chagrin, though, the 'Bubb' stuck; it suited him so exactly, especially when Pope made merciless play on its similarity with *Bubo*, or owl. 'Full-blown Bubo, puff'd by ev'ry quill,' wrote the satirist, in a passage that, for fear of legal problems, he later amended. In his moral essay on taste, however, he left a nasty quartet of lines that dealt with Dodington's employment of the architect John Vanbrugh to complete his uncle's palace at Eastbury in Dorset:

> See! sportive fate, to punish aukward pride,
> Bids Bubo build, and sends him such a Guide:
> A standing sermon, at each year's expense
> That never Coxcomb reach'd magnificence!

Coxcomb Bubo—'Coxcomb' was another epithet that stuck—was fat, pompous and egregiously self-important. He was a crawler, a toady, a bustling, lobbying worker for his own advancement in the place-hunting game. The Prime Minister, Sir Robert Walpole, to whom he wrote a squirming poem of praise, made him a Lord of the Treasury. But he was anything but a faithful follower and in the end he was dismissed from office. His faithlessness continued: he became a supporter of Prime Minister Henry Pelham (who made him Treasurer of the Navy) and then, when he realised what might be in it for him, resigned his office and took up with the opposition figure of Frederick, Prince of Wales. At this point —to the subsequent dismay of many who figured in it—he began to keep a diary, and one of its earliest entries was, 'October 12, 1749: Arrived at Hammersmith.'

With its name-dropping, franknesses, self-deceptions and total (or apparently total) recall of endless conversations with the highest in the land, Sillybub's *Diary* makes remarkable reading. It was published twenty-two years after his death by a relative of his heir, who took as his excuse for laying such hot stuff before the public the time-honoured one that it was educational. The editor also gave as good a summing-up as any of Dodington's public character: he was 'too experienced a courtier, to speak the same language to all people: on the contrary, he was studious to assimilate his politics to those of his correspondents, and to make his ideas apparently consonant to the opinions of those men, from whom he expected emolument.' (The writer added that he would be happy to 'insert all explanations' from readers who claimed Dodington had got things wrong; it was that sort of book.)

Yet the *Diary* is not totally a chronicle of intrigue. Here and there are passages as beautifully turned as:

> The ministry, of late years, had been like children round a fire, telling stories of spirits, till they frightened one another, that they dared not look behind them.

66

There is also the adventurous:

> At half past three, without going to bed, Mrs. Dodington and I set out in our post-chaise for Eastbury, where 'we arrived the same day, at six in the afternoon.

(At this time, Dodington was sixty-one; the note of pride in his own stamina is clearly evident.) And, in delightfully Pooterish vein:

> I went to town with design to go to the Prince's drawing-room in black, being in mourning for the Countess Temple. After a little time, the Earl of Hyndford was so obliging as to come and tell me, that, he believed, I had forgotten that they did not appear in mourning that day, it being coronation-day. So I was forced to slip away.

Through it all run the lists of the 'Top People' Bubo entertained to dinner at Hammersmith: Pelham himself, Lord Lincoln, Lord Ashburnham, the Marquis de Mirepoix, the Spanish and Sardinian ministers. 'Much wine, and as much good humour as I ever met with; both lasted till almost eleven o'clock,' runs one dinner entry. But the house where these jolly evenings took place was no longer the one Crispe and Peg Hughes had known. Dodington had done it up, getting rid of the cupola, hiding Crispe's precious bricks behind stucco and building a magnificent gallery for his statues and *objets d'art*. 'The floor', wrote Lysons in his *Environs of London*, 'was inlaid with various marbles, and the door-case supported by two columns, richly ornamented with lapis lazuli.' The door itself was of marble too, and the general effect, though grand, was ponderous in the extreme. Dodington was frequently told that the whole thing should be on the ground floor; the Duke of York went one better and kindly assured his host that it soon would be.

In the midst of all this splendour, Dodington ruled over a curiously heterogeneous collection of friends, associates and livers-in. They ranged from men of genuine distinction such as the novelist Henry Fielding and the poet Edward Young to a squalid physician called Thompson, who never bought new shoes till his toes were sticking through his old ones. Their host nicknamed the whole crew the Monks of the Convent; the house itself was *La Trappe*, or Trappist monastery. It was, however, a monastery with one permanent female occupant: Mrs Dodington. Mrs Dodington's married life can scarcely have been easy. Bubo had married her in 1725, but kept the marriage secret for a typically Buboesque reason: to an earlier love, a Mrs Strawbridge, he had given a promise, backed by a £10,000 bond, to marry no one if not herself, and only when the lady died in 1742 was he free of his obligation.

With intervals at Eastbury and at his London house in Pall Mall, Dodington lived at Hammersmith until 1762, socialising, intriguing and writing his diary. The peak of his career as a host there was noted in the *Diary* in detail:

> October 23, 1753: The Princess of Wales and Lady Augusta, attended by Lady Middlesex and Mr. Breton, did Mrs. Dodington and me the honour of breakfasting with us. After breakfast, we walked all round my gardens: we then came in, and they went into all the rooms, except the common dining-parlour: when we were coming down stairs, I told their Royal Highnesses, that there was one room, which I had forgotten to shew them; they desired to see it, and found a cold collation (for it was near three o'clock). The Princess very obligingly sat down, and we all ate a very hearty and very cheerful meal; she staid with us till the day began to decline, and behaved with infinite ease and condescension.

His ultimate triumph, though, came just after the *Diary* closes, in the spring of 1761. To his childlike and endearing delight, he at last got the thing he most wanted in the world: a title. He was made Baron Melcombe of Melcombe Regis. He died the following year, aged seventy-one, in his great Hammersmith bed whose gold embroideries showed signs of recycling to the close observer: tell-tale pocket-holes indicated that the bedcover had been made out of old jackets. Like that of the Baron himself, its glitter was slightly second-rate.

La Trappe passed to one of the 'monks', Thomas Wyndham, who honoured his benefactor by putting up a monument to him in the grounds. It bore an inscription that, even by the funerary standards of the day, was reckoned excessive:

> In his early years he was sent by K. George I envoy extraordinary to K. Philip V of Spain, 1715; afterwards appointed, in commission with others, one of the lords of the Treasury: twice treasurer to the navy to K. George II and privy counsellor: in 1761 created a peer, and of the cabinet to K. George III. He was raised to these honours (himself an honour to them) rather by his eminent merit and great abilities, after experience both in the senate and in the council, than either by birth or fortune: and, if wit and true humour can delight; if eloquence can affect the heart, or literature improve the mind; if universal benevolence hath its charms; no wonder he lived admired and beloved by all that knew him, and died by all lamented.

This testimony in stone later found its way to Wiltshire, where it too was recycled: it was pressed into service to commemorate, not the death of a grandiloquent second-rater, but the recovery of his king from madness. Meanwhile, La Trappe itself had one of its unwonted periods of calm and then, in 1789, the same year that George III recovered, bounced back into

36 Elizabeth, Margravine of Anspach. Portrait after Joshua Reynolds

public notice as the home of a lively society hostess called Mrs Sturt. She was soon to be followed by a lady who was livelier still.

It seems scarcely possible that a house that had been owned by one character as colourful as Dodington should so quickly become the home of a second. But Elizabeth, Margravine of Anspach, almost outclassed poor Bubo in terms of memorability. Like Margaret Hughes, the Margravine was an actress, although not a professional one; in compensation, however, her whole life seemed to have been on a highly dramatic plane.

She was a daughter of the Earl of Berkeley; legitimate, but highly unwanted by her family, who were hoping for a son. After birth, she was allegedly wrapped up in a piece of flannel, dumped down on a chair in the birth-chamber, and left completely unnoticed for several hours until her great-aunt nearly sat on her. The great-aunt galvanised the servants and the neglectful countess into activity, and the child survived. At the age of thirteen, she was taken to Paris by her mother, fell in love with a fellow British aristocrat and eloped. Her family got her back. Three years later, she married another aristocrat, the future Lord Craven. After bearing her husband seven children, she quarrelled with him, set off on a prolonged tour round the courts of Europe and finally met Christian Frederick Charles Alexander, Margrave of Brandenburgh, Anspach and Bayreuth. Elizabeth, still married, bided her time; she stayed on at Anspach, established a court theatre and tried her hand at writing plays. At last, in September 1791, came the news she was waiting for: Lord Craven had died. Within a month, she had married the Margrave; within three, the pair were private citizens and owners of a fortune, for Christian Frederick, well aware of the political situation in Europe, had sold his sovereignty over Brandenburgh and Anspach to Prussia, and got out while the going was good.

In England, the Margrave and his new Margravine found that the stuffier elements of society viewed the former Lady Craven with disfavour. Queen Charlotte, wife of George III, refused to allow her at Court. (The Margrave firmly supported his wife by refusing to pay court to Queen Charlotte.) Less damaging but more hurtful was the greeting Elizabeth received from her own three daughters: the pious trio delivered the most formal of notes telling her that respect to their dead father prevented them calling. However, Christian Frederick and his wife found no difficulty in attracting more progressive minds to Dodington's old home, which they bought in 1792 and renamed Brandenburgh House. The Margravine had a splendid time doing it over, jettisoning some of Bubo's arrangements (the gallery was transformed into a ballroom, its marble floor being replaced by one of wood) and altering others to fit her taste. Shortly after the changes took place, Lysons wrote that:

> Her Highness's well-known taste has been shown in the improvements and decorations of the house, which are both elegant and magnificent. The state drawing-room, which is 38 feet by 23, and 30 feet in height, is fitted up with white sattin [*sic*], and has a broad border of Prussian blue in a gilt frame. At the upper end is a chair of state, over which is placed a picture of the illustrious Frederick of Prussia, the Margrave's uncle; the whole covered with a canopy, which is decorated with a very elegant and rich cornice. The cieling [*sic*] of this room was painted for Lord Melcombe, by whom also the very costly chimney-piece, representing (in white marble) the marriage of the Thames and Isis was put up. The ante-chamber contains several good pictures, and some very beautiful specimens of needle-work.

The pictures *were* good; around the house were various Van Dycks and Fragonards, a Murillo, a Rubens and Romney's portrait of the Margravine. In the case of the needlework, Lysons was perhaps being polite; the main example was a copy of Murillo's *Boys in Play* worked by the Margravine in worsteds.

However, Elizabeth did not stop at mere alterations. The Margrave had a large and constantly growing library, supplied by sources he employed to scour Italy and Germany for rare books, whilst the Margravine herself was as interested in drama as ever. From one of its corners nearest the river, the house sprouted a 150ft long curving conservatory which terminated at the water's edge in an odd-looking little building like a ruined church. It was the Margravine's own private theatre, built in the Gothic style favoured by her friend William Beckford for his very much bigger Fonthill Abbey. A ruin it may have appeared from the outside— the towers were even topped with vegetation—but the appointments within were luxurious. The local historian Thomas Faulkner, writing in 1839, called it 'one of the most elegant and convenient private theatres ever built in this kingdom'. Attached to it were a coffee-room, a billiard-room and the Margrave's library, which had been moved out of the house.

The little theatre itself could seat seventy people comfortably and here, before select audiences, the Margravine exercised her dramatic talents to her heart's content. Her main assistant was a member of her former family who had not broken with her: her son Keppel, whom she had taken with her from England and, in spite of promises to return him when he was

37 Interior of the Brandenburgh House theatre

71

eight, had kept under her auspices. Together, they worked away at writing, producing and acting in a string of presentations with romantic names such as *The Yorkshire Ghost*, *The Smyrna Twins*, *The Princess of Georgia* and *The Robbers*. 'These pieces', Faulkner tactfully continued, 'derived their principal interest from the admirable acting of the Margravine and her son, both of them being excellent performers and passionately fond of music.' (Elizabeth, of course, always took the female lead; although well into her forties by now, her preference was for playing melting heroines in their teens.) The two actor-managers ensured themselves an audience at all times by allowing the Hammersmith tradesmen they patronised to attend rehearsals with their families, while on performance days Hammersmith Broadway was choked with the audience's carriages. Ensconced in his box at the back of the house and surrounded by diplomats and the like, the Margrave himself appears to have enjoyed the show as much as anyone.

Christian Frederick died in 1806, leaving his wife an inheritance of almost £150,000. She continued to live at Brandenburgh House for another thirteen years and then moved to Naples. Her departure cleared the way for her home to become the scene, not for third-rate dramatic pieces such as *The Ghost*, but for real drama, played before an engrossed audience of thousands.

On 29 January 1820, King George III died. His son, the Prince Regent, became George IV and, to the new king's horror, his estranged wife Caroline became his queen. Their marriage had been almost ludicrously wretched. They appear to have hated each other on sight: Caroline was dismayed at the prince's girth, while the prince himself had made his famous demand for some restorative brandy. After the birth of their only child, Princess Charlotte, the couple split up and the prince later tried to prove her guilty of adultery. The attempt failed but, after the prince assumed the regency, Caroline finally decided to move as far away from the continuing war with her husband as she could. Like Elizabeth Craven before her, she left England for the continent, and she did not return until the death of her father-in-law.

When she came home in June 1820 to demand the honour due to her, it was to find that public sympathy, alienated by George's behaviour, was rapturously on her side. Greeted by wildly cheering crowds, she stayed first in South Audley Street and then in Portman Street. Meanwhile, the king's big battalions were being lined up against her, and in July a bill was brought before the House of Lords that would, if passed, achieve a double end: it would find the queen guilty of adultery with the major-

38 October 1820: crowds throng to present loyal addresses to Queen Caroline at Brandenburgh House. The theatre can just be seen on the far left

domo she had employed on her travels and would annul her marriage. The second reading—the 'trial' of Queen Caroline—was due to start on 17 August.

The crowds in Portman Street got larger and noisier by the day and Caroline, anxious for more privacy, began to think of moving. At first she chose a villa in Barnes. But the arrangement fell through, and she decided to rent a house familiar to her vice-chamberlain, Keppel Craven: Brandenburgh. On 3 August, she moved in and Hammersmith welcomed her with ecstasy.

For the next few months, the place went mad. Every sector of society—the mechanics of London, the parishioners of Shoreditch, the paper-hangers and the bricklayers, the women of Manchester, the Oddfellows, the United Guildries of Perth—wished to present loyal addresses to the queen they felt had been so cruelly wronged, and they all came to Brandenburgh House to do it. The grounds were packed and the river was crowded with boats. Pick-pockets had a field day, and so did youths in the crowd who took advantage of the trampled state of Brandenburgh's hedges to invade the fruit garden. Guns banged all the time out of sheer excitement, and one unfortunate was killed.

The presentations themselves were on occasion richly comic. The brasiers and brass-founders, for example, had arranged a procession in which almost every member carried a product of his trade. There were some with coal-scuttles, some with candlesticks, and one little party staggering under the weight of an immense fire-extinguisher. The deputation that entered Brandenburgh House was led by three men dressed *cap-à-pie* in armour and, as Caroline's contemporary apologist, Robert Huish, reported, they had an embarrassing time:

73

The knights were evidently overladen with their harness, and it was with infinite difficulty they could be dismounted on their arrival at Brandenburg-house. Dismounted they were at length, and they marched at the head of the deputation into the hall of audience, where the principal knight advanced in front of the rest, bearing in his hand a large brazen *baton*, headed with the crown. Having arrived 'with stately step and slow', immediately in front of the chair of state he knelt and laid his *baton* at the feet of her majesty, on the steps of the platform. The *baton* was explained by his attendants to contain the address; and whilst some of them placed it in the hands of her majesty's chamberlains, others assisted the knight to regain his perpendicular.

The queen was graciously pleased to hand him her written reply; then the presenter moved off, clanking and looking 'very awfully'.

But, in spite of these moments of unintentional hilarity and Hammersmith's general air of fiesta, the underlying mood of the crowds was deeply serious. It is impossible to say what the effect on Britain might have been had the bill been successful. The monarchy was deeply unpopular, Caroline's trial was fanning the flames of republicanism and, if George had succeeded in divorcing her, the results could indeed have been far-ranging. The suspense mounted, for the proceedings continued into September and then, after an adjournment, to November. Caroline was lent a house in St James's as her London base, but she generally returned home to Hammersmith in the evenings, the usual crowds thronging the thoroughfare. By the end of August, they had added a triumphant new catch-phrase to their cheering: *Non mi ricordo* ('I don't remember'). Its involuntary originator had been a key witness against the queen, Theodore Majocchi, who under cross-examination destroyed his credibility by using it time and time again. The division on the second reading of the bill took place, and resulted in a narrow Government majority of twenty-eight. And the division on the third reading resulted in an even narrower one. 'The ministers', Huish reported with a flourish,

> just saved their reputation for majorities by nine men; but this was so obviously insufficient for public purposes, to say nothing of their own promises in bringing the measure forward, that the bill, upon their own proposition, was immediately thrown out. The abortive bantling would not live . . . it was sick from the first, and nine men held it tenderly at the font in vain. It gave a last gasp and expired.

The inhabitants of London rejoiced by illuminating their houses; the queen gave thanks in Hammersmith Church.

She also applied to be given a royal palace. But her husband turned the request down, so it was again from Brandenburgh House that she set out in July the following year in her disastrous attempt to attend the Corona-

39 Caroline of Brunswick, heroine of the real-life drama at Brandenburgh House. Portrait by L. Lonsdale

tion. She was applauded when she arrived but, as she and her party trailed round Westminster trying to secure admission to the Abbey, the applause was ominously mixed with laughter and boos. Already ailing, she fell seriously ill a fortnight later and, in a ground-floor corner room on the landward side of Brandenburgh House, died during the night of 7 August. By accident, the door of the room was locked before her coffin was taken through to Brandenburgh's great hall to lie in state; no one could find the key, and in the end the undertaker's men had to take the lock off.

Caroline's body left Hammersmith on a pelting wet day, again watched by a huge crowd. The king had insisted that the funeral procession should not go through the city, but riots broke out and, after the deaths of two onlookers, the cortège eventually passed Temple Bar *en route* for Chelmsford and Harwich, where a ship was waiting to take the dead queen back to Germany. Within the year, her house had gone too. The contents—naturally thought to be hers—were sold in February 1822, and in May the house's fabric came under the hammer. Crispe's bricks were sold off, so were Dodington's marble chimney-piece and door pillars and so were the chandeliers, fittings and machinery from the theatre. While it would be tempting to see the king's vengeful hand in this disintegration—demolishing a potential shrine to his late wife would not, after all, be so different from denying her funeral the honour that was its due—the reason was in fact banal. The Margravine, still alive in Naples, gave the explanation in her *Memoirs*. The house, she wrote, was now

> completely levelled to the ground, the dry rot having got into the timbers, and as I never intended again to reside there, after I had been so long in Italy, I disposed of a portion of the land which surrounded it, and by the sale, which proved highly advantageous, with my accustomed good fortune, I was considerably benefitted. I think what was sold produced more than three times the sum which was given for it.

Her gain, and the future's loss.

❧ *Brooke House*

Near the point where Hackney's Upper Clapton Road meets Kenninghall Road and on the site now occupied by a comprehensive school, stood a house with an enormous talent for contrasts and surprises. Its owners included both Henry VIII and a family called Monro, specialists in the care of the insane; its visitors—for shorter or greater lengths of time—included Mary Tudor, John Evelyn (naturally) and the mentally deranged of the Georgian, Victorian, Edwardian and inter-war periods. It was pulled around and improved, often to remarkable effect, at least once every century between the sixteenth and the twentieth; it was damaged by water and fire, by German bombs, British lead thieves and Hackney children, some of whom were chased over its roof-tops by the local police. It reserved its greatest trick, however, to the very end. When it was demolished in 1954-5, there suddenly appeared among the dust and rubble a medieval wall-painting that had been whitewashed for years and that, in delicate reds and greens, showed St Peter with the house's likely builder: one William Worsley, Dean of St Paul's in the latter years of the fifteenth century. The discovery of the picture, in the house's final moments, did more than anything else to indicate when the house might have been built, and by whom.

Joined with documentary evidence, the picture suggested that the building that came be called Brooke House, Hackney, dated back in part

40 The Tudor courtyard at Brooke House, drawn in 1844 by George Toussaint

to the late 1470s. However, the house did not achieve the architectural glories for which it was famous until the century following, when it was transformed into a 'double-courtyard' building, roughly in the pattern used so spectacularly at Nonsuch (see page 214). The man responsible for the transformation was, according to the London County Council survey of Brooke House, in all probability Thomas Cromwell, King Henry's right arm in the matter of the English Reformation, and architect of his marriage to Anne of Cleves. The rebuilding took place in 1535. Oddly, though, the following year Cromwell gave his creation back to the king, and it was here that the twenty-year-old Mary Tudor, at last browbeaten into accepting her illegitimacy, met her father after a gap of five years and was officially 'reconciled' to him.

Later in the century, the house came into the possession of a relative of Anne Boleyn, Baron Hunsdon, and, although his occupancy was also of short duration, it was he who was responsible for Brooke's outstandingly important feature: a magnificent plaster ceiling in the building's Long Gallery. The gallery, with its estimated length of 174ft, must have caused some envy among other Elizabethan householders with pretensions to style; Hunsdon's particular contribution was to ornament its ceiling with

41 The chief glory of Brooke House: its long gallery and the Hunsdon ceiling, drawn in 1842 as it would once have have looked by John Burlison. The caption to the original drawing points out that, by this time, the gallery was divided into several rooms

the swans, stags, gryphons and eagles of his family crests, all divided up into squares, octagons and roundels.

Hunsdon lived in Hackney from 1578 to 1583. By the end of the century, his house had become the home of a peer whose family, Charles I later said, was one of the three 'ancientist' in Europe. (In fact, it was the property of the peer's wife.) Edward de Vere, seventeenth Earl of Oxford, was a colourful character whose many failings were perhaps matched by his talents. It has been suggested that he was the author of Shakespeare's plays. He certainly supported a private theatrical company and he wrote poems that were highly praised by his contemporaries. That other attitudes to the noble earl existed is indicated by the gleefully scurrilous gossip recorded by John Aubrey in the seventeenth century: when bowing to Queen Elizabeth, de Vere had an accident of an audibly personal nature and hurried abroad to live the affair down. On his return seven years later—having allegedly spent the staggering sum of £280,000—he was welcomed by the Queen with the double-edged remark, 'My Lord, I hadd forgott the Fart.'

In spite of de Vere's renown for his breeding, his literary talent, his extraordinary spending sprees, and his behaviour, which at times verged on the downright frightful (the shyness after his Court accident was a-typical), the house he lived in came by its permanent name from a family that required a century to rise to the dignity of their own earldom. They were the Grevilles. Sir Fulke Greville, one day to become the first Baron Brooke, took over the property a few years after de Vere's death in 1604. He was succeeded in the barony by his cousin, Robert, who let the house. Both, like de Vere before them, were literary men: Fulke wrote poems, plays and the well-known biography of Sir Philip Sidney, while Robert's subjects were theology and politics. Robert's widow returned to the Hackney family home, whose appointments were coolly summed up by Evelyn. 'I went to Hackney', the diarist noted in 1654, 'to see my Lady Brook's [sic] garden, which was one of the neatest and most celebrated in England, the house well furnished, but a despicable building.'

The seventeenth century, in fact, saw plentiful changes to Brooke House: bay windows, a new wing and, regrettably, partitions that made extra rooms out of part of the Long Gallery. But, as Evelyn noted, the house was a difficult one to bring up to prevailing standards and, at some point in the second half of the seventeenth century, the Grevilles moved away. In interesting contrast, however, Hackney itself was on the up-and-up as a desirable area, and, by the time that Defoe described it in the first quarter of the eighteenth century, it was 'so remarkable for the retreat of

42 Brooke House's Georgian block. Drawing by George Toussaint

Wealthy Citizens that there is at this time near a Hundred Coaches kept in it'. Meanwhile, the alterations to Brooke House continued: more partitions (the house was now divided into separate lodgings) and, in about 1758, a whole new Georgian block, built where the house's former great hall had been. This latest addition was an elegant one, but its appearance also signalled a plunge in the building's prestige. From being a baronial hall, it had been transformed into an upper-class lunatic asylum, and an asylum it remained until World War II; an astonishing time-span that covered treatment methods ranging from the primitive (cold baths but, in view of the inmates' social status, no shackles) to the post-Freudian.

This was by far the longest settled state in Brooke House's history. The next and final episode was much shorter, and much more eventful. In 1940, Brooke House was hit by a bomb. Afterwards, the now-empty building (the occupants had been moved away) presented a dismal appearance: most of the northern end had gone, the timber framework of the older parts had been shaken by blast, the roof was damaged. Miraculously, the former Long Gallery had escaped unharmed and so had its beautiful ceiling. Rain, however, was slowly dripping down on to it through the gaps in the tiles.

It could have been worse. An officer of the Society for the Protection of Ancient Buildings reported in 1942 that, in spite of the difficulties posed by nineteenth-century mutilations to the structure, 'efforts should be taken to preserve the building as it stands at present so that further consideration can be given to the problem of its reconditioning when the time comes and the use to which it is to be put is decided.'

A decision on this point came, in fact, fairly soon: in 1944, the area in which Brooke House stood was bought by the London County Council, and the house itself later passed to the keeping of the LCC's education committee. The idea was to use it as a county college. The LCC moved in with repair-and-protection works but these, though continuing, proved vain. Lead thieves added insult to injury by lighting fires on the premises they had ransacked, while the scapegraces of Hackney led the police a merry dance over the roof-tops. The costs of restoring the building were, of course, formidable and, against a background of lament, the ultimate fate of Brooke House became increasingly obvious.

In a 1954 leader, the *Hackney Gazette* asked what was to happen to a building that had strong connections with royalty and was also the 'shrine of the Shakespeare Fellowship, formed to advocate the claim of another owner, Edward de Vere, seventeenth Earl of Oxford, to be the author of Shakespeare's works.' The Fellowship itself had not been idle in the matter: slightly earlier in the year, *The Times* had reported its request to the LCC that part of the building should be kept and separated from new building work. The *Star*, meanwhile, reported a local petition that the building should become a youth centre. But there was no prevailing against the economic facts of the situation and, on 25 March 1954, the London *Evening Standard* spelt out the house's death warrant:

> Brooke House, the sixteenth-century manor house at Hackney, acquired by the London County Council in 1944, is to be demolished. A report to be presented to the council next Tuesday says that temporary repairs after heavy bomb damage cost £6,000. 'It soon became clear, however, that in view of the condition of the house and also of the wanton damage and theft, the restoration of all except the already demolished wing at the north end must be completed or the house demolished,' the report says. That would cost at least £75,000.

The LCC survey team recording its features before they vanished, Brooke House started to come down that year, and revealed among the ruins the wall-painting it had been hiding for so long. This was not the first time in its career that destruction had brought an unexpected gain— the bombing had revealed early window frames and a large archway into the court—but it was the most important. The painting was cleaned, photographed, removed and transported to the Museum of London, where it remains. But the house in which its anonymous fifteenth-century creator had expected it to stay is now only a memory.

When, in the early 1830s, the astonishing Sophia Daw decided to return to her native country, she brought with her a French title, a fortune and the intention of buying a country house. The property she chose was the modest seaside house of Bure Homage in Hampshire, then owned by the diplomat Baron Stuart de Rothesay. The baron—who, as British ambassador to Paris, knew all about Sophia—saw nothing to prevent him accepting her offer: 'Well, why not?' he is recorded as saying, 'I do not think she murdered the Duke.'

The duke the lady of Bure Homage did not kill was one of the great nobles of France, the Duc de Bourbon. Sophia, by contrast, was the daughter of an Isle of Wight fisherman, so poor that both he and Sophia lived for nine years in Newport Workhouse. At the age of fifteen, she became a maid-of-all-work in a local farm; at seventeen, she ran away to London, fell on hard times, then retrieved her fortunes by becoming the mistress of an army officer. When her lover left her, he handsomely made a settlement in her favour of £50 a year. Sophia, by now aware of her own worth, promptly sold it and invested the proceeds in an education. At about the same time, she met the duke, possibly while she was working as a servant in a Piccadilly brothel.

Almost immediately, Bourbon took the country girl on the make under his protection. She and her mother settled in the London house he took for them, and Sophia worked hard at enhancing her mind. (Interestingly, she became proficient in Greek as well as in the modern languages that would be of practical use to her.) When the war with France finally ended in 1815, the duke established his English mistress in Paris and, to give her a place in society, looked round for a suitable husband.

In 1818, Miss Daw—now declaring that she was the middle-class widow 'of a fictitious William Dawes—became the wife of Adrian Victor, Baron de Feuchères. Although the couple lived under the Bourbon roof, and although Sophia's relationship with the duke continued unabated, de Feuchères evidently took some time to realise that he was being duped. His early suspicions were lulled when Sophia (supported by the duke) told him that she was Bourbon's daughter, and the baron did not separate from his wife until 1822. Sophia weathered the ensuing scandal, went on living with her duke, and queened it over the upper reaches of French society.

43 Bure Homage in about 1890. The 'Frenchified villa' had lost little of its continental appearance in the fifty or more years since it was built

During her relationship with Bourbon, she had become an extremely rich woman: at the time of her marriage, for example, she was worth over 214,000 francs, all of it proceeding from the duke. In 1830, however, she suddenly became richer still. The duke died under bizarre circumstances—his body was discovered hanging from the handle of his bedroom window by two neckties—and, under the terms of his will, his mistress stood to gain an estate worth ten million francs, or £500,000. She was, of course, suspected of killing him.

The whole story was retold when, after her own death, a complex sequence of litigation started in settlement of her affairs. As recounted in a law report in *The Times*, Sophia's connection with France ended shortly after the case of the dead duke came before the French tribunals. 'The baroness', the report went on,

> was fully acquitted; nor, said the learned counsel, does any doubt now exist in the mind of any reasonable person upon the propriety of that verdict. After this event the baroness seemed to take a great distaste to France and came to this country apparently with the intention of residing permanently here, as she made several purchases in this country, amongst others the estate of Burr [*sic*] Homage, near Christchurch.

The Hampshire house on which Sophia spent some of her irregularly gotten gains was, though small, an enchantingly pretty one. It had started out as a farmhouse belonging to the Highcliffe estate, but Lord Stuart de Rothesay—then Sir Charles Stuart—had enlarged it to make a comfortable home in England for himself, his wife and his two small

83

44 The celebrator of Bure Cottage: Louisa Stuart, later the Marchioness of Waterford. Portrait by F. Grant

daughters, Charlotte and Louisa. Louisa, who later became the Marchioness of Waterford, left a detailed description of her parents' improvements. As quoted later by Augustus Hare, she wrote: 'I do not think I ever saw a more original elevation than that of Bure Cottage—a complete oval, surrounded by a green verandah, covered with clematis and honeysuckle. The drawing-room was an extended oval, and I used to admire what, in those days, was a novelty—a paper representing Swiss scenes.' Outside, she went on, there was a shrubbery crossed by a stream, flowerbeds with tiger-lilies and rose-pink carnations, greengage trees whose fruit could be picked through the windows, and a fine view of the Isle of Wight.

Life at Bure Cottage, as it was then called, presented an idyllic picture of a seaside home in the first quarter of the nineteenth century. The two little girls had writing lessons in the dining-room from an elderly local cleric, rambled round the garden, gorged on the fruit, and played on the sands.

The idyll was interrupted, however, when Sir Charles was recalled to Paris, and it was dispelled beyond recall when Bure Cottage was shortly afterwards sold to the Baronne de Feuchères. According to *The Times*, Sophia's story was summed up (by a judge, no less) as a 'romance of real life, more extraordinary than any he . . . had ever read'; but the romantic ambiance created by the cottage's curving verandah and its sweet-scented creepers clearly failed to impress her.

Of the £500,000 left her by the Duke, Sophia brought only £100,000 to England, but it was more than ample for her plans. With a portion of it, she had the Stuarts' house demolished and built a much larger one, heavy with Grecian inspiration. Outside, rows of columns marched along the façade; inside, guests entering the hall were edified by an imitation of the Parthenon frieze. The new house, which survived until 1957, could hardly have been called charming, but it was certainly more modish than its predecessor. Indeed, it was majestic, and its disappearance would one day represent an important gap in British country-house architecture. (In 1963, the Royal Commission on Ancient and Historical Monuments labelled it as of 'outstanding importance' and described its extinction as a 'serious loss'. The site was used by the armed forces for offices; one Bure Homage remnant, the former lodge, is now a fruit shop on Bure Lane.) Unsurprisingly, however, it made no appeal to at least one of the site's former occupants. In a lament for her own lost house, Lady Waterford scathingly condemned the new building as a 'Frenchified villa such as you might see in the Champs Elysées'. Nothing, she added, was left from the Bure Cottage days except the lawn, the medlars and quinces planted by Sir Charles and the gate that led to the sea.

Ironically, though, it was the women from the small house who prospered, while *grande dame* Sophia's fortunes were at last faltering. At the period that the Bure Homage mansion was being built, Louisa and her sister were emerging from their schoolroom chrysalises as startling beauties, and both made excellent matches. But Sophia's own beauty had vanished. Swollen with dropsy, she lived in Bure Homage for only four years. Ill though she was, she showed that she had lost none of her social aplomb: a member of the local gentry who refused to visit her got a sharp reminder of his social duty when she refused to tell her employees to vote for him. But her illness finally became so severe that she sold her country house and went to London to be near her doctors. The next year, 1840, she died, leaving behind her an estate in England and France of £200,000, a string of litigants, and a memorial to money earned in the classic manner by a woman who had started life as a pauper.

Myths do not necessarily relate to the ancient past. Canons, the great Edgware mansion that stood on the site now occupied by the North London Collegiate School, became something of a myth in its extremely short lifetime. Built by an amiable fraud and temporarily the home of one genius, it had mythical status quickly thrust upon it by a second genius of equal stature, aided and eagerly abetted by popular opinion. In 1731, only eight years after the building was finished, it achieved abiding fame as a byword for false magnificence. Both fame and the consequent efforts to disentangle fact from fiction have lasted centuries longer than the house itself.

At the beginning of the 1730s, Alexander Pope wrote his fourth *Moral Essay*; addressed to Richard Boyle, Earl of Burlington, it dealt with the use of riches, and in it the poet delivered a scathing and elaborate attack on a grandee with more money than taste, whom he dubbed Timon. 'Timon's Villa' was conceived on the most spectacular and most uncomfortable scale, with howling winds coming off the lake and blistering heat bouncing back from the terraces. Pope's own views on the perfect garden were summed up in the dictum, 'In all, let Nature never be forgot.' Timon, however, tortured his trees into statues, created complete forests of real statuary, imprisoned his grounds within a confining wall, and bemused the already suffering eye with his relentless addiction to symmetry. Once indoors, Pope sharpened his claws still further:

> His Study! with what Authors is it stor'd?
> In Books, not Authors, curious is my Lord;
> To all their dated Backs he turns you round,
> These Aldus printed, those Du Sueil has bound.
> Lo some are Vellom, and the rest as good
> For all his Lordship knows, but they are Wood.

Timon's chapel was also a monument to style rather than content: painted saints sprawled on the ceiling's gilded clouds, and modish music, 'broken and uneven', led worshippers' souls heavenwards in the most cheerful way possible. The worshippers' bodily comforts were catered for by cushions; their sensibilities were in the cosy care of a dean who 'never mentions Hell to ears polite'.

After chapel came dinner. Uncomfortable luxury was here again the rule:

> But hark! the chiming Clocks to dinner call;
> A hundred footsteps scrape the marble Hall;
> The rich Buffet well-colour'd Serpents grace,
> And gaping Tritons spew to wash your face.
> Is this a dinner? this a Genial room?
> No, 'tis a Temple, and a Hecatomb.
> A solemn Sacrifice, perform'd in state,
> You drink by measure, and to minutes eat.

By now, however, the tour round Timon's villa was almost over:

> In plenty starving, tantaliz'd in state,
> And complaisantly help'd to all I hate,
> Treated, caress'd, and tir'd, I take my leave,
> Sick of his civil Pride from Morn to Eve;
> I curse such lavish cost, and little skill,
> And swear no Day was ever past so ill.

It is now generally thought that Timon and his horrible house were amalgams, a composite portrait based on a whole gallery of contemporaries with more money than sense. Pope himself was later at pains to deny any intended connection between Timon's villa and Canons, on one occasion making another attack in verse on the tale-bearer 'who sees at Canons what was never there'. But, at the time, the public thought otherwise. Several characteristics lampooned in the *Epistle to Burlington*, though present in many houses, were also present at the great mansion in Edgware. Laguerre, one of the painters to whom Pope had ascribed the chapel's saints, had indeed done much work at Canons, including some in the local church of St Lawrence, rebuilt by Canons' owner. The Canons grounds

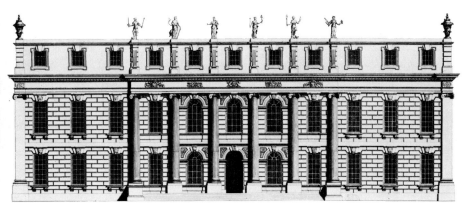

45 Canons, engraved by H. Hulsbergh, one of the very scarce surviving reproductions of Chandos's semi-legendary palace

46 More money than sense? James Brydges, first Duke of Chandos. Portrait attributed to H. van der Myn

did feature a grand terrace, a walled garden and a lake. There were quantities of statues. And in the middle of it all was Pope's Timon: His Grace the first Duke of Chandos, a man with money to burn.

The duke had been born James Brydges, son of a somewhat impecunious baron from the Welsh border country. Brydges made his way to the top in a classic fashion: he was energetic, he got to know the right people and he exploited to the full his ability to manipulate money. His great chance came in 1705 when, at the age of thirty-two, he was made Paymaster-General of the Forces Abroad. (The Duke of Marlborough was one of the influential friends he had made.) Brydges did what was then expected of someone in this position, but he did it with outstanding flair: what with the presents for services rendered, the mark-ups imposed on goods supplied and the personal returns on public money invested, the duke-to-be ended up with a fortune. One estimate put it at about £600,000, but an official inquiry into his dealings appeared to show that the much higher sum of £3 million was unaccounted for. However, nothing happened; Brydges' accounts were passed in the end, and the baron's self-made son from Herefordshire was created, first, Earl of Caernarvon and then, in 1719, Duke of Chandos.

By this time, he was already in possession of Canons, a Canons fit, and nearly ready, for a duke. It had come to him from the uncle of his first wife, Mary Lake, who died in the year before he left his paymaster's post in 1713. Less than a month after he did so, he started to turn the Elizabethan house he had acquired into a modern mansion. Shortly after that, he married again, and his second wife Cassandra, his first cousin, lived out the first decade of her marriage against a background of building works, decisions made and remade and rows with architects. In all, Brydges worked his way through at least three of these: William Talman, who was dismissed after some initial minor works and a subsequent fight over money; John James, who was too slow for Brydges' liking, and parted company with Canons after two years; and James Gibbs, who was probably responsible for the way Canons finally looked and who soldiered on with his rather difficult employer until about 1719.

Slowly, at a cost of about £200,000, the old Canons became the new one: an almost square stone-faced building round a court, adorned with columns and statuary and containing state rooms, living rooms for Their Graces, dressing-rooms for the same, their bedroom (just one; it had a white satin bed and a ceiling by the ubiquitous Laguerre), rooms for the domestics, a chapel and a library. This last was a magnificent room, the biggest on the first floor and positioned between the duke's dressing room and the duchess's with its adjoining ducal bedchamber. On his way to bed, Chandos would have had the chance to admire his collection of books and, among the wealth of *objets d'art*, the Grinling Gibbons carving of St Stephen's martyrdom, now in the Victoria and Albert Museum.

The general effect was indeed splendid, but, as the Bakers, biographers of both the duke and his house, point out, it was not as splendid as all that. 'People', they comment in *James Brydges, First Duke of Chandos*, 'have dizzily envisaged Chandos' palace as a creation vying with Blenheim, Castle Howard, and Hollywood. It was really nothing of the sort. The main building measured no more than 147 feet by 123 [puny when compared to, say, Gordon Castle]; its great dining-room was 15 feet 8 inches high, 45 feet wide, and 23 feet deep [not much bigger than the drawing room at Blyth Hall]; the state bedchamber was 18 feet 7 inches high, 21 feet wide, and 23½ feet deep.'

One of the odd things about Canons, and one that has certainly helped to confirm its mythical status, is the fact that very few pictures of the building appear to have survived and that, of these, none puts it in the context of its surroundings. For this reason, imagination can run riot. However, the deficiency is to some degree made good by contemporary descriptions of the palace, one of which appears in Daniel Defoe's *Tour Thro' the Whole Island of Great Britain*, published soon after the house was finished. Here he is on the subject of the grounds:

> The Avenues and Vista's to this House are extreamly Magnificent, the great Walk or chief Avenue is near a Mile in length, planted with two double rows of Trees, and the middle Walk broad enough for a Troop of Horse to march in Front; in the middle Way there is a large Basin or Fountain of Water, and the Coaches drive round it on either Side; there are three other Avenues exceeding fine, but not so very large; the Beauty of them all will double in time, when the Trees may be grown.

Still on the subject of the avenues, Defoe noted a curious optical illusion caused by the fact that the route to the main entrance in the south façade ran in one place towards the corner of the building. 'As it gives you the view of two Fronts, join'd as it were in one, the Distance not admitting you to see the Angle, which is in the Centre; so you are agreeably drawn in, to think the Front of the House almost twice as large as it really is.' This, perhaps, was one of the factors that gave Chandos's home its legendary reputation for grandeur.

Face to face with the building, Defoe noted the columns and statues shown in the Hulsbergh print. 'The whole Structure', he continued, letting himself go, 'is built with such a Profusion of Expence, and all finish'd

Laudatur et Alget
Juven . Sat .I.

47 (*left*) Daniel Defoe, who wrote that 'The Duke has spared no Cost to have every thing as Rich as possible.' Portrait by M. van der Gucht after J. Taverner and (*right*) 48 George Frederick Handel, Canons's most celebrated resident. Portrait by an unknown artist

with such a Brightness of Fancy, Goodness of Judgment; that I can assure you, we see many palaces of Sovereign Princes abroad, which do not equal it . . . the Duke has spared no Cost to have every thing as Rich as possible.'

No expense spared: this was the theme running all through Defoe's long account (and, of course, through its satirical counterpoint produced a few years later by Pope). Nothing but the best would do for the newly arrived Duke, and the rule applied to the smallest details. The doors to his state apartments were fastened with locks of gold or silver. His green-houses were full of devotedly tended pineapples. The grounds were protected by a private police force of Chelsea pensioner sergeants, ceaselessly patrolling the premises at night on the look-out for the foot-pads and ne'er-do-wells in which the Edgware area abounded. And His Grace's music was for a time composed by George Frederick Handel.

Canons was particularly famous for the music performed there by its resident 'concert'. Here is Defoe again:

91

> The Chapel is a Singularity, not only in its Building, and the Beauty of its Workmanship, but in this also, that the Duke maintains there a full Choir, and has the Worship perform'd there with the Best Musick, after the manner of the Chappel Royal, which is not done in any other Noble Man's Chappel in *Britain*; no not the Prince of *Wales's*, though Heir Apparent to the Crown.

The concert itself consisted of a range of singers from bass to treble, string and woodwind players and a trumpeter, of composers with various specialities and a chapel-master, or director. Handel came to Canons as resident composer in about 1717, stayed for at least two years and retained his connection with it for another year. It was there he composed the two Chandos *Te Deums* and the twelve Chandos anthems, which include 'O come let us sing unto the Lord'. It was there that he produced the masques *Acis and Galatea* and *Haman and Mordecai* (the latter was reworked later to become Handel's first oratorio, *Esther*). And it was there that he wrote his *Pièces pour le Clavecin*, among which is the so-called 'Harmonious Blacksmith'. Unfortunately for legend, however, it was not in the local parish of Whitchurch or anywhere else that he sheltered from the rain in a forge and gained the inspiration for the piece. Both the name and the delightful but wholly false tradition belong to the nineteenth century.

Chandos, as befitting someone whose fortune had derived from adroit book-keeping, had the most detailed records kept of the Canons household expenses; he was also a voluminous correspondent. So another of the odd things about Canons is the fact that nowhere is the production date for *Haman and Mordecai* mentioned. But records for plenty of other company occasions do exist: royalty, dukes, prominent figures from the political and financial worlds and local residents and family all called. But much of this hospitality took place against a background, not of a continuing rise to further glories, but its opposite. Chandos's activities in the Paymaster-General's office were only the first round of what was to be a lifetime of financial venturings. When the South Sea Bubble burst in 1720, Chandos reckoned he had made £900,000 and lost over £700,000 of it. Other mistakes followed; 'all he got by fraud is lost by stocks', as Swift commented nastily. However, the duke and duchess trimmed their sails to the wind, made savings and went on living at Canons. (The idea of building a London version of Canons in Cavendish Square was jettisoned, although the duke did erect two houses there and take over one of them.)

To Chandos's great grief, his wife Cassandra died in 1735. However, he was a man who treasured family life and, the next year, at the age of sixty-three, he brought his third duchess to Canons. Eight years later, he himself died, and although contrary to the Canons legend he did not die a ruined man, his passing also signalled the end of the magnificent house he had built. The next duke—his second son, Henry—was a different sort of character. While the fables about his father, however scurrilous, at least portrayed a man who thought large, the main one about the second duke concerned a squalid down-payment of £20 in a Newbury stableyard for a wife. (Her first husband, an ostler, had allegedly offered her for sale in the manner later made famous by Hardy's *Mayor of Casterbridge*.) In spite of his financial mishaps, the first duke ended up on more or less the right side of the ledger, but his son was nothing like as good a manager. The cause of subsequent events at Canons is a mystery, but the Bakers point out that Henry's ill-management and thriftlessness were probably at the bottom of it. He certainly worked fast: in 1747, three years after the old duke's death, a dispersal of fixtures and fittings began that would take bits of Canons all over the country. The grand marble staircase went to the Earl of Chesterfield's London house in Mayfair; when this, too, was demolished (in 1937), the staircase went to a Broadstairs movie-house that was bombed in World War II. The chapel windows, painted with scenes from the New Testament, went to Witley Court in Worcestershire. The portico is usually thought to have gone to Wanstead House (see page 261), although Lawrence Weaver, writing in *Country Life* in 1916, found part of it gracing Hendon Hall. A statue of George I on horseback, which had once stood in the middle of the lake, ended in Leicester Square where, in 1873, it finally succumbed to the attention of vandals.

At last, the building itself came down and, in the 1750s, a new owner built himself a new and smaller Canons from the wreckage (and on the foundations) of the first one. Even this newer building had a certain power to generate legend: one of its later owners was Major Dennis O'Kelly, owner of the superlative racehorse Eclipse. The story ran that the stuffed body of the late champion adorned the new Canons hall; in fact, skeleton and skin went separate ways, one to the Natural History Museum and the other, stretched out on a frame, to a local vet. As with the first Canons, so with this minute part of the second: the tale is one of glory, demise and final fragmentation.

The seventeenth-century diarist John Evelyn is often quoted in this book. He frequented many houses that have now vanished, and the detail in which he described them is pleasingly supplemented by his frank and often icy comments on their owners' taste. Inevitably, the picture he usually gave was of a single stage in a house's career, but there are some buildings whose history he witnessed from the very beginning to the very end. One of these is the second of the great Piccadilly mansions mentioned earlier: Clarendon House, also known as Dunkirk House.

According to Evelyn's fellow-diarist, Samuel Pepys, the name of the port attached itself to the building even before it was fairly up. Later, in June 1667, Pepys described how the house had been attacked by a window-smashing, tree-vandalising mob who stuck up an explanatory placard with the words:

> Three sights to be seen;
> Dunkirke, Tangier, and a barren Queene.

As the mob howled and the trees splintered, far more serious damage had been wrought at Chatham, where the Dutch, then at war with England, had attacked the fleet and burnt some of the country's best ships.

The Dutch war, the sale of the English possession of Dunkirk to France, the marriage of King Charles II to the barren Catherine of Braganza—all three national disgraces were, in the public mind, laid at the door of one man, and laid literally. The man was Edward Hyde, first Earl of Clarendon and owner of the mansion round which the London crowd had swarmed. Hyde was an important architect of the Restoration and had benefited enormously from its success: the benefits included an earldom, wealth, enormous power and the position of father-in-law in the royal house (his daughter Anne was the wife of the Duke of York, later James II). Clarendon House, which he started to build in 1664, was a spectacular symbol of his achievements; its alternative name was an equally clear indication of his standing with the public at large.

The house stood where Albemarle Street now runs and faced down towards St James's Palace. It had been built to the designs of a friend of Evelyn, Sir Roger Pratt. As young men, Pratt and Evelyn had known each other in Italy and, on returning to England, Pratt had become a highly successful 'gentleman architect'. His first triumph had been

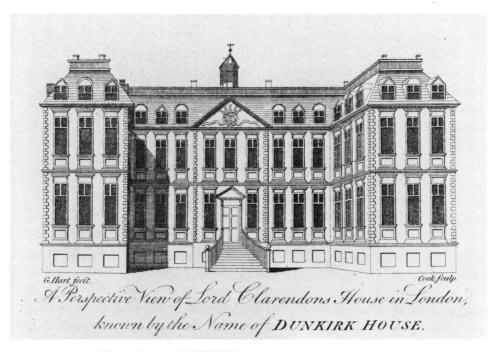

G.Hart fecit.

Cook sculp.

A Perspective View of Lord Clarendons House in London, known by the Name of DUNKIRK HOUSE.

49 Lord Clarendon's house in Piccadilly, also known derogatorily as Dunkirk House

50 Edward Hyde, Earl of Clarendon. Portrait by D. Loggan

Coleshill, the house he created for his cousin, Sir George Pratt, and Clarendon was his most prestigious commission to date. (It was perhaps unfortunate that the materials purchased by the earl for the building included some that were originally designated for repairing the predecessor to Wren's St Paul's.)

Evelyn first mentioned Clarendon House on 15 October 1664, when he dined with Clarendon and his wife at their then home in the Strand.

> After dinner my Lord Chancellor and his lady carried me in their coach to see their palace . . . building at the upper end of St. James's-Street, and to project the garden. In the evening I presented him with my book on Architecture, as before I had done to his Majesty and the Queen Mother.

(Planning or 'projecting' gardens was one of Evelyn's great delights.) In January 1666, he was writing to Clarendon's son, Lord Cornbury, as follows:

> I acknowledge that I have never seen a nobler pile . . .. When I had seriously contemplated every room (for I went into them all), from the cellar to the platform on the roof, seen how well and judiciously the walls were erected, the arches cut and turned, the timber braced, their scantlings and contignations disposed, I was most highly satisfied.

For obvious reasons, Evelyn could not be absolutely frank on this occasion and, as his *Diary* reveals, his real opinion of the house was, 'a goodly pile to see to, but had many defects as to the architecture'. He was not as overwhelmed by his old friend's talents as the letter to Cornbury implied. However, the business of fitting out the building interested him keenly, and he compiled a list of English notables whose portraits should, he urged, hang in the mansion's galleries: the subjects included Sir Walter Raleigh, the Earl of Leicester, Lady Jane Grey and the Venerable Bede.

On 26 April 1667, Evelyn stated that the house was at last finished: 'My Lord Chancellor showed me all his newly-finished and furnished palace and library.' It had taken £50,000 and 300 men to build, and the result was a stately building glittering with windows. In front of it, between the house and the street, lay a vast court, the immensity of which is emphasised in one contemporary print by the solitary figure of a manservant exercising a dog. It was bounded by the customary high wall of the period and in front of this grew the trees that suffered at the hands of the rioters.

Pepys, attracted by Evelyn's reports of Clarendon House, visited the building while the work was in progress and forecast that it would indeed be glorious. In the minds of the cognoscenti, the forecast was amply

51 The site of Clarendon House on Piccadilly as it is today. The Qantas office marks the south-east corner of Clarendon's former domain

borne out, and Clarendon himself was delighted with his new mansion. He went further than that: he loved it, and it is easy to picture the pride with which he showed his old friend Evelyn round its apartments. But the London public felt otherwise. It was firmly believed that the earl had financed his building project with the aid of a huge bribe received during the Dunkirk affair; the mob rumbled and grumbled and, two months after Clarendon had happily taken the diarist on his tour of inspection, it erupted. The Dutch were in the Medway laying waste to the

97

English fleet, London was in a panic; the necessary scapegoat was duly found.

Clarendon's house survived the attack, but Clarendon's career plummeted. In August, he was forced to give up office, and his enemies in Parliament and at Court gathered round for the kill. Late in the year, Evelyn paid him a last visit and drew a pathetic picture of a beaten man: 'I found him in his garden at his new-built palace, sitting in his gout wheel-chair, and seeing the gates setting up towards the north and the fields. He looked and spake very disconsolately. After some while deploring his condition to me, I took my leave. Next morning I heard he was gone.' The fevered accusations against Clarendon failed but his flight to France was immediately confirmed by an official order banishing him. He died in exile in 1674. Clarendon House passed to his son who, plagued with debts, sold it to the second Duke of Albemarle for half the amount the mansion had cost to build.

Albemarle, who renamed the house after his dukedom, was the son of the renowned General Monk and a hard-drinking, high-living wastrel. He galloped through his patrimony and inevitably the house changed hands again. 'It fell', Evelyn reported, 'to certain rich bankers and mechanics, who gave for it and the ground about it £35,000; they design a new town, as it were, and a most magnificent piazza.' The duke went off to Jamaica on a hare-brained scheme to raise a sunken Spanish galleon; improbably, he succeeded, but died shortly afterwards. His wife, however, lived to become the mistress of another great London house, if under rather different circumstances (see page 210).

Nineteen years after he had witnessed the building of Clarendon House, Evelyn was present at its end. On 19 June 1683, he and Clarendon's son happened to drive down Piccadilly, and at the top of St James's Street drew level with a scene of great activity. 'When passing', the tactful diarist recalled,

> by the glorious palace of his father, built but a few years before, which they were now demolishing, being sold to certain undertakers, I turned my head the contrary way till the coach had gone past it, lest I might minister occasion of speaking of it; which must needs have grieved him, that in so short a time their pomp was fallen.

In September, he was back, watching a 'little army of labourers and artificers' laying foundations for the buildings that the new owners planned to erect on the site. 'It is said,' he noted, 'they have already materials towards it with what they sold of the house alone, more worth than what they paid for it. See the vicissitudes of earthly things!'

Two outstanding creations can be accredited to Henry Fiennes Pelham Clinton, second Duke of Newcastle under Lyme. The first was Clumber House, one of the great mansions built in the area of Nottinghamshire dubbed the 'Dukeries' by virtue of the number of ducal estates it contained. The other was the thick-set, amiable breed of spaniel that bore the house's name. In this case, however, the dog it was that lived; the house vanished in 1938, pushed into oblivion by heavy taxation.

Both started their careers at roughly the same time, in about 1770, two years after Henry had inherited the dukedom from his uncle. The duke was a man of rural tastes, and he was also undaunted by the general view that his new estate, Clumber Park, was a rabbit-ridden heath. He started building, choosing as his site the spot occupied by a ducal hunting lodge. And, as his architect Stephen Wright was producing his designs for a classical building of white stone, flanked by a square wing at each corner, Henry busied himself with the smaller of his two projects: mating spaniels to basset hounds, culling the failures and training the rest to the gun.

The new breed throve; so did the building and, towards the end of the decade, it was ready to take its place alongside Welbeck and the area's other great residences. Since Wright had to incorporate the old hunting lodge into the centre of the building, the rooms here were not particularly grand. However, the apartments in the flanking wings made up for this, particularly the large dining-room. After later alterations, a *Country Life* of 1908 described this apartment in terms that showed the effect Wright had originally achieved.

> It is a pity that, at the partial rebuilding of the house, two new features were added to this room. One of these is a huge and somewhat pretentious door and doorway of mahogany, with curved and carved pediment whose crude colour and florid decoration kill the beautiful old doors with their restrained ornament and subdued tone. Again, the original ceiling is one of great beauty. Its beams and the ribbing or framework of its panels are delicately worked in plaster scrolls raised and gilt. They thus form a full and sufficient decorative design which demands a plain background. That, no doubt, it originally had, but it is now confused by the elaborate and highly-coloured painted ornamentation which covers the ceiling.

Delicacy and restraint may have been the hallmark of the building's interior, but outside the second duke was determined to go all the way. The house was already sited on the banks of a small river, the Poulter; at the cost of £7,000, the river was dammed to form a lake almost two miles long. At the same time, the heathland was reclaimed, the rabbits evicted, and sheep and forest trees were brought in in their place. One near-contemporary, with a charming turn of phrase, wrote that the whole effect 'paradised the mind'.

Henry died in 1794 and, after a year (during which a short-lived third duke came and went), the Poulter paradise came into the hands of its most famous, even notorious, owner: Henry Pelham Fiennes Pelham Clinton, fourth Duke of Newcastle from the age of ten. This second Henry was a great acquirer of *objets d'art* and children (he had eleven; his wife died giving birth to a final two). He was also an ardent loather of mobs, parliamentary reform and the general idea that his social inferiors should have a voice in the running of things. His adult career started, oddly enough, in jail when, fresh from Eton, he went on a young gentleman's tour of Napoleonic Europe and was imprisoned by the French for four years. On being freed, he assumed the role expected of him by becoming a twenty-four-year-old Lord Lieutenant of the county. He also put the ducal finances on a sound basis by marrying a wife, *née* a Miss Mundy, who injected £190,000 into the family funds.

Although he could have settled back to live happily among his offspring, possessions and honours, the third owner of Clumber House also possessed a talent for controversy. He disapproved of both Roman Catholics and Dissenters, and he said so. He made no secret of his distaste for the way in which refugee monks and nuns were allowed to take shelter in Britain. In 1830, he heard that a group of his tenants at Newark had voted contrary to his wishes. He threw them out, and justified himself with a sentence that summed up all the feelings of Property Outraged: 'Is it not lawful for me to do what I please with mine own?'

Unsurprisingly, his property suffered drastically the following year when, aroused to fury by his opposition to the 1831 Reform Bill, the people of Nottingham set fire to his other great house, Nottingham Castle, and burned it to ashes. Reactionary though he may have been, the duke was by no means lacking in courage. Instead of staying in London, where the shutters of his house protected him against the stones of the London mob, he came dashing up to Clumber to face the worst. He made his preparations as best he could—his house was fortified, his possessions hidden, his family tucked away in a dwelling in the grounds—and waited. The mob, however, never came; it is hard to imagine whether the colours-to-the-mast duke was thankful or sorry. Either way, he went on fighting reform in all its manifestations—indeed, he took a positive pride in his

52 Clumber House as the fourth Duke of Newcastle knew it, in 1826. The size of the flag
seems in keeping with the duke's attitude to his possessions

firmness of attitude—and, in the end, he reaped a harvest that even he
must have regretted. He refused to countenance two Dissenters as local
magistrates, and told the Lord Chancellor of his decision in the rudest of
terms. He was invited to withdraw his letter; he refused again and, as a
result, was sacked from the lord-lieutenancy.

Although the fourth duke suffered financially at the passing of the
1832 Reform Act (he estimated that loss of control over six boroughs had
cost him £200,000), he still had a fortune large enough to allow him to
beautify Clumber as best he thought fit. In 1840, the expenditure of
£350,000 brought him one of his great ducal neighbours, Worksop
Manor, partially rebuilt after a fire and then left in a half-finished state.
Newcastle dealt with his acquisition in a traditional way: he plundered it
for its materials, having first transferred its paintings, books and statuary
to Clumber. Further additions to the Clumber collections were made by
his successors and, by the third quarter of the nineteenth century, the
house's contents included paintings by Rembrandt, Rubens, Van Dyck,
Poussin, Gainsborough, Holbein and Breughel. Amongst other treasures
were three Caxtons, a first folio Shakespeare, a medieval Book of
Hours that had once belonged to Isabel of Brittany, four Roman altars,
a marble fireplace that had come from William Beckford's even more
remarkable treasure-horde at Fonthill Abbey and, outside on the lake, a

101

three-masted frigate, whose function was principally to enhance the view.

The fourth duke's main effort in the building line had been a mausoleum for his wife, whose last ill-fated childbed had taken place in 1822. In 1857, his successor called in Sir Charles Barry to enlarge the house. But, just over twenty years later, a disastrous fire forced the seventh duke, or rather his trustees since yet again the duke was under age, to start building afresh. The fire, in addition to destroying many of the Clumber treasures, ravaged the central part of the building; when the flames were brought under control, the building's wings stood up round a hollow shell while the surviving books and statues lay in snow-covered heaps by the lake.

The trustees were faced with a considerable problem, for the sixth duke (who had died a month before the fire) had been a highly extravagant spender and had made notable inroads on the estate. However, the ducal family pulled through: 'Their rent roll is vast', commented a Mr Jacks in 1881 in his guide to Nottinghamshire mansions, 'and if the Dukes of Newcastle cannot buy pictures like those which were destroyed in the last fire, they have been enabled to rebuild their house on a sufficiently magnificent scale, and at a very considerable cost to repair the damage that had been done to brickwork and masonry and to internal decoration.' The man in charge of the operation was now Charles Barry, first son of the great Sir Charles, and his solution to the loss of eighteen rooms in the heart of the house was a boldly simple one, inspired by plans made by his father: he replaced them with an enormous entrance saloon with balustraded galleries, tessellated pavements and abundant niches for the rescued Clumber statuary.

53 Clumber refashioned, taken in 1907

The seventh duke, in whose name Clumber had been recreated, died in 1928 at the age of sixty-four. A decade after his death, Clumber itself went too. The years between the wars (and especially the 1930s) saw a continuing dispersal of the house's contents: a bowl specially made for a Renaissance Pope, pictures, Isabel's Book of Hours. The final clearance took place in 1937, by which point the Earl of Lincoln, heir to the eighth duke and inheritor of Clumber from the seventh, was living in the smaller and less echoing surroundings of the vicarage next door. In May the following year, the local press reported that he planned to build himself a new house by the lake, and the same papers also stated that the demolition of Clumber had begun. 'The decision', the *Guardian* and the *Journal* said, 'completely to demolish the mansion has been taken with great reluctance by the present owner, the Earl of Lincoln, but it is necessitated by heavy taxation.' Scarcely more than a century had elapsed since the fourth duke had barricaded his home against all comers, but such basic methods of defending one's own seemed to belong to an unimaginably distant past.

❧ Deepdene

In 1969, a demolition took place in Surrey that, in architectural terms, was somewhat akin to having an eye-tooth out. The house demolished— Deepdene, on the fringes of Dorking—was one of the most notable British houses of the nineteenth century designed in the deliberately assymmetrical style called Picturesque. Surrounded by a spectacular garden, it was famous for the way its design married house and garden at a period when the majority of older country houses firmly kept the two apart. And, most remarkable of all, it represented a stylistic bridge between two other famous buildings that, on the face of it, seemed wildly dissimilar: Fonthill Abbey in Wiltshire, the astonishing Gothic creation of William Beckford, and Osborne, Queen Victoria's seaside home in the Isle of Wight (see page 233). At the outset of its career as a building of note, Deepdene was the home of the extremely wealthy writer and collector, Thomas Hope; at the end of it, just before its final change of hands to developers, it was being used by British Rail office staff. The rhododendrons for which the grounds were noted are present today, but the park is now bisected by the A24, while the site is occupied by an office building also called Deepdene House. The disappearance of its predecessor, commented Nairn and Pevsner in the 1971 edition of *Surrey* in the *Buildings of England* series, was a 'disgraceful and depressing story'.

It was the gardens rather than the house that first brought the estate into lasting notice. 'I went to Dorking', wrote a visitor in 1655, 'to see Mr Charles Howard's amphitheatre, garden, or solitary recess, being 15 acres environed by a hill. He showed us divers rare plants, caves, and an elaboratory [laboratory].' The visitor, of course, was the diarist John Evelyn; it would have been surprising if, as a garden enthusiast who had been born in the area, he had not gone to call. John Aubrey, writing slightly later, described how the garden's 'hope' or valley was planted full of cherries, myrtles, orange trees and syringas, and contained no less than twenty-one different varieties of thyme. The house at the heart of all this scented beauty was, however, rather plain; it was, Aubrey went on, 'not made for grandeur, but retirement: a noble hermitage, neat, elegant, and suitable to the modesty and solitude of the proprietor'.

In the eighteenth century, the grandson of Evelyn's host at Deepdene succeeded to the dukedom of Norfolk, and his own successor rectified the plainness of the house by pulling it down and building a Palladian man-

54 The duke's Deepdene, with some of Hope's additions. Note the tower. From Prosser's *Select Illustrations of the County of Surrey*

sion in its place. Thomas Hope bought it at the beginning of the nineteenth century and, in the century's second decade, set about creating a Deepdene Mark III.

Unlike the duke, he did not pull down the earlier house; instead, it became the core of a building that spread in a pleasingly irregular way in all directions. Gone was the preoccupation with symmetry that had until very recently dominated the British idea of how a great house should look. New ideas were in the air—ideas that were the architectural equivalent of the Rousseauesque cults of nature and sensibility—and Hope, always abreast of contemporary thought, was extremely receptive to them. With help from the architect William Atkinson, the Palladian mansion acquired a neo-classical carriage front with a semi-circular porch, battlements on the skyline and a tower that G. F. Prosser's contemporary account of Surrey houses described as 'constructed in the Tuscan or Lombard style'. On one side of the house, to the east, a separate kitchen block was built; round the corner to the south, another wing grew up that brought the garden right into the house via a sequence of conservatories.

Mixed though the details may have been in terms of style—and this indeed was Hope's intention—the overall emphasis was on the architecture of the Mediterranean. However, a link has been deciphered with that most un-Italianate of buildings, Fonthill Abbey. James Lees-Milne,

55 Deepdene in its final form; the view from the south-west

writing of Beckford's later building work at Bath, acknowledges that Beckford was here influenced by the product of the Hope/Atkinson partnership. 'But conversely', he goes on, 'Hope and Atkinson had been influenced by Beckford in that The Deepdene was a late outcrop of the Picturesque harvest of which Fonthill Abbey had been perhaps the earliest, albeit a Gothic one.' The link with Queen Victoria's Osborne was present, too, and in a very obvious shape. The house would grow much more Italianate as the century went on, but the already present tower was a feature that became a favourite with the Victorians, and one that Thomas Cubitt, who was one day also to settle in the Dorking area (see page 110), repeated twice over in the seaside house he built for the young queen and her husband.

To have created Deepdene was by any account an achievement of some magnitude. But it was far from being Hope's only one. The activity that probably brought him the greatest fame in his lifetime was his writing, notably on aesthetics and architecture. (His *Household Furniture and Internal Decorations, Executed from Designs by the Author* commanded widespread attention, including that of Beckford.) But he also produced the Byronic novel *Anastasius, or Memoirs of a Modern Greek*. Written at the close of the eighteenth century, this moved Byron himself to tears of envy and the public to much admiration.

In addition to producing his own very real contributions to the arts, Hope also collected those of others. Indeed, he went further and encouraged others to produce them. One of his protégés was the artist and sculptor John Flaxman, whom he commissioned to illustrate Dante's *Divine Comedy*. Another was the Danish sculptor Bertel Thorwaldsen, whose career might have foundered without him. When Hope and Thorwaldsen met, the Dane had been studying in Rome and had come to the end of his grant. The only thing that stood between him and a forced return home was a model he had produced for a statue of Jason and the Golden Fleece. There were no takers, until Hope, filling in time while a travelling companion extricated himself from a tangle over passports, visited the young sculptor's studio. He approved of the model, commissioned it to be executed in marble and set Thorwaldsen on the road to international success.

The *Jason* came to Deepdene, where it occupied a prominent position in Hope's new sculpture room adjoining the conservatory. So did the works of other sculptors, ancient and modern; so did the Hope Diamond, once the property of Marie Antoinette and one of the largest blue diamonds in the world. And so did paintings by Watteau, Veronese, Raphael, Correggio and Sir Joshua Reynolds. But the building that housed them was, by the middle of the century, not quite the one that Hope had created, for his son Henry enlarged it in 1840 and emphasised its Mediterranean look still further. However, many of the Deepdene traditions continued. The collecting went on and so did the encouragement of endeavour in the arts: Benjamin Disraeli conceived his political novel *Coningsby* at Deepdene, wrote part of it there and dedicated it to his host. In the older Hope's days, Deepdene was open to view by interested members of the public; unusually for the period, the tradition was maintained even after the younger Hope's death. And the gardens were, as always, magnificent: 'The Dene itself, a long steep glade, carpeted with turf, and closed in by a woody amphitheatre, opens close to the house,' wrote James Thorne in 1876 in his guide to the environs of London.

> The lower part forms a flower-garden; and the whole scene, with its occasional cypresses and sunny patches of greensward, is of almost unequalled beauty. A walk leads to the upper part, through a beech-wood, in which much of the undergrowth consists of self-sown rhododendrons . . .. A large tulip-tree on the lawn fronting the house should not pass unremarked. It measures 10ft in circumference.

In the 1890s, Deepdene was let to Lily, Duchess of Marlborough who, in 1895, married Lord William Beresford, and whose visitors in Surrey

56 A further manifestation of the picturesque: Thomas Hope in oriental dress. Portrait by W. Beechey

included the Prince of Wales and the young Winston Churchill. Later guests at Deepdene were at the other extreme of respectability: the house was sold in 1920 and, by the thirties, it had become a hotel famous for the neon sign on the roof, the illicit liaisons that flourished in the bedrooms and the witchcraft allegedly practised in the grounds. Its then tenant was one Peter Mazzina who had as backer the notorious honours-peddlar Maundy Gregory. Mazzina went bankrupt in 1936 and, a few years later, the Deepdene Hotel was bought by the Southern Railway Company.

In 1965, a reporter from the *Dorking Advertiser* visited Deepdene and drew a tragic picture of contrasts between past and present.

Decades of vandals have been at work in the house. Tall, thin panelled doors have been ripped off their hinges. Others have had ventilation panels cut into them. Layer upon layer of cream and brown paint has been encrusted indiscriminately over everything, burying fine wood carvings, marble and gilding alike. The fine mahogany bookcases now hold files, their light, concave shelves replaced by fittings heavy enough to take ledgers . . .. Nobody now knows which was the Etruscan room with its unique collection of vases, or the Pompeiian room which once held the statue of Minerva found in 1797 at the mouth of the Tiber. Only the entrance hall can still be identified. The niches, each of which once held Roman statues, are now used by messengers. The fine double staircase is now blocked in with hardboard. And the gallery it leads to, once lined with paintings by Rubens, is now full of wooden racks stacked high with more files.

He added that the railwaymen could not be given all the blame; the house itself had done its bit by shedding gold leaf from the canteen ceiling into the workers' teacups. In 1966, however, the workers all left and, after standing empty for almost two years, Deepdene was sold for development. The office block that, among much controversy, replaced it won a commendation from the Concrete Society, particular note being taken of the way the building fitted into its surrounding landscape; unexpectedly, the key characteristic of the old Deepdene had managed to survive.

If the nineteenth century's pursuit of wealth and progress had ever been officially elevated to a religion, the builder Thomas Cubitt would have been one of its leading saints. As it was, he was one of its commercial heroes. He produced, not machines, but districts: large parts of Belgravia, large parts of Bloomsbury and parts of Clapham and Brighton. He built workshops, villas, and the homes of royalty; Osborne (see page 233) was one of his creations, as was part of Buckingham Palace. More importantly still, he fulfilled all the demands that the Victorian period made of those whom it wholeheartedly revered.

He had, for example, started at the bottom, as a journeyman carpenter. In his obituary, his professional journal, *The Builder*, commented that 'the uncertainty attending such a position made a deep and lasting impression on his mind, and stimulated him to unceasing exertion, in order to obtain a more independent position.' The result of his exertion was that he became a millionaire. He was also public-spirited: he worried over smoke abatement and helped to found Battersea Park; he was extremely generous to his employees, to schemes such as the Great Exhibition (for which he offered a financial safety-net) and to good causes. And—a minor requirement, but one that the Victorians found helpful when dealing with self-made men—he showed himself aware that wealth should be accompanied at the very least by the status of a country gentleman.

In fact, he left compliance with this last point rather late, and it was only in the last decade of his life that he bought the house and estate of Denbies, above Dorking on the opposite side to Deepdene and within commuting distance of London. The most noticeable features of his purchase were its woods and the views through and over them: Box Hill, Dorking itself and the South Downs. Just outside the grounds lay Ranmore Common where, according to John Dennis's *Hand-book of Dorking*, 'the eye wanders over an ample surface of wild heath land, about which several small cottages are scattered at intervals, while far beyond this foreground, is an extensive landscape, and if the tourist look in the direction of London, he will see St. Paul's Cathedral and Westminster Abbey.'

Denbies itself was a two-storey Georgian mansion which even its most ardent admirers appeared to find small and pokey. Writing in the 1820s, G. F. Prosser was tactful, but the best he could manage was, 'the apartments, though not spacious, are convenient'. But the house compensated to some degree for its deficiencies by boasting a collection of remarkable previous occupants, of which the first was the most remarkable of all. He was Jonathan Tyers, proprietor of the famous Vauxhall Gardens during the eighteenth century and a man of complicated tastes.

The pleasure gardens of Vauxhall had been in existence under their earlier name of Spring Garden since the early years of the eighteenth century, but it was Tyers who, in 1732, revived them and took them to the peak of fame. Success came immediately and patrons united in praise of the music, the illuminations, the charming groupings of trees, walks and pavilions. Until 1752, Tyers was only Vauxhall's tenant, but in that year he purchased the gardens outright. Two years later, he signalled a further access of wealth by buying the former home of a Surrey farmer called Denby and rebuilding it as a gentleman's residence. The house became a run-of-the-mill Georgian establishment, but the garden was something else again. Tyers, to the amazement of all who penetrated the domain, turned it into a sort of 'anti-Vauxhall', with mementoes of death rather than life, pain rather than pleasure. His London business had been called Spring Garden; a wood he planted on the estate was named Il Penseroso, after Milton's poem. Ornaments of the gardens included a

57 Denbies I, home of Jonathan Tyers and the Denisons. From Prosser's *Select Illustrations of the County of Surrey*

111

58 Denbies II, the mansion that builder Thomas Cubitt built for himself

statue of Handel playing a lyre. Il Penseroso, however, was adorned with life-size statues showing the Christian and the Unbeliever in their last moments. A small temple, Prosser recalled, was decorated with 'many inscriptions of a serious character', while two human skulls, male and female, grinned down from a pedestal at the end of one of the walks. Tyer's final comment—if it was a comment—on the vanity of worldly success was yet another statue: it represented Truth trampling the mask of illusion underfoot.

The creator of these bizarre surroundings lived to enjoy them (and, just possibly, the joke) for another thirteen years. But they were not appreciated by his successors, who tore them down. After some brisk changes of hand, the house was bought by a Mr Joseph Denison, who gave his name to the hill on which Denbies stood, and who reacted to wealth and success in a far less twisted fashion than Tyers had done. He was fixated by lamb; the alleged reason was that, when he had come to London as a penniless young northerner, his first dinner had been scraps left over from a leg of roast mutton. In his later years at Denbies, he had roast mutton served every day, and even went to the point of selecting the joint himself; Dorking inhabitants were quite used to the sight of this painstaking old buffer trudging back home up the hill, leg of mutton in his arms. He was followed at Denbies by his son, a Member of Parliament and another pleasant character, who let Dorking residents wander round the grounds and the former Penseroso.

Cubitt bought his Surrey estate in 1850. He already knew the area well, for he had built the successor to Richard Sheridan's home at neighbouring Polesden Lacey. The views, the woods (of which he was to plant more) and the nearness to London all appealed to him and, as a self-made man himself, he can scarcely have failed to appreciate the behavioural quirks of his predecessors in the house. He himself, however, planned to express his ultimate reaction to success in the far more conventional manner of leaving a country estate worth having to his heirs. While the grounds offered immense possibilities, the house did not and, by 1854, a new Denbies was standing behind and above the soon-to-vanish old one.

While Tyers had, a century before, commemorated his great work by turning its standards upside down, Cubitt did no such thing. Indeed, the country home he built was all of a pattern with Osborne and with his big London houses. It was, in fact, a bay-windowed London mansion dropped down on a Surrey hill. However, he made up for his lack of compromise in this direction by improving the country estate round him as enthusiastically as any eighteenth-century duke. He had scarcely taken over when the first of thousands of conifers were planted, to be followed by further thousands of hardwood trees. Some of them were firmed into place by the most illustrious but one of all his clients, Prince Albert. But this royal interest was to be a source of mixed feelings to the builder himself. The story grew up that Denbies was intended as a holiday home for the royal couple's eldest son. Cubitt, much embarrassed at this presumptuous linking of his name with that of the Prince of Wales, did his unsuccessful best to kill the rumours right up to the year of his death. *The Builder* also tried: 'We can state positively that there is no truth in the story, and that the residence is being created for a private family', ran an entry in its 'Miscellanea' columns in April 1855. But the rumour outlived Cubitt, who died eight months later at Denbies of cancer of the throat, aged sixty-seven. In his will, written over thirty sheets of parchment and a record in its time for length, he left Denbies to his widow, then to his sons in succession.

The Builder's obituary concluded: 'There are few men, perhaps, having so large an intercourse with the world, who have made so few enemies, and who may be said to be so generally respected . . . . As we said at starting, we have lost a great builder and a good man.' Over a century later, this reputation is still essentially intact. His house, however, is not. After World War II, its owner—the third Baron Ashcombe, Cubitt's

59 Thomas Cubitt. By an unknown artist

great-grandson—converted the Denbies laundry and gardeners' premises into a smaller home and moved in. The great house, with its total of almost a hundred rooms, was demolished in 1953-4. Between the floors, the demolition teams found a final reminder of the great builder's unceasing exertions in the shape of a small but important adjunct to a good building: a sound-proofing layer composed of mound upon mound of century-old seashells.

❧ *Derwentwater House and Panmure House*

One of the essential qualities of a myth is its capacity to travel, and the direction the journey takes is usually clear. Its starting point may still be unknown and its uttermost ramifications still unresearched, but, with the great myths at least, the general line of travel has been well charted. It is the small, local myths that provide small, knotty mysteries. Why, for example, should a legend involving two rebellious earls, two wretchedly anxious women and two sets of gates that remain closed for ever emerge in places so culturally dissimilar as a great Scottish estate and a one-time village on the western environs of London? Over 400 miles separate Angus and Acton; not far, admittedly, for a well-travelled tale. But where did this one start, and why did it come south (or north)?

The agent involved in the journeying is, however, reasonably easy to guess, for this is a Jacobite story with its roots in the rising of 1715. In the Scottish variant, the chief characters are the fourth Earl of Panmure and his wife; their English parallels are James Radcliffe, third Earl of Derwentwater, and his countess. Both men became involved in the struggle to put a Stuart back on the British throne; both women, according to tradition at least, heroically tried to cope with the aftermath. One succeeded; one had, in essentials, already failed. The gates in both cases belonged to the houses in which the women were living at the time: Panmure House, a mansion a mile or so from Muirdrum on the Forfar road, and a much less magnificent establishment on a site now between Acton's Newburgh Road and Horn Lane.

The background to the Scottish account starts earlier, in the sequence of the 1715 events. When Panmure left his family home to join the Earl of Mar on this luckless enterprise, he ordered that the gates through which he had ridden should be kept shut until he came again. In November, he was wounded at the Battle of Sheriffmuir, and only escaped through the help of his brother, Harry Maule. It is at this point that the tale begins to acquire its legendary aura, for a familiar figure in the Scottish folk tradition appears on the scene: the beggarman who is not what he seems. Walking on the lawns to the west of Panmure House, Countess Margaret saw a ragged figure approaching, recognised him and had him hurried indoors. The earl had indeed come again, though not in the way he had hoped. But to open the gates, of course, would have been unthinkable, since his only hope was to keep his presence secret until he could escape to France.

The Right 🛡 *Honourable*
James Earl of Derwentwater.

SPERAND TIMERE EST.

1714.

G. KNELLER. *Baron.* pinx.

G. V. Sculp.

Sold by the Bowles next to the Chapter house in S.t Pauls Church Yard

Consumed with anxiety, the countess hid him under the mansion's great staircase until transport could be arranged. The earl left, reached freedom and died in exile without returning. And the gates stayed shut for ever.

The English version of the tradition is a tragic one. The Earl of Panmure managed to avoid paying the price for his involvement in the rising. But Derwentwater, one of the English Jacobites, was made hostage at Preston, imprisoned in the Tower (his wife voluntarily joined him there until threatened by an outbreak of smallpox) and impeached for high treason. In spite of the countess's repeated pleas for royal clemency, her twenty-seven-year-old husband was beheaded on Tower Hill on 24 February 1716. He had requested that his body should be taken back to the family's Northumberland home at Dilston. But, lest a martyr's shrine be created, the request was refused, so arrangements for his burial went on in great secrecy. His body was spirited away after the execution and, on the first stage of its journey north, it·was taken to a house the countess had rented in Essex. However, she was not living there herself; according to Acton tradition, this very young and heavily pregnant woman spent the appalling hours of 24 February at a local house built a century earlier and owned at one point by the Parliamentary general Philip Skippon. And, again according to tradition, the dead earl's body was not taken to Essex but to the same Acton house. The coffin entered the estate through a set of iron gates on its eastern boundary. The gates were closed behind the furtive cortège and the earl's body was buried in the grounds, where it lay until disinterred a few days later and carried to Northumberland. The countess also left, moved from one part of the country to another and had her baby—a girl. And the gates at Derwentwater stayed shut for ever.

Apart from the fact of its existence, little is known about Derwentwater House, as it came to be called. The countess was firm-minded enough to return there four years later, when she paid for a special peal of bells at the nearby church on the occasion of her young son's birthday. The house survived until early in the next century, when it was pulled down and replaced by a villa in the classical style. Panmure, however, survived until 1955, and unlike its counterpart near London acquired a second layer of celebrity that had nothing to do with the great Jacobite drama.

60 (*opposite*) Jacobite hero: James, Earl of Derwentwater. Portrait after Godfrey Kneller
61 (*overleaf inset*) The refashioned Panmure from the west, showing the lawns where the Countess Margaret once walked. The coops are for pheasant chicks. 62 (*overleaf*) Panmure House in the moment of demolition

The house to which the fourth earl never officially returned was a mansion that the second earl had started to build in 1666 near the site of an earlier Panmure. This, Panmure Castle, was a massive stronghold—twelfth century in its oldest parts—with walls 6ft thick. They were not thick enough, however, to withstand the onslaught of General Monk who besieged and destroyed it in 1651. Its successor presented a far from military appearance. Its only remotely defensive adjunct consisted of the towers that stood at each end of the front of the building, and even these were finished, not with battlements, but with the graceful lines of an ogee roof. These decorative curves remained a characteristic of Panmure until the very end. But by the time that end was approaching, there were many more of them, together with a great central tower. There were also 87 rooms, almost 400 windows, a library, a gasworks, a laundry (with ironing and mangling rooms) and a ballroom that ran the full width of the house.

The changes dated back to the mid-nineteenth century when the architect David Bryce turned the house back to front, hugely increased its size and transformed it into a paradise for a sporting gentleman and his friends. 'Everything about the house betokens enlightened management', commented an admiring contributor to the *Arbroath Herald* in 1890.

> The house and stabling are upon a very extensive scale; the super-abundance of cover gives shelter to a quantity and variety of low ground game that is scarcely credable [*sic*], there is an extensive tract of moorland, well stocked with grouse, and there are few places in Scotland better adapted for riding to hounds.

Details such as these were very much to the point for Fox Maule, Lord Panmure and owner of the house when it was rebuilt, was a sportsman on an epic scale. His preferred weapon was the shotgun; during a single three-day shooting party in 1870, he and his guests accounted for almost 4,000 partridges and a mixed bag of 993 hares, 131 rabbits, 10 snipe and a woodcock. 'At that time', the *Herald*'s man went on after giving these bags, 'there was much less cover than there is now'. Nearly three million trees had been planted in the interim.

The reworked Panmure was, in fact, a house that simply begged for the statistician: there were more than 30 main bedrooms (and 15 more for servants), stabling for 18 horses and thousands of feathered and furry corpses passing through the game larder. But among this profusion is a figure given by the *Scotsman* as late as the 1950s that sounds an ominous note. Panmure had 130 rooms in all (the total had gone up since the 1930s count), but only two of these were bathrooms, albeit bathrooms with marble baths. The house had exquisite ceilings and magnificent oak panelling, so magnificent, in fact, that newcomers to the house sometimes had trouble spotting the doors amongst all the carved intricacies. But, as the *Scotsman* pointed out again, there was no electricity. The private gasworks, too, had gone, its gasometer being sold for scrap before World War II.

A further figure with an ominous ring was supplied by Frederick Ferguson, factor to the Panmure estates at the time the house was demolished. The moulded ceilings in the main room—in which thistles and crowns were entwined with initials of members of the family—would, he had been advised shortly before, have cost over £5,000 to renovate, and that in a relatively small room.

The death of Panmure was an event that started well before World War II and arguably before the First. Fox Maule was the last owner to live there, and from the late nineteenth century onwards the house was only occupied to the full in September and October, when it was let for shooting. Apart from two permanent housekeepers, it was still unoccupied, though largely furnished, until just before World War II. Like many other houses with a future appointment with the bulldozer, it was used by troops during the war itself. Afterwards it was discovered that, in addition to the wear and tear caused by this wartime occupation, there was dry rot in one of the towers and the greenish-blue slates on the roofs could be crumbled in the hand. In 1951, the imposition of heavy death duties led to the sale of the estate, and the new owners, a trust, spent the next four years trying to find a possible buyer for the house. Deputations from national bodies, convalescent homes and schools came, saw and shook their heads; the place was so big, and required too much restoration.

In 1955, the inevitable decision was taken: the carved oak and other fittings were removed, charges were placed and, stage by stage over the next year, Panmure House vanished from the landscape. The site was sown with grass and by the end of 1956 cattle and sheep were grazing over it.

A few fragments, however, were left, among them the garage block and the chapel; these are now used as a storehouse and a social club. And the famous gates still remain, repainted but as tightly closed as ever, a memorial to a road that no longer goes through them and to a tradition that, for some inscrutable reason, finds an echo in a minor key at the other end of the country.

Every year, the crews of the Oxford and Cambridge boats race past the site of one of the most famous necromancer's dens in Europe. This same den was also home to a large and lively family, the scene of a prolonged confidence trick and, if Elizabethan standards are applied, a sixteenth-century version of the Massachusetts Institute of Technology. For here, near the river bank and slightly to the west of the church, lived the most famous resident in Mortlake's history: Dr John Dee, mathematician, astronomer, astrologer, alchemist and seeker after psychic truths.

In his time and for long afterwards, he was also the area's most notorious inhabitant. The local children were quite panic-stricken by him, since he was 'accounted a conjuror'. Various tales of his strange powers were preserved for posterity by a carpenter's daughter who, as a girl, was a friend of one of Dee's own children. At one point, the two girls contrived to lose a basket of clothes; many years later, Goody Faldo of Mortlake recalled with awe that her friend's father controlled the weather, distilled strange substances in his house—and found the missing clothes basket.

John Aubrey, the recipient of these confidences, added other details in his *Brief Life* of Dee that demythologised this figure of local terror. Dee the conjuror was a respectable man with respectable relations; in fact, Aubrey's great-grandfather was his cousin. Dee, though a passionate inquirer into the Other World, was also passionately interested in this one—his works included a treatise on sea power. Dee, the children's bogey-figure, was anything but intimidating in appearance: 'Hee had a very faire cleare rosie complexion; a long beard as white as milke; he was tall and slender; a very handsome man.' And even the locals allowed that the wizard of Mortlake was also a pillar of the community: 'He was a great Peace-maker', Aubrey's report goes on; 'if any of the neighbours fell out, he would never lett them alone till he had made them friends.' But, even here, local gossip could not resist adding yet another instance of his uncanny powers of insight. He had warned one neighbour against another, 'who he sayd was a Witch'; centuries later, this popular image of Dee the magician still remains relatively untarnished. He continues to be thought of as a sort of Elizabethan Merlin, while his home, if thought of at all, emerges reeking of the fumes of alchemy.

In spite of its lurid reputation, however, Dee's house at Mortlake was far from spectacular. Both its name and its exact position appear to have

63 Dr John Dee, the conjurer of Mortlake. Portrait by an unknown artist

been forgotten, but it probably stood on or near the site now occupied by the Red Lion Garage in Mortlake High Street. The adjective most often applied to it is 'rambling', and ramble it certainly did: there were work-shops and laboratories and extensions, punctuated by tall chimneys that were doubtless watched intently by the doctor's suspicious neighbours. It was not without its elegant appointments, though; one room, observed as late as 1817, still displayed its sixteenth-century decoration of carved roses, painted red and white. The place had originally belonged to Dee's mother. By the time Dee himself moved in at the age of forty or so, he had become a scholar of international standing and enjoyed close links with Queen Elizabeth I and her court. A degree of elegance was therefore needed in his company apartments.

123

In all, the building was to house no less than three Mrs Dees, for the old lady (who later formally presented the house to her son) went on living there, sharing the premises with a short-lived first daughter-in-law and then with a second. It was the second, *née* Jane Fromond, who gave the doctor his large family of eight children; she also presided over a complicated *ménage* that included her husband's assistants, the domestic staff and a highly productive but troublesome medium, Edward Kelley or Kelly.

It seems that initially she disliked Kelley intensely, but this was not her only problem. Her children got into mischief on the river bank. ('Rowland', Dee noted in his diary on 5 August 1590, 'fell into the Tems over hed and eares abowt noone or somewhat after.') More disturbingly, the family nurse went mad and tried to commit suicide by throwing herself down the household well. The Conjuror of Mortlake saved her but, three weeks later, she succeeded in her intention by cutting her throat. And the Conjuror himself, while on speaking terms with the highest in the land, was perennially in a state of financial embarrassment. On one occasion, when he was visited by the Polish nobleman Albert Laski, he imploringly told the authorities that he could put either food or plate in front of the Prince, but scarcely both; to feed his visitor properly, he would have to sell some of his dining equipment. On another, much more serious one, he told a Royal Commission appointed to consider his financial state that he was all but destitute, and backed the claim up with a moving account of his debts and dismal prospects.

The constant money worries were, if anything, made keener for Dee by his knowledge of his own worth. Although no stranger to the arts of self-salesmanship, he had a genuine superiority complex. Equally genuinely, his sense of superiority was securely founded on fact. Such were his achievements and reputation that the Mortlake house became a centre for some of the leading figures of the day. Dee, himself a mapmaker and author of a series of books on 'the perfect art of Navigation', was visited by seafarers of the order of Sir Humphrey Gilbert, Sir John Hawkins and Thomas Cavendish. The geographer Gerardus Mercator had made some of his instruments; others included a quadrant once owned by a long-dead friend, Richard Chancellor. A visitor who worked in a different line of country was Gerard, of *Herball* fame, while the historian and antiquary William Camden not only supervised the studies of Dee's son at Westminster School but himself pored over the contents of Dee's magnificent Mortlake library. Unsurprisingly, the house and its owner also attracted beginners in the various branches of learning that

Dee commanded, and Jane's unwieldy establishment always included several of her husband's pupils.

However, this hive of industry was not frequented by scholars alone. At a period when astrology was taken extremely seriously, Dee's abilities in this direction caused him to be regarded as a sort of technical adviser on state security. Before he moved to Mortlake, he had, among other duties, been called in to name a suitable day for Elizabeth's coronation, and to advise the panic-stricken court when a wax model of the Queen was discovered with a pin through its heart. Queen and courtiers were therefore frequent visitors at Dee's Thames-side house, and the visits were carefully noted down by the householder. 'The Quene's Majestie', runs a *Diary* entry for 17 September 1580,

> cam from Rychemond in her coach, the higher way of Mortlak felde, and whan she cam right against the church she turned down toward my house: and when she was against my garden in the felde she stood there a great while, and than cam ynto the street at the great gate of the felde, where she espyed me at my doore, making obeysains to her Majestie; she beckend her hand for me; I cam to her coach side, she very speedily pulled off her glove and gave me her hand to kiss; and to be short, asked me to resort to her court.

While Dee could not help but be gratified by such public interest, it was also to tire and distract him. More engrossing were visits, or alleged visits, from quite a different company of beings: the spirits Uriel, Il, Madimi, Galvah, Jubanladec and others, all produced through the medium Edward Kelley. The activities at Dee's home were, by any standards, remarkable enough, but it was Kelley's involvement that lifted them into the category of the truly extraordinary. Dee, hot for knowledge, would seat his assistant at a table—a specially made table adorned with seals bearing mystical patterns—in one of his most private back rooms. Kelley stared into the crystal globe in which the spirits were usually said to appear, while his patron, pen at the ready, conducted a three-cornered conversation with whichever visitation turned up. Kelley would report the apparition's reply, although Dee sometimes thought he heard it for himself. He could not, however, proceed further than aural contact; the visions in the globe were Kelley's alone. Between them the pair received statements of the Almighty's purpose, prophecies, practical advice (a book that Dee had lost was pronounced to be in Scotland) and warnings against enemies. One spirit even promised to finish Laski's pedigree, a work Dee had had no time to complete himself.

Current opinion of Kelley is that he was a complete charlatan; poor Dee was therefore taken for a prodigious ride. But one of Kelley's

pronouncements was, to say the least, an amazingly lucky shot. It was made in Lübeck on 15 November 1583 at a time when the Dee family and the master's medium had set off with Laski on what was to be a six-year stay in Europe. Jane Dee's brother, Nicholas Fromond, had taken over the house in Mortlake; as far as Dee knew, all was well there until, during a seance, he heard otherwise. A spirit dressed in sables and enthroned on a chair set with precious stones came out with the astonishing news that Fromond was in prison. 'They examin him', the manifestation continued.

> They say, that thou has hid divers secret things. As for thy Books, thou mayst go look at them at thy leasure. It may be, that thy house may be burnt for a remembrance of thee too. Well, if they do, so it is; if not, as thou wilt. I have told thee my phansie, and given thee my counsel, and offered thee my help, and desired to do thee good.

In fact, the house escaped conflagration. But a mob had indeed broken in, run riot through the wonderful library and caused over £600 worth of damage to Dee's books and instruments. The suspicious inhabitants of Mortlake had taken their revenge at last; given Dee's notoriety in the district, it was reasonable on Kelley's part to guess that they might.

When Dee and his family finally returned to England (without Kelley), they were desperately poor. Friends helped out, the Royal Commission gave a kindly ear to his tale of achievements and woes and a grant of a hundred marks was forthcoming. The visitors returned in droves, but Dee had now wearied of them. In 1596 he moved to Manchester where he had secured the post of Warden of Christ's College. While he was there, his wife died. Elizabeth I died too, and James I was to show himself no friend to the ageing supernaturalist who continued to be plagued by money worries. In the end, Dee came back to Mortlake and, with the mother of Goody Faldo in attendance, died there in 1608.

Afterwards, Dee's workshops were pulled down and the ground put to less controversial use: it became the site of the famous Mortlake tapestry works, at which five of the Raphael Cartoons were copied on to fabric. The house, also now shorn of notoriety, entered a period of humdrum existence as first a residence and then as a girls' school. By the 1870s it had gone. Mortlake High Street, however, still remembers the district's most famous inhabitant. On the opposite side of the road, next door to the church, stands a second John Dee House—a four-storey block of modern flats.

64 (*opposite*) Alchemist at work, with client: how members of Dr Dee's profession were perceived by the public at large

❧ Easton Lodge

Among East Anglian casualties of World War II was the deer park surrounding a stately home that, thanks to the efforts of one of Britain's oddest great ladies, had become a suitable setting for royalty, a fun-fair, a composer's retreat, Independent Labour Party summer schools and for an informal menagerie. The house was Easton Lodge in Essex whose former owner was Frances, Countess of Warwick—one-time mistress of the future Edward VII, passionate lover of animals and good causes, and one of the most startling early converts to the Labour movement.

The park became a war victim when, shorn of 12,000 oaks, hornbeams and firs, it was transformed into Great Dunmow airfield. In 1946 the house itself was, for the second time in thirty years, damaged by fire. Two years later, all but its stable block and former servants' quarters was demolished. With it went oddly assorted memories of society love-making and of the Salvation Army, of game pies and orders for nesting-boxes. But Easton Lodge in its totality was a monument to an oddly assorted character.

Frances ('Daisy') Maynard was, from her birth in 1861, a member of the Upper Ten Thousand, the ruling class of Britain. Due to her lack of brothers, she also became one of Britain's richest heiresses four years later, and the property she inherited included the family home at Little Easton in Essex, a Victorian mansion built round a genuinely Elizabethan core. At one point in her youth, she was expected to marry into the royal family. Her choice fell on the heir to the Earl of Warwick instead, but she later got the best of both worlds by becoming, not a royal bride, but a royal mistress. During the last decade of the nineteenth century, the Prince of Wales regularly featured on the guest lists of Frances's house parties at Easton Lodge and Warwick Castle. A long-surviving memento of the relationship was the bed in which, according to information given to the countess's biographer, Margaret Blunden, Frances would in later life indicate she and the prince had taken their pleasure.

The house parties themselves were luxurious affairs. The novelist Elinor Glyn, one of Frances's Essex neighbours, commented in her autobiography that 'Easton in the 'nineties was the centre of all that was intelligent and amusing in the society of the day.' A usual total of about twenty guests—foreign princes as well as home-grown ones, ambassadors, politicians and a wide selection from the British aristocracy—enjoyed walking, shooting, conversation, spectacular meals and (in a discreet way) each other. Two innovations, in particular, increased their comfort: efficient heating and an enormous tea that, according to Mrs Glyn, consisted of 'every kind of lovely muffin, crumpet, scone, cake, sandwich, jam, honey and Devonshire cream as well'. This was eaten sitting round a big table in schoolroom style, and it appeared to be Frances's own invention. In other households, guests were still juggling teacups, plates and thin bread-and-butter from hand to hand, without the benefit of somewhere to put them all.

These pleasant arrangements were, however, counterbalanced to some extent by drawbacks in other directions. There was a scarcity of bathrooms and an overflowing abundance of Frances's pets. These included dogs, monkeys, a young elephant (which followed its owner into the dining-room) and an ant bear (which attacked footmen's legs). Given the presence of this private zoo, it was hardly surprising that a prank played by the Prince of Wales himself should have been successful. As the countess wrote in her memoirs,

> My children were so accustomed to strange animals that they never feared the advent of a new pet, however wild. When the Prince of Wales once happend to come to see us at Easton on a first of April, and sent a message to the schoolroom to Guy and Queenie, my two eldest children, to say that he had seen a bear in the garden and urging them to come down and look for it, the children made all haste to obey. They searched in vain for the bear, and on their return through the stable regions they met the Prince who enjoyed telling them it was All Fools' Day.

The house parties and all they stood for represented one side of Frances's character. The pets, on which she lavished attention throughout her life, represented another, and this natural tendency of hers to identify with the helpless explains to some degree how the socialite of the 1890s became the Socialist of the twentieth century. The process was gradual, but as the old century moved towards its close the signs steadily accumulated.

Frances's friends, for example, included both the Prince of Wales and the campaigning journalist W. T. Stead, the Duke of Manchester and the founder of Britain's first farmworkers' union, Joseph Arch. Again, like many society ladies of the period, she was a strong supporter of charities and philanthropic schemes, but her scope extended far beyond the charity bazaars beloved by her contemporaries. In 1902, when she and her landscaper Harold Peto started immense gardening works at Easton, she made a good a shortfall in local labour by bringing in what a contemporary *Country Life* called 'about seventy Salvation Army waifs'. The waifs—they were, in fact, adults rather than children—bivouacked for the

65 Easton Lodge, of sixteenth-century, seventeenth-century and (largely) nineteenth-century origin. Photograph from the Spalding Collection

66 House party at Easton Lodge in about 1890. Frances is in the centre, wearing a dark jacket and furs. Next to her, with cigar, is the Prince of Wales. Photograph from the Spalding Collection

duration on the lawns in front of Easton's windows and were given the cricket pavilion as a recreation room. When they and the gardeners departed, they left behind them terraces, shrubberies, an artificial valley, a Japanese teahouse on a newly formed lake and a balustraded lily-pond that, even though it looked like a large stone play-pen, was on balance approved of. The countess herself was extremely pleased: the improvements, she said, were 'singularly successful . . . the men were first-rate'.

Frances's good works in connection with the land did not stop at beautifying her own domain. In 1897, she founded a co-educational school on the estate that aimed to provide a secondary education that prepared pupils for life in a farming community. Another of her schemes involved the founding of a horticultural college for women. Anything but a blue-stocking herself, she held views on the importance of education that would still be respected today; anything but prudent over money, she felt an emotional bond with those for whom prudence was a necessity.

Starting from this emotional base, Frances drifted slowly towards the socialist movement and finally embraced it publicly in the early years of the new century. Thereafter Easton Lodge gatherings developed a flavour completely different from that of earlier years. George Bernard Shaw visited and laughed at the nest-boxes put up by his nature-loving hostess. Gustav Holst lived in a house in the park, where he wrote *Egdon Heath* and *A Moorside Suite*. H. G. Wells was another neighbour; other house guests included Ramsay MacDonald and Beatrice and Sidney Webb, who came when, in the early 1920s, the countess took her hospitality into a new field by offering her home as a study centre to the Labour Party. The arrangement was tried out for a year, during which Beatrice Webb made a note of some potential difficulties. 'The Countess', she wrote in her diary in 1924,

> continues to live here in her own apartments; a picturesque, floridly ornamented and lavishly equipped great barn adjoining the main structure of the house; and when she is in residence, she acts as hostess. After ten days' observation I *doubt* the feasibility or desirability of the arrangement. The house is far too gorgeous in its grandiose reception rooms and large extravagantly furnished bedrooms. Owing to the devastation (by fire) of 28 bedrooms during the War, there is an absurd disproportion between the *number* of the bedrooms (there can only be 30 guests and this entails a proportion of married couples occupying one room) and the plenitude and magnificence of the reception rooms. Then there is a grave disadvantage in having the Countess on the premises.

(The fire referred to took place in 1918, and destroyed the last remaining fragments of the sixteenth-century mansion round which the Victorian Easton had been built. The 'barn' was, in fact, the converted and still-existing stable block into which Frances had by this time moved.)

The offer was not taken up but, undeterred, the countess threw the house open for the Independent Labour Party summer schools, then offered it to the Trades Union Congress. Again, though, the scheme fell through. Try as she would, Frances's family home obstinately remained in the ownership of the propertied classes.

On 27 July 1938, the first of *The Times'* obituaries for the day recorded the countess's death at Easton and, among her activities, listed both the offer of her home to the Labour movement and her foundation of a bird sanctuary there. Of the second, more successful project the countess herself had once written:

> I fear we cannot educate the elderly; we must begin with the young. We must interest them and instruct them; give them sympathy, and forbearance will come. I was advised that schoolboys might do damage in the park, and that the sanctuary might be desecrated. I am convinced that this is not so.

As things turned out, it was not marauding schoolboys that the park at Easton had to fear.

The end of Lambert Simnel's bid for the English throne is familiar from a hundred illustrated histories for children. There is the wretched lad, slaving away in Henry Tudor's kitchens. The aftermath tends to be forgotten, however: the ten-year-old royal imposter grew safely into adulthood, was promoted to the post of royal falconer and then, with a sound background in service behind him, moved into the teeming household of Sir Thomas Lovell at Enfield, called Elsyng, Elsing or Elsynge Hall. He was still alive in 1524, when Sir Thomas died; he attended the funeral of his late employer who omitted Simnel from his will.

This moderately happy ending has, though, a curious aftermath of its own which also involves Elsyng and an imposter with royal pretensions. That the two stories—each remarkable enough on its own—should in some ways be linked seems, in this writer's view, inescapable.

Elsyng—the site of which is north of Forty Hall, close to Maiden's Bridge—had probably been built in the mid-fifteenth century and by Sir Thomas's day was a big place; six priests were needed to meet the spiritual demands of his establishment. As such, it made a suitable present to a monarch. Sir Thomas's successor, the Earl of Rutland, granted his Enfield property to Henry VIII as part of a land deal, and it stayed in royal hands until just before the Civil War. While it was visited several times during the sixteenth century by the adult Queen Elizabeth, its chief contemporary claim to fame was as a nursery. Henry had it refitted to receive his two younger children, then aged eight and four, and it was here that six years later they heard that their father had died. Young Edward rode away to London (the journey was expected to take four hours), while Elizabeth moved into the household of her stepmother, Catherine Parr, and there started the long and hazardous period of waiting that ended in her own accession in 1558.

The new queen gave the keepership of Elsyng to a connection of her mother's family, John Astley, and it was Elsyng's keeper who allowed another eight-year-old to grow up in the house where Henry's two children had once lived. Indeed, this same child would later recall that Astley (whom he called Ashley) had himself paid for him to receive a suitable education for a gentleman: music, the use of arms, classical and modern languages and dancing. He also stated that he was the queen's own son by the Earl of Leicester. His name was Arthur Dudley.

67 The employer of imposter Lambert Simnel: Sir Thomas Lovell of Elsyng Hall

Scandal stories about Elizabeth's alleged child-bearings were not uncommon in England. This particular one, however, surfaced in Spain, where Arthur, aged about twenty-seven, arrived at the end of 1586 and told a wonderful yarn about his concealed birth, his fostering by one of Astley's lieutenants, Robert Southern, his time at Enfield, his discovery of his identity and his subsequent lively adventurings round Europe. The Spaniards, who had picked him up on suspicion of being a foreign agent, treated these outpourings with much reserve; Arthur might or might not be the person he claimed, but he was also clearly a man who had to produce some answers in a hurry. Tantalisingly, he then dropped out of recorded history as abruptly as he entered it.

Today, it is anyone's guess as to where Dudley's tale departs from fact and becomes fiction. His mistake over the keeper's name is not as glaring as it first appears, for John was not the first Astley of the period to have the 'Ashley' alias. Arthur, whatever his parentage, may well have lived at Elsyng for part of his childhood and youth. On the other hand, he may have pulled the name out of the hat of his sub-conscious memory. But the coincidences are intriguing and, whether Dudley grew up at Elsyng or not, it seems entirely possible that he knew of its old connection with another spurious claimant to royal blood. It also seems likely that this information provided at least part of the inspiration of his tale to the Madrid authorities. In a left-handed, shadowy way, Lambert Simnel rode again.

Well before Dudley was called on to exercise his inventive powers, though, Elsyng, by now also called Enfield House, was starting to lose its claim as a suitable residence for a queen. The last major occasion on which Elizabeth used it was in 1568, and even then the visit had to be preceded by speedy repair works. (Someone had the pleasing inspiration of turning the windows of the royal apartments into a sort of glass Visitors' Book: the panes were engraved with the arms of her noble guests.) Afterwards, the place went badly downhill in the manner of all unused houses. Cracks developed in the walls, pipes leaked and dripped and the lead and glass were stolen. In the next century, Charles I sold it with its park to its keeper, the Earl of Pembroke, for £5,300. The earl died in 1650. The extent to which the property declined still further from its once-royal state can be judged by this advertisement, published shortly afterwards:

> At Enfield-house are several wholesome bathes erected, wet and dry, cold and moist, for several diseases; the rates are easy, and the price low; let them repair to the Coach and Horses, Drury-lane, where they shall have speedy passage every day. The coachman's name is Richard How.

The advertisement was quoted by the Rev Daniel Lysons, who wrote his guide to the environs of London at the end of the eighteenth century. By this time, Elsyng Hall had completely disappeared from view. And, although its site has now been pinpointed and its history researched, it still retains a sort of invisibility. No pictures of it have ever come to light and like Arthur Dudley, who may or may not have grown up there, it remains in the last resort faintly mysterious.

❧ Emral Hall

Among the quirks and delightful boundary accidents that were abolished during the 1970s were two outposts of Flintshire that at no point touched their parent county. The smaller of the two—Marford on the road from Wrexham to Chester—was completely surrounded by Denbighshire, while the other was eight miles away to the south-east, on the English side of the Dee. As its anomalous position dictated, it was called Maelor Saesneg or Maelor of the Saxons, and it was an extraordinary place for boundaries altogether: neighbouring Denbighshire actually owned two meadows inside 'English' Maelor. Boundaries apart, Maelor of the Saxons was renowned for connections with Owain Glyndwr, for its once enormous monastery (as big as a walled town) at Bangor-is-y-Coed, for cheese and for a building that, by the twentieth century, was seen as the most important country house within the intricate confines of the whole county. Flintshire itself and its topographical oddities endured up to the reorganisation of local government in 1974; the house, however, had predeceased it by thirty-seven years.

Emral Hall at Worthenbury—the first Emral Hall—came into existence in the thirteenth century, built by the English wife of a local quisling. Emma of Emral Hall was the widow of Gruffydh ap Madawe, a Welsh lord who, in spite of his position, turned his back on his people and sided with the English crown. After his death, his sons were put in the guardianship of four English nobles. Emma, meanwhile, prudently built herself a strong stone house. None of them enjoyed their possessions for long, however; the four sons, less than mysteriously, went missing, while in about 1277 Emma had her Flintshire lands confiscated. Emral passed to a Shropshire family called Puleston and, with a few gaps, it was the Pulestons who continued to own it until the twentieth century.

The gaps were mainly caused by war—as, indeed, were the circumstances that caused Emral to be handed from one early Puleston to another. The first of them came by it because he was a key figure (and evidently a more useful one than Gruffydd's relict) in Edward I's campaign against the Welsh. The second of them lost it because Edward, by then involved in war with France, had appointed him collector of a war subsidy among the fiercely resentful Welsh; they caught and hanged him. A later Puleston married a niece of Owain Glyndwr (who himself had married a daughter of the neighbouring Hanmer family), joined Glyndwr's rebellion against

Henry IV and was killed. Emral was temporarily confiscated but, by the middle of the fifteenth century, a Puleston was back in possession, carefully making a will that bequeathed 6s 8d for the repair of Worthenbury Chapel and £20 apiece to his two daughters, 'to marry them'. Slightly later, the Pulestons fought in another civil war, this time on the side of the Lancastrians. One of them was impeached afterwards, but their house continued to remain within the family.

The Tudor Pulestons flourished; so did their successors. One indication of the comfortable state of their finances is the fact that they built a new Emral Hall in place of, and probably on the foundations of, the old one. It is not known exactly when the rebuilding took place, but the most likely time is the first quarter of the seventeenth century. Even more debatable is the date of the house's main glory, the plasterwork ceilings in its principal rooms. Were they really the work of a pre-Commonwealth plasterer, or were they executed by a later craftsman whose skills were a generation behind the times? The otherwise copious Emral records are, for some unaccountable reason, silent on the whole question of Emral's rebuilding. But whichever Puleston was responsible for commissioning the work in his handsome new saloon and dining-room, he produced something quite extraordinary. The saloon ceiling, in particular, has been estimated by *Country Life* to have scarcely any parallel. The Signs of the Zodiac, which formed part of it, are a common enough motif, but the great figure of Hercules, heroically working through his twelve labours, is practically unknown in ceiling decoration.

It was, perhaps, not surprising that guesses about the creator of Emral's main architectural fame should concentrate on the period of Emral's most famous owner: the seventeenth-century Judge John Puleston, Serjeant-at-Law, Chief Justice of the Common Pleas, Chief Justice of Lancashire. The judge was, of course, involved in the civil war of his own period and, rather freakishly for his immediate neighbourhood, was a Parliamentarian. Relations between him and his neighbours were strained to the utmost by the turn events took in the locality. During the war, Puleston complained to Parliament that the head of the Hanmer family (friends with the Pulestons since the Glyndwr period and earlier) had invaded his Flintshire possessions, appropriated goods to the value of £6,000, set soldiers to collect Puleston rents and driven out Puleston's children, 'sucking their nurse's breast', to be thrown on to public charity. The Parliamentarians, however, shortly took Emral back and captured Hanmer's house with it.

Even for a tense period, the Pulestons of the mid-seventeenth century seemed to have an outstanding gift for tension with those close to them over matters of belief. The judge differed in his views, not only from his neighbours, but also from his sons, and the family row rumbled on well after his death, with the sons' former tutor, Philip Henry, acting as the judge's luckless stand-in. In *Noblesse oblige*, Nancy Mitford commented that the relationship between local landowner and local divine had led to 'some of the most ringing rows of all time'; at Emral, the relationship deteriorated to the point at which the landowner's heir and the divine actually came to blows.

Philip Henry had arrived at Emral in 1653, a Nonconformist in the making just down from Oxford. He spent an uncomfortable few years in the judge's warring family and then moved out into a house specially built for him by the judge. It had cost £800, a fact that cannot have helped to endear him to the judge's heir, Roger. The judge died two years after the move; Henry preached a funeral sermon at Worthenbury on the virtues of aiding God's ministers, and was clearly anxious to go on preaching there. But Roger Puleston, then aged twenty-two, had other views. He did not merely disagree with the Worthenbury minister; he actively loathed him. As Henry himself once noted with remarkable candour, 'Roger Puleston assaulted mee in wrath, whereby my unruly passions being stirred, I strook again and hurt his face.' Retiring from the fray, Roger waited until the Restoration, put pressure on the returning church authorities, and at last had the satisfaction of sending a serving-man to Worthenbury Church, where he read the formal notice of Henry's eviction from his job. The poor minister lived on in the parish for some years, treasuring memories and trying to win back an annuity settled on him by the judge and done away with by the judge's son. But he was unsuccessful; all he ended up with was a down-payment of £100 and an invitation to dinner with Roger's widow and her second husband.

At the very beginning of the eighteenth century, Emral was repaired. From 1724 onwards, it received a drastic face-lift that, from all but one angle, converted it into a different house completely. In 1726-7, Sir Thomas Puleston, Roger's grandson, paid £160 for the front of the house to be rebuilt; earlier, new wings had been extended from the front to form a three-sided court. The intention was Palladian; the actuality unorthodox, even lumpish. But the result went further than being merely pleasing. As *Country Life* again pointed out, it gave Emral an idiosyncratic character that reflected not just fashions in architecture, but the social and economic history of a whole area.

The Pulestons did not stop at changing the exterior appearance of the building. Internal additions included carved oak wainscotting throughout most of the hall and, on the 6ft wide main staircase, a charming pair of small gates in wrought iron that had a function not unlike that of child gates on modern staircases. The Emral stair-gate, however, forbade passage not to children but to Puleston dogs. There were additions outside, too: more wrought iron gates, a pair of ornamental sentry boxes guarding the bridge over the Emral Hall moat, a new set of stable buildings, an ice-house and a dog kennel. The kennel was the work of another John Puleston who, in about 1775, experienced a resurgence of the ambiguous family attitude to religion and tore down the hall's own medieval chapel. He built the dog kennel from the remnants. Within the year, he was dead of a riding accident in which he had dashed his head against the new kennel's walls. The death, the neighbourhood felt, was clearly a case of divine retribution. The Rev Sir T. H. Gresley Puleston, local rector for a large part of the nineteenth century, did not go quite as far as that, but in his account of the parish he did recall that was a 'very singular thing that trees planted on the spot always refused to grow'.

With John's accident, the direct Puleston line ceased, but the nephew who inherited Emral adopted the family name and was later given a baronetcy to add to it. Life at Emral briefly became very grand. The new baronet was a friend of the Prince Regent and host at Emral to Prinny's brother, the future William IV. Later in the century, in 1861, further lustre was shed by the discovery in an attic of a unique packet of manuscripts. A throw-back to the Pulestons' fighting past with the Lancastrians, they were a collection—the only one in existence—of contemporary copies of letters written by the queen of Henry VI, Margaret of Anjou.

68 The eighteenth-century front court of Emral Hall. By the nineteenth century, when this picture was taken, the sentry-boxes by the gates had received a thatch of ivy

But the year of the discovery was also the year in which Emral's fortunes began to change for the worse. After the second baronet's wife died some years before, the baronet himself took against the house. For several years he let it, but the last tenants left at the beginning of the 1860s and thereafter Emral stood empty. (The third baronet, whose funds were low, preferred to concentrate his resources on life in London.) A *Country Life* contributor visited it in 1897 (the first year of the magazine's existence) and found it in a state of desolation:

> Its once beautifully-painted staircase walls have lost all trace of the subjects of the decoration, and the banisters and rails of the black oak staircase have been kicked out and carried away, together with pieces of the oak carving, notably from the fireplace in the drawing-room. The lofty panelling of this room is much disfigured with names and dates cut by unthinking visitors who used to visit the hall without permission, entering by broken windows, with evidently no object but spoliation. Almost every room can still be climbed into, but the floors and the staircase leading to the upper chambers are in places very rotten.

It sounded like the end, but about the turn of the century the unbelievable happened. A Puleston by marriage, the wife of the third baronet, found that the family fortunes had so recovered that she could restore the family home. The work was started, destroyed by a disastrous fire in 1904, restarted and finally finished. When the second *Country Life* contributor visited in 1910, he was presented with a building worth writing about. When the Royal Commission on Ancient Monuments (Wales) published their report on Flintshire two years later, Lady Puleston had died but they remarked that Emral was probably the only country mansion of importance in the county.

The tragedy is that, within twenty-five years, much of her effort had gone for nothing. In 1936 the house and estate were put up for sale. Among those who attended to buy fragments of Emral was Sir Clough Williams-Ellis, creator of Portmeirion. Sir Clough called his Italianate fantasia of a village his 'home for fallen houses'; Emral was shortly to join the list of the fallen, and he salvaged as much of it as he could. The house (although not the stables and ice-house) vanished, but much of the glass, the oak panelling, the grate from the saloon and the Hercules ceiling (sale price £13) made their way in numbered lots to Portmeirion's town hall. The fact that they can still be admired today is perhaps the only cheerful aspect of a story that should have ended well and did not.

69 (*opposite*) The oldest part of Emral Hall: the west front

✣Gordon Castle

Unlike most of the houses dealt with in this book, Gordon Castle near Fochabers appears still to belong to the here-and-now. The castle of today, however, is only a fragment of the former structure: an enormous building, almost 600ft long, built in the late 1760s by one of Scotland's richest dukes and ruled by one of Scotland's most celebrated duchesses. And this building, in turn, contained a fragment of yet another vast edifice; one that Defoe, writing in a period when size was *de rigueur* in ducal residences, described as 'a very noble, spacious and Royal Building; 'tis only *too large* [author's italics], and appears rather as a great Town than as a House.' Taken together, the two structures and their missing elements carry the historian back to the fifteenth century. Even then, the Gordon's ancestors were in the habit of thinking big.

The first Gordon Castle was the building that dominates the scene today—a six-storey tower that George Seton, Lord of Gordon and second Earl of Huntly, raised on the remains of a still earlier tower. It was protected from unwelcome attentions by a marsh called the Bog o' Gight and the tower's function was also partly defensive. Like the other fortress of Alloa Tower (see page 29), it was added to by the builder's successors (earls, marquises and then, by decree of Charles II, dukes) and its military function had become obscured by the time Defoe visited and found that 'as a Castle much is not to be said of it, for old Fortifications are of a small Import, as the World goes now'. Obscured, but only just; the memory of the 1715 rising was still very fresh at the time and so, in Moray, was that of the taking of Gordon Castle by the Earl of Sutherland in pursuit of a Roman Catholic and Jacobite Gordon, heir to the first duke. Defoe continued urbanely that the second duke, who had inherited in 1716, the year the castle was surrendered, had been 'embroil'd a little in the late unhappy Affair of the *Pretender*; but he got off without a Forfeiture, having prudently kept himself at a Distance from them till he might see the Effect of Things'.

Prudent he may have been, but the future second duke had been lucky as well, for his initial involvement in the '15 had run to the raising of over 2,000 troops for the Earl of Mar's force, and to accompanying them to Sheriffmuir. His rebel-raising example was followed during the '45 by one of his sons, Lewis. But his wife, a daughter of the Earl of Peterborough (see page 238), had by now changed the family's religious allegiance to

Protestantism and his successor, the third duke, put a damper on Lewis's efforts by refusing to call out the clan. Gordon Castle's days as a house of war were now over.

The fourth duke, called Alexander like his grandfather, also had an unruly younger brother: the highly embarrassing Lord George Gordon, instigator of the riots that had London quaking in 1780. But Duke Alexander himself, one of the best looking dukes in the country and probably the richest, was a totally different character, though a curiously divided one. In his public persona, he did everything a duke should—raise regiments, serve as Lord Lieutenant and marry (for the first time round, at least) suitably. In private, he was a homely, pleasant character, with a string of modest and endearing achievements to his name. Using a wealth of local idiom, he wrote the song 'There's cauld kail in Aberdeen'; he was an addict of the turning-lathe and solved the problem of occasional presents to friends by giving them all snuff-boxes of his own making. He even extended his present-making to a pair of gold earrings which he took to London and presented with a flourish to Queen Charlotte, wife of George III. They were a tremendous success, so much so that the duke, clearly delighted, began to joke about getting further orders from all six royal princesses.

70 Gordon Castle with, at its centre, the original (and still existing) tower

The new Gordon Castle was also his creation, but this, at least in the eyes of later generations imbued with notions of romanticism, was less successful. The duke retained the old tower with its battlements, but the massive four-storey block that he built round it, with wings and pavilions, did not appeal to visitors of the nineteenth century such as R. Carruthers, a local newspaper-owner. This mansion 'of the modern school', designed by John Baxter, caused Carruthers to shake his head; its style, he commented in 1843, was to be regretted, 'for the old, rude, and varied Gothic, with its round towers and battlements, would harmonise better with the associations connected with the spot and the family that so long possessed it'. However, Carruthers overflowed with praise for the castle's surroundings; the Bog o' Gight had gone, and Duke Alexander had again demonstrated his down-to-earth capabilities by laying out the grounds with devotion and skill. There were now hawthorns over 30ft high, horse-chestnuts twice as big and huge plantations of hollies. In his own time, however, the duke's own favourite had been a willow, the first tree he ever planted. As a four-year-old child, growing up in the castle in the 1740s, he had stuck a willow-twig in a tub standing in a puddly, swampy spot near the old house. Easiest of trees to grow, the willow took root at once, even though its container was floating around on the swamp's moving surface. The tub finally rotted, the tree anchored itself for good and the duke, who now looked on it as a symbol of his fortunes, carefully left it undisturbed when the castle was rebuilt.

Another tree that Carruthers noted years later was a lime so enormous that 'his grace might dine a regiment under its boughs'. This, however, had been the favourite, not of Duke Alexander, but of his wife. The fourth duke had his willow; Jane, the fourth duchess, had her lime, which she transformed into an outdoors boudoir by having its branches trained and propped up. Against strong competition from other members of the ducal family, it is Jane who remains easily the most celebrated. In London, she was the the Tories' answer to her contemporary, the Duchess of Devonshire. (One of her special haunts was Brandenburgh House, home of the Margravine; the two ladies were on the closest of terms.) In Edinburgh, she ruled the fashionable roost. She was, Burns said, 'charming, witty, kind, sensible'; she was also unorthodox, tough-minded, foul-mouthed and on occasion unfaithful to her husband. One of the best remembered facts about her is the hat-trick she pulled off in connection with her daughters' marriages; three of them left the altar as duchesses. One of the best remembered legends concerns her system of recruiting soldiers for the regiment her son was raising: the report was that she arrived at

71 Alexander, fourth Duke of Gordon. Portrait by J. Moir

country fairs, sword in hand and Highland bonnet on her head, and offered the King's shilling to recruits from between her teeth.

While Jane was skilled at arranging marriages for her daughters, she was not successful in maintaining her own. Deepening rifts culminated in estrangement; reconciliation was tried, but failed. Jane built a Scottish seat of her own—a villa miles further up the Spey valley, near Kingussie— and in 1812 was buried there. She died, however, in the less seemly surroundings of a London hotel, where her corpse lay in state, on view to

145

72 The legend-making Jane Maxwell, the fourth duke's first wife, in 1786. Portrait by John Brown

all comers, for several days. 'From the great want of judgment and attention with which the body was exposed, for above a week after her death, to the curiosity of all who thought fit to go into the hotel, it became quite indecent', commented a contemporary indignantly.

In 1820, the duke—then well into his seventies—was married again, this time to a Fochabers woman called Jane Christie. This other Jane had already borne numerous ducal offspring but, when Alexander regularised their union, the new duchess was too self-effacing to take her place in the ducal home. The reason, the duke once explained to a friend, was that 'were she established at Gordon Castle, she is sure that my friends would not come to the castle, and she should never forgive herself if she were the means of preventing any of my friends from visiting me as they have always done'. To her husband's great distress, she died four years after the wedding; Alexander himself died three years later still.

The fifth duke—the former Marquis of Huntly, for whom the first Duchess Jane had helped to raise the Gordon Highlanders—succeeded in being much more resplendently ducal than his father. He was a byword for conviviality in both Moray and London (when he was once urged to move an address in the House of Lords, he replied that he would be charmed—as long as all involved adjourned to the City of London

146

Tavern). And the style he kept up at Gordon Castle was dazzling. An earlier visitor than Carruthers, an American called N. P. Willis, found himself amazed by the social routine that prevailed at the castle in 1833:

> Dinner was announced immediately, and the difficult question of precedence being sooner settled than I had ever seen it before in so large a party, we passed through files of servants to the dining-room . . . . The number at dinner was seldom less than thirty, but the company was continually varied by departures and arrivals: no sensation was made by either one or the other. A carriage drove to the door, was disburdened of its load, drove round to the stables, and the question was seldom asked, 'Who is arrived?' You are sure to see at dinner; and an addition of half a dozen to the party made no perceptible difference in anything.

The hospitable duke, who had to sell large parts of the family property to meet his expenses, was also the last of his line. On his death, Gordon Castle went to the family of the dukes of Richmond, into which one of the first Duchess Jane's daughters had married. In 1876, however, the title was revived, and the owners of Gordon Castle became the new dukes of Gordon as well.

The house created by Duke Alexander lasted in all its magnitude until the mid-1950s. Troops used it during World War II; afterwards, the weather made such drastic inroads on the structure that a new owner— Lt Gen Sir George Gordon Lennox, colonel of the Gordon Highlanders and a descendant of both the castle's ducal familities—decided to demolish the main block and one of the wings. The other wing was left as were the stables and laundries and the old tower, nucleus of both the eighteenth-century building and its predecessor. And some new buildings were added to protect the tower at its base. The Gordon Castle of today, therefore, occupies an interesting position, halfway between irrevocably lost and painstakingly salvaged. It is possible to wonder how many other buildings, irrevocably lost *in toto*, could with luck, skill and application have been made to fit into this pattern.

147

In the centre of Perth, on the corner of Tay Street and South Street, stands the handsome block of the Sheriff Court, adorned with columns and in one window a towering display of tomato plants, witness to the skill of some horticulturalist within. On the opposite corner is another building devoted to public activity: it houses the Procurator Fiscal's Office and the Tay River Purification Board. Immediately behind them is a rather dingy area that has as its centre the Speygate car-park. Dingy the area may be, but it once contained a building that is possibly the most famous of all Scottish lost houses. Its appearance was ordinary enough, and so were the reasons for its disappearance: it was pulled down in 1807 to make way for county buildings and a prison. But the events that took place there have given Scottish history one of its greatest enigmas. The house itself belonged to the earls of Gowrie; the mystery is usually known as the 'Gowrie conspiracy', and it has been baffling historians and criminologists for almost four centuries.

Although its details are extremely complex, the heart of the matter is simple and concerns the 'conspiracy' label itself. Did young John Ruthven, third Earl of Gowrie, and his even younger brother Alexander really conspire against their sovereign lord, James VI of Scotland? Or was it the other way round: did James, soon to become James I of England, lay a plot of astonishing subtlety against a difficult and potentially dangerous nobleman, and catch two fish in the same net? Or was there a conspiracy at all; was the whole business the product of accident, hot temper and a massive subsequent dose of whitewash? We can theorise but we still do not know. And Gowrie House, the interior layout of which could have thrown important light on the truth, is no longer there to help us.

Like the classic murder mystery of fiction, the Gowrie conspiracy involves a sizeable cast, a locked room, layer upon layer of obfuscation and a bystander who reappears at a key moment and clears everything up. (Was he, however, the right bystander?) It also demands the help of a sequence of maps. Although the action ranges from Falkland to Edinburgh, and possibly even further afield, the main events took place here, within the L-shaped main building of the Gowries' mansion in Perth, and within a single day, 5 August 1600.

The day started with James and his followers hunting deer at Falkland and one of those present, the Duke of Lennox, later bore witness to the opening events of the tragedy. Early in the morning, he saw young Alexander Ruthven, who had just ridden over from Perth, talking to James by the stables. After the hunt, the king told Lennox to accompany him straightaway back to Perth, where he wanted to speak to Alexander's twenty-three-year-old brother, the earl. The king then hurried off without even changing horses; Lennox, more prudently, changed his, buckled on a sword and hurried after in the company of about twenty other nobles, royal retainers and servants. When he caught James up, he found him again in conversation with young Ruthven. 'And shortly after the Deponent's [one who makes a statement] coming to the King,' said the Duke in a statement read at the subsequent judicial proceedings, 'His Highness rode a-part, and spake with this Deponent, saying, Ye cannot guess, Man, what Errand I am riding for; I am going to get a Pose [horde of gold] in Perth; And Mr. Alexander Ruthven has informed me, that he has fund a Man, that has a Pitchard full of coined Gold, of great Sorts.' James had recounted an amazing story: the younger Ruthven, he said, had discovered a suspicious character lugging a pot of gold pieces round the Perth environs the evening before. He now had the man under lock and key at Gowrie House and had invited His Majesty to come and investigate the matter in secret. Not even Ruthven's brother, the earl,

73 (*left*) Victim, plotter or unknowing bait for a trap? James VI of Scotland, survivor of the Gowrie Conspiracy and 74 (*right*) John Erskine, second Earl of Mar and childhood friend of James: how much did he know? Portrait attributed to Adam de Colone

must know about it. Lennox's reaction to this tale was, unsurprisingly, 'I like not that, Sir, for that is not likely.'

The royal party rode on, and within a mile of Perth Alexander Ruthven hurried ahead to the town to let his brother know of the king's unexpected visit. But was it unexpected? According to another witness—Andrew Henderson, one of Gowrie's household officials—the earl had had plenty of notice, for Henderson himself had accompanied Alexander Ruthven to Falkland and had hurried back to Perth earlier with the news of the king's plans. The only thing was that no one at Falkland could remember having seen him; at Gowrie House itself, someone had noted his absence and, on asking where he had been, was told 'two or three miles above the town'. Henderson, who played, or was made to play, a key part in the whole affair, had an explanation for this inconsistency. Whether it holds water remains to be seen.

Whether or not the Gowrie household had had ample warning of the royal visit, the atmosphere that surrounded the visitors on their arrival appears to have been one of complete surprise and confusion. By now, it was about midday and Gowrie, summoned from his meal to meet the king, hastily told his steward to find some royal provender. The steward bustled round, found a grouse, a fowl and a shoulder of mutton and ordered the cooking to start. James and his party waited in the Great Hall on the first floor of the building. The king asked for a drink but this, said Lennox afterwards, seemed 'a long Time a-coming'. Meanwhile, there was a fair amount of coming and going among the Gowrie household and the earl, in particular, seemed uncomfortable and preoccupied.

After an hour, the meal appeared (the mutton, though hurried on, must have been very underdone). The king went into the dining-room next to the hall where, with the fidgety Gowrie in attendance, he was served in solitary state. The rest, still in the hall, ate slightly later. Towards the end of the meal, James sent in a grace-cup, via Gowrie, with the message that he drank his health to them. Then the king himself entered with Alexander Ruthven; they crossed the corner of the hall and vanished up the main staircase to the second floor. Lennox made to join them but was told by the earl that 'His Majesty was gone up quietly, some quiet Errand'. It was at last time for the king and young Ruthven to inquire into the pot of gold business; Lennox did not enlighten the earl as to the errand's true nature but joined him and some of the other royal followers in the garden.

Until now, the action had been leisurely; puzzlingly so, in view of what the King's business at Gowrie House was supposed to be. From this point, however, things began to speed up. James accompanied Alexander

75 The scene of the crime. In the plan of the first floor, D marks the room where James ate, H the great hall, Y the main entrance and staircase, and T the black turnpike. In the plan of the second floor, A is the long gallery, C the gallery chamber and X the small turret room. Plan reproduced from the *Transactions* of the Literary and Antiquarian Society of Perth, 1827

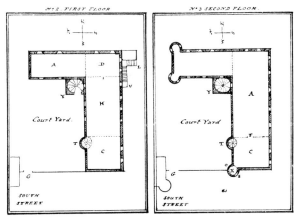

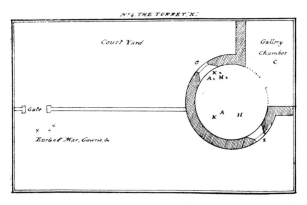

Ruthven upstairs, having—so he said later—asked for the courtier Sir Thomas Erskine to be brought up to him. It turned out, as he also said later, that Ruthven did not carry out the request. The king and Ruthven moved down the second floor's long gallery, where the Gowrie art treasures were arranged, entered the gallery chamber at its far end, and then the little circular room in the turret which hung over the street. It is at this point that Gowrie House itself could have given us some useful information. In his own account of what happened upstairs at Gowrie House, James spoke of going through three or four rooms, and of Ruthven locking each door behind them. But in all other accounts of what took place afterwards, only two doors appear to have been locked: those between the gallery and the gallery chamber and between the chamber and the turret room. So where did the extra doors (and extra rooms) spring from? Since the issue of Jame's truthfulness or lack of it is at the heart of the mystery, anything that definitely accords with or contradicts his story would help to assess it as a whole. Unfortunately, such aids are thin on the ground, and the evidence of the building itself would have been highly

151

welcome. As one 'conspiracy' commentator, Andrew Lang, has said, 'Could we see Gowrie House, and its "secret ways", as it then was, we might understand this problem of the locked doors.'

At all events, the door between the gallery and the gallery chamber certainly was locked. James said it was locked by Ruthven, and Ruthven was soon in no position to contradict him. If Ruthven had indeed locked it, the king might well have been somewhat surprised, and his surprise would have mounted when—to return to his own story—he entered the turret room and found, not the owner of the gold, but a dark stranger with a dagger in his belt. The stranger looked rather miserable; but James had little time to wonder about this, for Ruthven locked this door too, grabbed the stranger's dagger, held it to his sovereign's chest and, daring him to make a move, furiously reminded him of how his own father, the first Earl of Gowrie, had met his end. (The late earl had been a leader of the raid of Ruthven [see page 29]; he was pardoned afterwards, but continued plotting brought him to the scaffold.) The king, in whose name the execution had taken place, retorted that he had been a minor at the time. He implored Ruthven to see reason, reminded him of the consequences of regicide and promised to keep quiet if Ruthven would let him go. The stranger grew more miserable than ever. Ruthven, confused, said he would go and fetch the earl. With a final threat, he went, locking the door behind him. The stranger, left alone with the king, denied all knowledge of what was afoot; he had, not long before, been locked into the turret himself, in all ignorance of young Ruthven's plans. In an effort to make amends, he then opened one of the turret windows—the one giving on to Speygate outside.

Suddenly, Ruthven came bursting in again. The king, he cried, 'behoved to die'. He pulled out a garter and reached out to tie James's hands. James twisted away, grabbing Ruthven's sword hand. Ruthven, with his free hand, snatched at James's mouth to stop him crying out. The desperately struggling pair lurched towards the window and, at last, the king was close enough to lean out and shout, 'I am murdered! Treason! My Lord Mar, help! Help!'

For the King's actual words, we have more than his own story; we have witnesses. There are outsiders' accounts, too, for much of what had been happening downstairs until this point, and for what happened afterwards. Whether their testimony throws much light on the inner meaning of the events at Gowrie House is a matter of conjecture.

Left to their own devices, Gowrie and the courtiers enjoyed themselves in the garden until the earl's equerry, Thomas Cranstoun, hurried up with the news that the king had already left. The earl, flustered, called out for his own horse, then accompanied Lennox into the house, out into the court and to the front gate, where the porter was asked if the king had gone. The porter said he had not, nor had James yet left by the back gate because the porter held the keys. Gowrie, now angry as well as flustered, went back into the house to find out what was going on. Almost immediately, he came out again with the news that the king had indeed departed and then, puzzled and at a loose end, most the company drifted out into the street. And—so Lennox went on—as they were wondering what to do,

> this Deponent heard a Voice, and said to the Earl of Mar, This is the King's Voice, that cryes, be where He will: and so they all looked up to the Lodging, and saw His Majesty looking furth of the Window, wanting His Hat; His Face being red, and an Hand gripping his Cheek and Mouth; and the King cry'd, I am murdered! Treason! My Lord Mar, Help, help!

Lennox, Mar and most of the others ran back through the court, up the main staircase of the house, down the gallery to the locked door at the end, and were brought up short. They battered and thumped, but it would not give; they smashed at it with a ladder, but the ladder broke into pieces. They used hammers and succeeded in making a hole in the panelling but they still could not get in. However, one of the king's retinue was more successful in bringing aid. John Ramsay, a twenty-three-year-old page to the king, had not joined the others in the street on hearing his master had left; instead, he had gone for his horse in the stables, where he heard the king cry out. (Interestingly he had been the nearest of all his fellows to the king earlier, while the preliminary scuffle was taking place in the turret: he and another man had wandered up to the gallery in search of James and had stayed there for a while, looking at the pictures.) On hearing the king's voice, Ramsay ran back into the close and instantly noticed a way into the building that the others had missed: the door giving on to a narrow spiral staircase called the Black Turnpike, closer to the street than the main entrance. He raced up it and, in the words of his own statement,

> hearing an Struggling and Din of Men's Feet, he ran with his hail Force at the Door of the Turnpike-Head, which enters to the Chamber at the End of the Gallery; the Deponent having in the mean time His Haulk [hawk] on his Hand, and having dung [pushed] open the Door, he sees His Majesty and Mr. Alexander Ruthven in others Arms, striving and wrestling together, His Majesty having Mr. Alexander's Head under his Arm, and Mr. Alexander being almost on his Knees, and his Hand upon his Majesty's Face and Mouth; and His Majesty seeing the Deponent, cry'd Fy! strike him laigh [low], because he has an Pyne [mail] Doublet upon him.

153

Ramsay dropped the hawk, pulled out his dagger and, instead of striking low, stabbed his struggling junior in the neck and cheek. Then James bundled the wounded Alexander back down the turnpike stair and Ramsay, seeing Sir Thomas Erskine through a window, yelled at him to come up and help. The king smartly stood on the leash of the agitated hawk to prevent her escaping; Ramsay, drawing breath and looking round him, was vaguely surprised to see that they were now alone. On entering, he had—or later said he had—seen 'a Man standing behind His Majesty's Back, whom he noways knew, nor remembers not what Apparelling he had one'. Now, however, the man had gone.

Down below, meanwhile, the Earl of Gowrie himself had become involved in the affray. As the courtiers in the street below the turret window raced back into the building, Erskine (who, whatever Ruthven had told him to do, had by this point joined the main throng) turned, noticed the earl and pounced on him with the words, 'Traitor, this thy deed'. The earl, struggling in two pairs of Erskine hands—Sir Thomas's brother had joined in—replied, 'What is the matter? I ken nothing'. Then Gowrie's servants separated them and Erskine went into the court. In obedience to Ramsay's cry, he started up the turnpike, but climbed no further than five steps when young Ruthven came hurtling down into his arms. Erskine did not wait to check what had happened. 'This is the traitor', he cried to the men following him. 'Strike him!' Erskine's companions—a servant and a doctor—fell on Ruthven, who collapsed, protesting his innocence. The three men did not stop to watch him die; they raced up instead to the gallery chamber, where they found Ramsay and the king. For safety, they hustled James back inside the turret room from which he and Ruthven had been carried in their fight. Locking the door on him, they then turned to face the Earl of Gowrie, Cranstoun, and the other Gowrie men who had followed them up. Fighting broke out immediately. Erskine, Cranstoun and the doctor were wounded, while Ramsay, engaged with the earl, panted out that Gowrie had killed the King (who was, of course, invisible in the turret). Horrified, the earl halted for a second—and Ramsay ran him through. The Gowrie party fled.

By this time the town was in turmoil. The town bell was ringing, people were streaming from their homes and crowds were in the street outside, asking—like the poor earl before them—what the matter was. The king's life was in danger; Gowrie, Perth's provost, was dead; rumours ran in all directions and received their final expression in the shouts and screams of the people surging round Speygate and the Gowrie court, brandishing fists and weapons. In the gallery chamber above them, the king had emerged from the turret room and had finally been reunited with the Lennox party (the gallery door had at last been broken in). An anxious voice outside called inquiries about Gowrie, and was brusquely told he was well. The king fell to his knees to give thanks for his delivery from evil, and his nobles reassured the mob from the window, telling them to go home. James showed himself too and, hurried on by the threat of being charged with treason, they went. The affair at Gowrie House was over.

Two young men lay dead: noblemen of Scotland, killed by their sovereign's retinue; hosts, killed under their own roof by their guests; creditors, killed by their debtor's agents (James owed Gowrie £80,000, a sum spent on behalf of the crown by Gowrie's father). Clearly, the king needed to give an explanation of what had happened. He immediately did so, and later filled it out. The pot of gold story was told, with stress on young Ruthven's urgency and strange demands for secrecy. The walk down the long second floor of Gowrie House was described, with door after door closing behind plotter and victim. Out came the tale of the events in the turret chamber: the armed and wretched stranger, James's homily, young Ruthven's attempt on the royal life. It was all so odd, and in places so inconsistent, that the king's account was greeted with doubt by many, from his own wife downwards. Six leading Edinburgh preachers refused to give specific thanks for James's delivery from treason, saying that the presence of treason was not certain. Other people asked why James (already, on his own showing, suspicious of Ruthven) allowed himself to be led through all those closing doors. Others again wondered how the king—a shambling and notoriously faint-hearted thirty-four-year-old—could have put up such a fight against a strong young man of nineteen. Poor Cranstoun, with two more Gowrie men, was tortured and executed. But even in his agony he said nothing to indicate the existence of a Gowrie conspiracy against the king; his announcement of the king's departure had just been a mistake and nothing more.

Abroad, the French were roaring with laughter at the whole affair, while London was soon to be toying with the theory that the 'conspiracy' had in fact been the product of complete accident. There was no denying that, from the official Scottish point of view, some corroboration of the king's tale would have been most desirable. But the only living witness of the turret room scene was the mysterious stranger, who had not been seen since. Various individuals were accused of being the man, but never successfully. And then, suddenly, the stranger himself came forward. He was Andrew Henderson, who had been missing since the day of the killings. On 11 August, the king's chaplain included in his sermon the astonishing news that Henderson had contacted him; that Henderson's account bore out the king's; and that Henderson had left the gallery chamber just after Ramsay had entered it. Soon, Henderson himself—who was not dark, but had a brownish-red beard—turned up, full of self-justification.

The tale he told was, if anything, even odder than the king's. It started with the fact that he had been to Falkland and returned early to Perth with the news of the king's coming. He had lied about where he had been, he said, because Gowrie had told him to keep quiet about his errand. Later, while the king was dining at Gowrie House, the earl had taken Henderson to Alexander Ruthven in the gallery chamber and told him to do whatever Ruthven wished. Ruthven directed that Henderson—who, at Gowrie's earlier instance, had put on a secret mail doublet and was carrying a sword and dagger—should go into the turret chamber and stay there, locked in. He remained like this for half an hour, in understandable distress of mind. At last, in came Ruthven and the king, and events proceeded more or less as the king himself had narrated until the entry of Ramsay, for whom Henderson said he had unlocked the door. As Ramsay sprang to James's defence, Henderson quietly left, walked out through the court, and went home.

In spite of Henderson's appearance, however, the Gowrie controversy raged on. In England, a former ambassador to Scotland, Sir William Bowes, soon launched his theory that the entire incident had arisen by accident: the king and Alexander Ruthven might have had words about the activities of Ruthven's father; the king might have taken fright and cried 'Treason!'; Ruthven might have done his best to shut James up and the rest followed automatically. Soon, too, the Ruthven version of the case was written and circulated anonymously. According to this, James—far from being the victim—had been both the plotter and the lure; it was easy for him to impose his presence on the Gowrie household, to command Alexander Ruthven to enter what would be the death chamber and to bring Gowrie to his side for a like purpose.

James meanwhile, went briskly ahead with the official aftermath of the case. The younger Ruthven boys had been pursued (in fact, they escaped). Now the bodies of the earl and Alexander were produced and posthumously tried, with statements from all the witnesses, for treason. They were found guilty. Their corpses were hanged, drawn and quartered, and the ghastly fragments nailed up in Edinburgh, Dundee, Stirling and, of course, Perth. Their possessions were forfeited to the crown and their very name extinguished. The turret, scene of their alleged crimes, was

156

demolished and 5 August declared a day of national rejoicing. One of the Gowrie estates, Dirleton, went as a reward to Sir Thomas Erskine, who later became the Earl of Kellie; Ramsay got a knighthood and was later also created an earl. Other favours awaited the rest of the king's helpers in and outside the turret chamber, and Henderson was not the only one who ended up the richer. Nor was that the end: when James came to the throne of England in 1603, he was able to seize one of Gowrie's younger brothers and imprisoned him for almost twenty years.

Later still, in 1608, a set of letters turned up in the possession of a down-at-heel notary from Berwickshire which seemed to indicate that Gowrie had indeed been conspiring against the king with a rakehell laird, now dead, called Robert Logan. The notary, George Sprot, was taken, accused of guilty prior knowledge of the Gowrie conspiracy and tortured; under torture, he broke down and said that the letters were all forgeries, composed by himself for purposes of blackmail. This confession was suppressed, and Sprot was treated to the soft side of the well-known 'hard and soft' interrogation method: he was removed from his dungeon and given medical treatment. The hoped-for result was finally achieved. Sprot went back on his confession and said that one letter of Logan's in his possession, which he quoted from memory, was genuine. That was enough. Another 'proof' had been found to support the king's story. Sprot was whisked to the gallows without delay, and Logan's estate was later forfeit. In fact, all the letters have been shown to be forgeries.

This strange sequel to the affair, though on the face of it helpful to the king's case, did not bring the controversy to a halt. Nothing has. The three basic theories—a Gowrie plot, James's plot and accident—were all formed, as we have seen, very early on, and have continued to be hotly debated. There are, obviously, fundamental objections to all three: the Gowrie theory founders on both lack of evidence and the sheer craziness of attempting action against the king in a house filled with his followers. The king's neurotic cowardice is a stumbling-block to the idea that he used himself as bait in a royal trap. And the pot of gold fable is a serious obstacle to believing the accident hypothesis.

A modern Gowrie commentator, George Thomson, suggests that James's own followers were not perhaps as innocent as they seemed even if James was too cowardly to have led them. This writer would go further, and make the suggestion that the King unknowingly acted as bait in a trap set, not by himself, but by his nobles. There is, in particular, something about the movements of John Ramsay and Sir Thomas Erskine that might well, if it were possible, bear further examination. They are so often

76 Gowrie House in 1827, drawn from memory by R. Gibb and engraved by W. H. Lizars. The block on the right of the archway is where the action of the 'conspiracy' took place; note the lack of the turret. South Street is now continued across the site of the archway

slightly removed from the main throng; they make such speed towards the two Ruthvens when the action finally erupts; they are so quick to attack without asking questions. But, of course, no one thought at the time to examine them further: Ramsay was a royal page of honour, while Erskine was of the family of Mar—lifelong friend of the king, keeper of Stirling Castle and official guardian of the young Prince Henry. Mar himself is another character who, during that important lull after the meal, stayed slightly apart from the main throng. As he told the trial himself, he 'passed not to the Yeard, in Company with the Earl of Gowrie, but passed to a Chamber where the King dined'. One may well wonder whether it was Mar who confirmed the news of the king's departure when Gowrie vanished into the house to find out what was happening; he was in the dining-room, close to the main entrance and nicely positioned to deal both with inquiries from without and disturbances from above.

Is it possible that some of the king's followers, for reasons unknown, 'set the Ruthvens up': inveigled them into a hare-brained plot against James and then, when the co-plotters were fully committed, stepped in as saviours and wiped the Ruthvens out? It is possible, but then so is almost anything about the Gowrie case. The Perth house of the Ruthvens kept its secret for two hundred years and, presumably, will keep it for ever.

On 19 March 1865, an informal meeting took place at Marton Hall, near Middlesbrough, between Victorian capital and Victorian labour. The representative of labour, a Mr Thomas, had the urgent hope of finding some way to end a lock-out that paralysed the town and threatened to reduce its work-force to desperate poverty. The representative of capital, Henry Bolckow, was chairman of the firm Bolckow and Vaughan, one of the town's leading ironmasters and also Thomas's employer. He had the same end in mind as his employee. Both knew that Middlesbrough— whose fortunes were as closely wedded to iron production as those of boom towns elsewhere were to gold—would die if trade collapsed, and both were pulling against the wishes of colleagues in other parts of the country. Against Thomas and the rest of the Teesside ironworkers were those of North Staffordshire, whose pay demands had precipitated the dispute. Against Bolckow were the other members of the Ironmasters' Association, agitated by the prospect of paying on a national scale what the Staffordshire ironworkers had demanded. Middlesbrough and its 19,000 residents were caught in the middle of the quarrel; at Marton, Bolckow and Thomas aimed to sink their differences.

The lock-out had been in force for a week when the ironworkers met to discuss their next moves. While the others ate lunch, Thomas slipped out and made off to Marton, south of the town. Like other Bolckow and Vaughan workers, he had been there before, since Bolckow was a strong believer in worker participation and often used his elegant new home as the setting for these proceedings. When Thomas returned to the workers' meeting it was successfully to propose a motion that they should dissociate themselves from the factions within their union that had promoted the dispute. Bolckow, on his side, had again tackled the Ironmasters' Association and, this time, his pleas for peace were heard. By the end of March, Middlesbrough was again belching out the smoke that, as its mayor proudly told the Prince of Wales later in the century, was the gauge of its life, prosperity and place in the world.

More than anyone else, it was Henry Bolckow who had been responsible for both the smoke and the life. Born in 1806 of Junker parents in Mecklenburg, Bolckow came to England in 1827, when the population of Middlesbrough was about forty. When he died in 1878, it was nearing 56,000. Between these two points lay a history involving the discovery of local iron ore, its massive exploitation, an 'iron-rush' that attracted workers from all corners of the country, and an alien ironmaster who successively became a mayor, a fully naturalised British subject and a Member of Parliament. As a memorial to their achievements, Bolckow and his partner John Vaughan left a whole industry behind them. On a smaller scale, they also left schools, a park and their two great houses: Marton Hall, scene of the Bolckow-Thomas negotiations, and Gunnergate Hall, Vaughan's home two miles away.

Marton and Gunnergate stood for more than mere affluence. They were symbols of a relationship that had started in the 1830s, soon after Bolckow had arrived in England. The pair met in Newcastle upon Tyne, where Bolckow was working in the corn trade and Vaughan, seven years his senior, was an ironworks manager. They were courting two sisters, a Miss Poole and Mrs Hay, a widow whom Bolckow married in 1840. (Miss Poole married Bolckow's friend the same year.) The links between the two men then continued, for Bolckow, whose speculations in corn had been highly successful, had money to invest, and Vaughan had the technical ability to make the investment work. The two households moved to Middlesbrough and founded their first ironworks on Vulcan Street, a business partnership that survived all beginners' trials and, in 1850, struck it rich.

According to local mythology, Vaughan was wandering through the Cleveland Hills on a shoot when he tripped over a block of stone. The story adds that he looked at it carefully, realised what it was and thereby laid the fortunes of both his firm and the district. In fact, the discovery of great quantities of ironstone took place in a more mundane fashion. Bolckow and Vaughan instigated a careful survey of ironstone deposits in the area, tested the results and chose Eston, on which they secured the mining rights. Within weeks, the first few tons of iron were mined; within months, the weekly total had climbed into three figures, then four. The iron rush was on. Ahead lay the massive increase in Middlesbrough's population, its incorporation as a town and, in 1865, the transformation of the Bolckow-Vaughan partnership into a limited company.

Although Bolckow differed markedly from many captains of Victorian industry, one way in which he reacted to success was entirely typical of the class as a whole. He moved out of town. He and Vaughan used to live in the same house in central Middlesbrough—not quite over the shop, but at least near it. In 1853, however, he bought the manor of Marton and started to build on the site of an earlier mansion that had been burnt down. The resulting Marton Hall, with its views of the sea, was not as grand as it one day became, but it was still large enough to allow Bolckow to live in the style required of him. In the year of his purchase, he had become both Middlesbrough's first mayor and one of its Justices of the Peace and, though rather a shy man, he plunged into his civic duties with energy. Vaughan continued to live in the Middlesbrough house he had shared with his friend. But in 1860 he too moved out and bought the stylish modern residence, built only three years before, of Gunnergate Hall. The partners now had a new common interest: both were landed gentlemen.

Sadly, this new link in the chain that held the two friends together was relatively short-lived. Vaughan died in 1868, leaving Gunnergate to his son Thomas. The extent of the fortune also inherited by his son quickly became apparent when Thomas started refurbishing works that, in the words of the local *Evening Gazette*, amounted to a 'complete revolution'. Indeed, hardly anything was left of the original structure. 'At present,' the *Gazette* went on, 'there are being erected magnificent dining, drawing and billard rooms, with spacious sleeping apartments and dressing rooms above. The style may be called an adaptation of the Gothic.'

John Vaughan never lived to play the role of stately-home owner; Bolckow, however, did, and fitted himself to it in rather the same way as the Rothschilds did in the south, although on a smaller scale. In Middlesbrough, he was ironmaster and civic worthy; at home in Marton, he was a gentleman of culture, taste and benevolent intentions. He financed

77 Gunnergate Hall, home of John Vaughan and remodelled after his death by his son Thomas

schools in Marton and in Middlesbrough. He collected pictures and manuscripts; his collection included the journal kept by Captain Cook during his expedition in the *Endeavour*. Cook himself had been born in a tiny thatched cottage that had stood in the grounds of Marton Hall; Bolckow, fascinated by the historical associations of his home, had Cook's birthplace restored.

In the same year that John Vaughan died, Bolckow became both Middlesbrough's first-ever Member of Parliament and a host to royalty. The royal visit took place in connection with the ironmaster's presentation of a park to the town. The Queen had signified her gracious approval of the request to name it after her late husband, and one of their sons, Prince Arthur, travelled north to open it. On 10 August, Bolckow and the Archbishop of York welcomed the prince to Marton. The next day, archbishop and ironmaster accompanied His Royal Highness to the park (the local Sunday School children, lined up in the market place, burst into a well-rehearsed National Anthem as the carriage passed). Bolckow made his formal presentation and the prince, in the words of the *Illustrated London News*, responded 'in graceful terms'. The archbishop said a prayer, the prince planted a tree, guns banged and the royal visitor was then conducted to lunch and a tour round the ironworks. He escaped late in the evening, *en route* for Scotland and the company of his family.

The Marton that received Prince Arthur on his overnight stay was no longer the establishment that Thomas, the ironworker representative, had visited three years before. Bolckow had—just in time as it turned out —started building again and, when he had finished, the result put Gunnergate in the shade. The Marton exterior, with its dome and lantern, was French in inspiration; the inside, Italian. There were marble pillars, a marble staircase and a black-and-white marble floor stretching across the hall. Bolckow, as his park project indicated, was fond of gardens. Here he could enjoy a hundred acres of ground, complete with lakes and rare trees, with a charming hexagonal conservatory at one end of the hall that brought the garden into the house. This, too, was a stately home of Cleveland, an even statelier one than its neighbour.

Both houses, in fact, soon came into the possession of a single owner: Carl Bolckow, the old ironmaster's nephew and heir. Marton came first, on Henry Bolckow' death. Three years later, Carl bought the Vaughan house, its contents having been sold off earlier. But in 1888 Carl himself was observed to be selling off his uncle's superb collection of pictures, and at about the same time Gunnergate was bought by the same Middlesbrough mayor who staunchly supported the town's smokiness: Raylton

78 Marton Hall, the tycoon's dream

Dixon. The reason for these abrupt changes of ownership lay not in Carl's inadequacy as the new chairman of Bolckow and Vaughan, but in forces quite beyond the Teessiders' control.

In the 1850s, the engineer Henry Bessemer had introduced to the world the process he had worked out for producing steel cheaply. Another process with the same result, known as the 'open hearth', came in a decade later. Steel from then on was to be the new king. The Bolckow company did its best to meet the challenge, but there was one grave snag. Both the Bessemer and the open hearth processes only worked if the iron ore used was low in phosphorus, and Cleveland iron, like most of the British deposits and many abroad, was highly phosphoric. Yet again, however, Bolckow, Vaughan & Co rose to the occasion. After some years of importing non-phosphoric ores from abroad, the company gave encouragement and trial space to two cousins, Sidney Gilchrist Thomas and P. C. Gilchrist, who claimed that they had discovered a way of processing phosphoric ore into steel. Their claim was true and, in 1879, the Bolckow firm became the first British manufacturers to use the Gilchrist-Thomas process. The move should have led to the happiest of endings but, by a savagely ironic twist, it did not. What was good for Bolckow-Vaughan was also good for all the steel producers overseas who had large supplies of phosphoric ore at their disposal. They, too, invested in the Gilchrist-Thomas process and, almost overnight, the Teesside steelworkers were in hot competition with firms on the Continent and in the USA. Carl found

163

79 Henry Bolckow: ironmaster, art collector, philanthropist and and Member of Parliament

himself in difficulties, and as a by-product of these Gunnergate and the Marton art collections had to go.

Carl was not, on the whole, a lucky person. Less financially astute than Henry had been, he made inroads on his inheritance through financial ventures that did not pay off. Bolckow, Vaughan & Co continued to adapt and prosper, but the big house at Marton stood idle and empty for a long time. A sale of furniture was held in the summer of 1907, followed by a sale of books. During World War I, it was used as a base for troops, a role that has frequently shown itself during the past century to be an ominous sign. There were further sales in 1923 and 1924 and then, later in 1924, Marton itself was sold. The buyer, Thomas Stewart, turned out to be a man whom the long-dead Henry Bolckow would have taken to his heart, for he presented his purchase to the public. The grounds were renamed after him: Stewart Park.

Gunnergate had meanwhile been standing empty ever since Dixon's widow had left it. In 1946, it came down. Marton Hall survived much longer, and it was only in 1960 that demolition was begun, interrupted by fire, and completed.

One now looks in vain through the Middlesbrough telephone book for the name of Bolckow, Vaughan & Co. The firm was bought by Dorman, Long in 1929. Only a colonnade remains of Marton Hall, while Middlesbrough itself has swamped the countryside between Hall and Tees. Middlesbrough itself is Bolckow's monument.

On the last day of his tour with Samuel Johnson from Edinburgh to the Hebrides and back, James Boswell tried to lure his companion into a final venture. On 9 November 1773 he wrote in his journal of the tour:

> I wished to have shewn Dr. Johnson the Duke of Hamilton's house, commonly called the *Palace* of Hamilton, which is close by the town. It is an object which, having been pointed out to me as a splendid edifice from my earliest years, in travelling between Auchinleck and Edinburgh, has still great grandeur in my imagination.

But Johnson was in no particular mood to dally; he agreed to inspect the building from the outside, but refused to go in. Instead, the pair hurried on to Edinburgh and arrived the same day after an absence of almost twelve weeks. 'I cannot express how happy I was on finding myself again at home', the journal-keeper added.

For nearly two centuries before Johnson hastened Boswell on, the palace of the Hamiltons (or castle or house—the name changed frequently) had been attracting the attention of travellers in the Clyde valley, and it continued to do so for another century and a half. Indeed, one of its remnants still does, for the domed building so strikingly visible from the M74 is the mausoleum erected by the tenth Duke of Hamilton, who had a passion for building and was obsessed with the hardware of death. The palace itself went through several changes of appearance: it started as a rather bleak-looking structure round a court, was transformed into a U-shaped mansion with sash windows (very modern at the time of their installation) and Corinthian columns, and finally acquired a whole new front of even more classical splendour, with three times as many columns and a double staircase. At no point during its metamorphoses did the building look outstandingly beautiful. But, as Boswell's memories indicate, it was splendid, imposing, grand—and its contents grew to be of almost fabulous value. While Gowrie is perhaps the most important of Scotland's lost houses, the great mansion of the dukes of Hamilton is without doubt the best known.

The building's history began in 1591, when the Hamiltons had recovered enough from the turmoil of Mary Stuart's reign and its aftermath to rebuild a family home on or near the site of an earlier Hamilton seat called The Orchard. The builder was not the nominal head of the family (who

80 Hamilton Palace: the old north front, engraved by Sturer and Greig shortly after the Wordsworths' visit

bore the French title of the Duke of Chatelherault) but his younger brother; the duke was incurably mad—as a result, so tradition said, of having been turned down years before by Queen Mary—and it was Lord John Hamilton who was in charge. The new house, four-square amid the smaller homes of the Hamilton burghers that crowded round it, was one of the foundations on which the family's restored fortunes were to rest. Another was the friendship between John and King James VI, for in the last year of the century the king made John a marquis. Two generations later, the Stuarts ennobled the Hamiltons still further: the third marquis, a widower with only two young daughters to follow him, was made a duke by Charles I. The elder of the daughters, eleven-year-old Anne, was living at Hamilton Palace when she heard the news of her father's ennoblement. Only eight years later, she became—in her own eyes at least—its owner. Her royalist father had been executed in the same year as the king, while the second duke, her uncle, had died of wounds received at the Battle of Worcester. Scarcely half a century after Lord John Hamilton had set to work to repair the Hamilton fortunes, a similar task now faced a nineteen-year-old girl who, though Duchess of Hamilton in her own right, had had her lands confiscated and her family seat handed over to a Parliamentarian army leader, while she camped out in a nearby house.

By good luck, determination and plain mother-wit, she won through. In 1656 she married the Earl of Selkirk (on her side, at least, it appears to have been a love match) and between them they managed to claw back the

166

Hamilton possessions. They also brought up a large family in their regained palace at Hamilton, which had gathered some additions and extra corners since it had first been built. But this was not the sum total of their aims. Given the financial difficulties in the early days of their marriage, it is perhaps unsurprising that the duchess and her duke (he was given the dukedom for life) should want to turn their home into something really splendid when time and money allowed. Other Scottish peers, of course, felt the same, and visits to the court of their king in London ensured that their ideas of splendour were of a most up-to-date nature. Throughout his life, the Duke of Hamilton kept bringing back to Hamilton Palace items that reflected this modernity, such as chocolate, silver candlesticks wrought in the latest style and a French servant who specialised in making sweets. By the last quarter of the century, the time had come for the house itself to be modernised and, in 1682, the Scottish architect James Smith was employed to draw up plans.

The Hamiltons were by now experienced rebuilders—they had already transformed one of their other possessions, Kinneil Castle—and they began their major works on the palace very modestly, by putting up some new stables. While this was happening, the plans for the main building were being changed and changed again and, by the end of 1691, the final scheme was more or less ready. The square formed by the building was to become a U; its southern side would vanish completely, and the eastern and western sides would be rebuilt. The northern side would remain, but the main entrance would now be within the open court formed between the two wings. Work on the west wing—the first to be rebuilt—was nearly over when, in 1694, the duke died. But the duchess, as determined at sixty-two as she had been in her early twenties, continued with her massive scheme. The east wing went up, a mirror-image of the one built earlier, and finally the north wing (which, in a last-minute change of plan, was almost entirely reconstructed) joined the two. Outside, the new palace looked severe; almost as bleak, despite its Corinthian columns, as its sixteenth-century predecessor. Inside, however, miracles of richness had been worked on the ceilings by master plasterer Thomas Aliborne and on the panelling, chimney-pieces and great staircase by wood-carver William Morgan. Motifs that appeared time and time again included the Hamilton cinquefoils and, on the staircase, the entwined letters W and A.

Anne outlived her William by twenty-two years, easily time for the palace to be completed. A few years after she died, her creation was visited by Daniel Defoe who, in his *Tour*, interestingly refers to the existence of yet further plans that would have turned the shape of the palace buildings from a U into an H. However, he was impressed enough as it was, both by the house and the exalted state of those who live in it:

> The Front is very magnificent indeed, all of white Freestone, with regular Ornaments according to the Rules of Art . . . . The Apartments are very noble, and fit rather for the Court of a Prince than the Palace or House of a Subject; the Pictures, the Furniture and the Decoration of every Thing is not to be describ'd, but by saying that every Thing is exquisitely fine and suitable to Genius of the great Possessors: The late Duchess, whose Estate it was, was Heiress of the Family, but marrying a Branch of the House of *Douglass*, oblig'd him to take the name of *Hamilton*, so to continue the Estate in the Name; and it has sufficiently answer'd that End. That Match being blest with a truly glorious Succession of six Sons, four of whom were Peers by Birth, or Creation.

Dealing later with the question of the fourth duke's death, Defoe pointed out that the estate had actually remained in the hands of Duchess Anne throughout the duke's lifetime, and added, with his usual diplomacy, 'whether this might not be the better for the present Heir, I shall not determine, let others judge of that'. In fact, it had indeed been the better

81 The Duchess Anne's dining-room, a photograph taken at the end of the nineteenth century by Lafayette. By this time it had become the palace breakfast room

for him—much better, as even the late duchess herself might have agreed. James, fourth Duke of Hamilton and heir to all his parents' hard work, was not heir to their qualities. He was an irresponsible, live-for-the-minute character to whom notions of family and family inheritance were completely alien. If he had lived to inherit from his mother, the estate he would have in turn handed on to his own heir would in all probability have been tiny. In 1712, however, he died in the duel recreated in Thackeray's *Esmond*, stabbing his opponent Lord Mohun to death seconds after Mohun had fatally slit one of his own arteries. After a period of numbed grief, the poor duchess yet again collected her resources and went on as usual, preparing for the time when she would hand over a prosperous estate to her grandson.

As both Defoe's and Boswell's accounts indicate, Hamilton Palace was typical of the British great house in that visitors (armed, of course, with suitable indications of gentility) were allowed to inspect both the grounds and the interior. And the interior was well worth visiting, not just for its magnificent carving and the charming plasterwork but also for its furniture and pictures. (The latter were housed in a special gallery that took up all the first floor of the U's cross-bar.) Unfortunately for connoisseurs, however, the staff's notions of gentility were on occasions rather inconsistent—as, thirty years after Boswell's visit, another group of literary sightseers found out. They were William Wordsworth (who had visited the interior two years before), Samuel Coleridge and Wordsworth's sister Dorothy. Their aim was to see the pinnacle of the Palace's art collection: *Daniel in the Lions' Den* by Rubens, on which Wordsworth published a sonnet in 1835.

Dorothy took against the palace from the start. 'It was', she wrote afterwards, 'a large building, without grandeur, a heavy, lumpish mass.' However, the trio confidently marched across the courtyard and arrived under the portico by which William had entered on his earlier visit. From this point, the trip went sadly wrong.

We were met by a little mean-looking man, shabbily dressed, out of livery, who, we found, was the porter. After scanning us over, he told us that we ought not to have come to that door. We said we were sorry for the mistake, but as one of our party had been there two years before, and was admitted by the same entrance, we had supposed it was the regular way. After many hesitations, and having kept us five minutes waiting in the large hall, while he went to consult with the housekeeper, he informed us that we could not be admitted at that time, the housekeeper being unwell [drunk?]; but that we might return in an hour: he then conducted us through long gloomy passages

169

to an obscure door at the corner of the house. We asked if we might be permitted to walk in the park in the meantime; and he told us that this would not be agreeable to the Duke's family.

The little group trailed away in the heat—it was August, dry and dusty —and then, having filled in the time, came back. This time, they went to the right door, but to no avail, for the porter—who again kept them waiting—finally told them that they could not go in, 'giving no reason whatever'. That night, William relieved his feelings by dashing off a letter to Lord Archibald Hamilton; Dorothy went to bed with a headache.

The recipient of Wordsworth's letter was the brother of the next and last Hamilton to subject the palace to major building works: Alexander, the tenth duke. Dorothy's sour comments indicate that some rebuilding was badly needed: even in its heyday, the new south front had been somewhat austere, while the north front retained from the earlier building must indeed have seemed heavy and lumpish by later architectural taste. Working from plans drawn up for the fifth duke almost a century before by William Adam (father of Robert), the tenth duke had a whole new north front created in the 1820s, with apartments of matching grandeur behind it. Both the addition and the statistics involved were a delight to the compilers of local guidebooks. One, published in the 1850s, commented:

> The harmonious beauty and grand proportion of this noble facade make it a luxurious eyefill to all observers, learned and unlearned. Its length is 264 feet, height 60. The portico has two rows of six columns each, 25 feet high, and fully 10 feet span, formed of a solid block of stone, quarried in Dalserf; each block required 30 horses to draw it . . .. The new palace took 28,056 tons stone, drawn by 22,528 horses; 5,535 tons lime &c., drawn by 5,196 horses; slates, 22,531, bricks 62,200, drawn by 731 horses. The stables (only half-finished according to plan), took 9,337 tons of materials drawn by 6,177 horses.

So much stone, so much lime, such amazing numbers of sweating, striving beasts; like serfs of the Middle Ages, the inhabitants of Hamilton were left in no doubt of the greatness of their lord. (Another indication of his grandeur was the fact that their homes had now been cleared well back from the palace's environs, a process started in the eighteenth century; the tenth duke himself bought up and destroyed a whole street.) Alexander also made alterations to the palace's interior. He had a passion for black marble and the reworked Hamilton Palace soon acquired black marble mantelpieces, black marble floors and a new grand staircase of gleaming black from floor to landing. Not content with adding such funereal touches to his home, he went on to start building a Hamilton

82 (*top*) Hamilton's south front, the work of the third duke and his duchess and 83 (*above*) the new north front, created by Duke Alexander

mausoleum in the palace's grounds. He died in 1852 before it could be finished, but not before he could choose his own manner of entombment. The coffin he selected for himself—its destined place in the mausoleum was of course a block of black marble—was a sarcophagus he had bought years before on behalf of the British Museum under the impression that it had belonged to an Egyptian queen. Its original occupant, however, turned out to be a lady of no distinction at all, so the duke, who was a great art collector, entered into negotiations on his own behalf, paid the museum the amount he owed and took the sarcophagus away with him. As he grew old, his interest in the object increased and, according to tradition, he used to scramble into it and lie down to see if it would fit.

Until, with its embalmed contents, the sarcophagus was transported to the Hamilton Mausoleum, its home was the tenth duke's London house in Portman Square. The majority of his art treasures, however, were kept at Hamilton Palace, adding themselves to those of his ancestors and added to in turn by a spectacular bequest to his wife. She was Susan, one of William Beckford's daughters. After the builder of Fonthill died in 1844, Duke Alexander had a special T-shaped room created to house his late father-in-law's library of almost 10,000 volumes, ranging from the classics to books on the occult.

Hamilton Palace also housed a Beckford portrait gallery: there was Romney's painting of the Misses Beckford as children, further Romneys of Beckford himself and a Reynolds of Beckford's august father, twice Lord Mayor of London. But the Beckford showing was tiny compared with the rest. There was of course, Hamilton after Hamilton (notably a Reynolds of the sixth duchess, *née* Elizabeth Gunning, whom eighteenth-century crowds had mobbed for her beauty). There was Rubens' *Daniel*, da Vinci's *Laughing Boy*, Poussin's *Entombment of Christ*, Giorgione's *Ascension* and a tail-end of other attractions that the directory quoted above summed up as 'gems by Titian, Rembrandt, Guido, Carlo Dolce, the Carracci, Spagnoletti, &c'. The new rooms in the north front were hung and carpeted with tapestry. Visitors passed through a maze of buhl cabinets, massive vases, and tables made of anything from marble to Sèvres china. One of these was worth £4,000. The plate, which included a tea-service made of gold, was valued at £50,000. Under the tenth duke and his immediate successors, Hamilton Palace was an Aladdin's Cave of unbelievable and, indeed, almost unguessable splendour: the Hamilton print collection contained some items that had never been valued, since no one had ever unfolded them.

Alexander did not devote all his wealth to the collection of fine art; he had a complicated water-supply installed at the palace, along with fire-fighting provisions. Gas came too, from a private gasworks. And William, the eleventh duke, in 1861 turned his attention to an area which had previously been somewhat lacking in interest and created almost an acre of formally laid-out flower gardens below the palace windows. But the art-collecting continued on a grand scale, as a *Hamilton Directory* for 1878-9 makes clear:

> The present Duke when recently in Venice, acquired two magnificent bottle-shaped vases, composed of tortoise shell inlaid with ivory, and studded with turquoise and other precious stones. The vases are four feet in height. They are placed on pedestals two feet in height, supported by three negroes in a kneeling posture. His Grace, at the same time, procured two figures of negresses, five feet in height, beautifully painted in full Eastern costume; mounted on pedestals two feet high, and which are placed on the Eastern staircase. [The duke referred to is the twelfth].

The social life at Hamilton Palace was on a scale to match: guests from the mid-century onwards included Queen Victoria's mother, the Duchess of Kent; the Queen of Holland; the Empress Eugénie; and the Prince of Wales. The prince, who visited in 1878, brought a string of foreign royalty, aristocrats and friends with him. One of them, the Prince Imperial of France, caused everyone's heart to stop by mounting an unbroken Clydesdale horse and thundering around the stud yard at nearby Merryton, where the royal party were making a tour of inspection. Afterwards, the whole lot went on a shooting party and accounted for a bag of over 5,000 pheasants, partridges, hares, rabbits, woodcock, deer and 'sundries'.

Although other royal visits were to follow, this sporting occasion, which culminated in a ball at the palace, really marked the end of the great days of Hamilton Palace. Alexander, with his collecting and building schemes, had run into debt and the debts, like the collections, had not decreased. It was the twelfth duke who finally decided on a solution: to

84 The tenth Duke of Hamilton

sell off the greater part of what his family had so carefully and expensively amassed. The sale itself took place in July 1882 at Christie's and enriched the vendor by £397, 562. Among the items sold was the *Daniel*, but the twelfth duke bought it back and reinstalled it in the now depleted collection. A reasonable amount, however, did remain in the Hamilton galleries, including the pictures of the Beckfords and of the sixth duchess, the other family portraits, the pillars brought from the Dead Sea, the statue of Venus found at Pompeii and a jewel case that had belonged to Mary Queen of Scots.

Barer but still grand, the house continued to dominate the Clyde valley by Hamilton. Life there, however, was never quite the same again, and the palace began to stand idle more and more often. In its insidious way, the usual decline from great home to deserted wreck had begun. Just how long the sequence would have taken to run its full course is, though, a matter of guesswork, for a crisis was hastened when the building started to develop problems of its own. H. Avray Tipping, *Country Life*'s leading writer of profiles of great houses, wrote a detailed account of the palace in 1919, but his three Hamilton articles were the building's obituary. Almost his first words were:

> The doom of Hamilton Palace is imminent. Its situation and condition join with its size in procuring its condemnation by general consent. It is in the midst of the Lanarkshire coalfield, and the numerous and proximate pits not only destroy its amenity, but actually threaten its structure. Subsidences in the park have been followed by ominous cracks in the walls. Pick and shovel work nearer and nearer, so that the time seems to be approaching when inhabitance may become not merely disagreeable, but dangerous.

By this time, the thirteenth duke had moved out for good. Another amazing sale took place at Christie's, the Hamilton Trustees decided that the building should be demolished and, in 1922, the Hamilton Town Council bought the grounds. The demolition squads moved in on Hamilton Palace, and stayed through almost the whole of the decade.

The site today—still called the Palace Grounds locally—is part of the Strathclyde Park and is occupied by a complex of playing fields. Further afield in the park are nature reserves, a bowling green, a caravan camp and the only palace now in sight: an inflatable affair for children labelled 'Castillo el Sid'. Further afield still are multi-storey flats, factories, a slag heap and, along with the mausoleum, the only obvious reminder of the Hamiltons—the pinkish length of their Adam hunting-lodge, Chatelherault, on a hill. The inhabitants of Hamilton have now come back to the territory from which they were cleared.

Although the family name of Barrett is indelibly connected with London's Wimpole Street, an equally indelible connection exists with the estate of Hope End in the modern county of Hereford and Worcester. Indeed, the family's most famous member, Elizabeth, lived at Hope End considerably longer: twenty-three years of her childhood and youth, as opposed to the eight spent at Number 50.

The Barrett Moulton-Barretts who came to Herefordshire in 1809 were, in fact, a very young family. Elizabeth herself, eldest of the children, was three, while her father—far from being the heavy paterfamilias of later fact and legend—was a headstrong young man of only twenty-four. The place he had bought was a self-contained estate ('hope' means a closed valley) that contained as its focus an uncompromisingly plain mansion dating in part from the seventeenth century. It had, as he saw, possibilities, both as a home for his still small brood and as a reflection of his remarkable personality.

Plain though the house might have been, it had dramatic associations before the Barretts's ownership. It was from a ball given here that the occupant's daughter and heiress, Sarah Pritchard Lambert, was persuaded to elope by a real-life bad baronet. Like Cinderella, she left her dancing slipper behind in the drive and, in pouring rain, had to make her way to the rendezvous half-barefoot. The pair moved into the house (evicting Sarah's father in the process) but the match turned out badly; Sarah was chased away in her turn and Hope End was finally sold to the Barretts.

Mr Barrett had no use for the romantic associations of his purchase. He took off the top floor and transformed the remains into stables. At the same time, however, he built a new mansion that was as ornate as its predecessor had been plain. Elizabeth's father may have lacked imagination where the feelings of others were concerned, but Hope End II showed that he was anything but lacking in flights of fancy. It was an amazing structure, topped and ornamented with an array of Turkish motifs— domes, spires, crescents. (Even the stables acquired a domed gateway and minarets.) The interior was just as breath-taking and just as odd: the fame of the doors, inlaid with mother-of-pearl, lasted long in the neighbourhood, and so did the way windows were positioned over fireplaces.

It was in these extravagantly picturesque surroundings that nine more Barrett children were born, bringing the total to twelve. Of these, all but one survived childhood, a remarkably low mortality rate for the period. But however healthy it may have been as a nursery, Hope End must have had a certain gloominess even before it was touched by the emotional tensions and storms that visited it later. It was, for example, visited all too frequently by real ones: the hills in that part of Herefordshire make it a great place for thunder, and the 'Turkish' ironwork on the house's roof acted as an unintended lightning conductor. Then again, there was its position in the valley: an observer, Allan Bright, who could just remember the building, commented in 1923 that the situation was almost sunless and quite without view. (The prime site, he added, had been occupied by Hope End I.)

Further obstructions to Hope End II's outlook were provided by the trees clustering thickly in the grounds, which had been planned by the landscape architect John Claudius Loudon. Barrett was a keen landscaper himself, just as he was a keen follower of other country gentleman's pursuits. He 'farmed largely, was an active magistrate, became for a year High Sheriff, and in all county contests busied himself as a Liberal', wrote Robert Browning in a preface to the 1887 edition of his wife's works. 'He had a fine taste for landscape-gardening, planted considerably, loved trees . . . and for their sake discontinued keeping deer in the park.'

For the young Elizabeth, however, the boskiness of both the estate and the general landscape was a greatly loved aspect of Hope End, if only one among many. Over twenty years after she had left them, she remembered the trees of her childhood home in her long novel-poem, *Aurora Leigh*:

> . . . past the lime, the lawn,
> Which, after sweeping broadly round the house,
> Went trickling through the shrubberies in a stream
> Of tender turf, and wore and lost itself
> Among the acacias, over which you saw
> The irregular line of elms by the deep lane
> Which stopped the grounds and dammed the overflow
> Of arbutus and laurel . . ..

An earlier poem, *The Lost Bower*, described her surroundings further afield and returned yet again to the 'glamour past dispute' of a place where trees shut out the sky:

> Few and broken paths showed through it,
> Where the sheep had tried to run,
> Forced with snowy wool to strew it
> Round the thickets, when anon
> They, with silly thorn-pricked noses, bleated back into the sun.

85 The Barretts' Hope End, drawn by a later occupant, Mrs Heywood, and produced as a lithograph by local artist Philip Ballard

The sheep could not get in; Elizabeth did, and in the poem she recalled her childhood discovery of a secret glade within the wood, like a natural garden—a garden she was never able to find again. But this small adventure was also the herald of much greater losses: those of the acceptance, confidence, dash and good health of her childhood and early youth. Her good health came to an end at the age of fifteen, when a riding accident led to serious illness and a prolonged absence from home. The other blessings withered away under the combined influences of growing up and her family background.

If, for Elizabeth, Hope End had the qualities of a Paradise Lost, it arguably represented something quite different for her father. Among Mr Barrett's characteristics was an unusually outstanding gift for imposing his own outlook on the world whenever the latter did not suit him—and Hope End II was a product of this gift. He saw nothing incongruous in erecting an Oriental extravaganza of a building in one of England's greenest, lushest counties. Much later, he would react with equal lack of compromise to Elizabeth's marriage: he simply cut her out of his life for ever. Long before this happened, though, his family were well aware of the costs to themselves of his ability to force dream-worlds on others.

86 Elizabeth Barrett Browning in later life. Portrait by M. Gordigiani

Relatively recently, a search for Elizabeth's imploring letters to her father after her marriage led to the discovery of a diary she kept shortly before she and the rest of the family were to leave Hope End for good. In this *Early Diary*, the twenty-five-year-old girl (she was twenty-six in the year of her departure) shows herself as lively and ailing, high-minded and caustic, delightful and exasperating by turns. She reads voraciously, especially from the classics; she also goes mushrooming and plays with her

178

pet squirrel, which takes chestnuts from her hand but has a tendency to smell. She gives lessons to her young brothers, receives visitors (and is chagrined when she forgets to offer a caller luncheon), nurses her nerves with 'aromatic vinegar' and is chased by a bull. Two constant themes, however, run through this variety: her friendship with her Malvern neighbour and mentor, the blind scholar Hugh Stuart Boyd, and the looming threat of the Barretts' departure from Herefordshire.

In the 1820s, the Barrett fortunes had begun to fail. It finally became obvious that Hope End would have to be sacrificed, but Papa, true to character, succeeded in obliterating this uncomfortable fact from the surface of his relationships with his children. Elizabeth later recalled that he never once mentioned it to them. Instead, they learned about the prospect of leaving Hope End from outside sources—gossip, 'for sale' advertisements, people coming to view—and Elizabeth's diary is full of the misery caused both by the threat of moving and its uncertainty. To some degree, she was forced by her insecurity into playing her father's obscurantist game. On being told by a friend that Hope End had been advertised by name, she wrote, 'I wd. & cd. ask no particulars. I was so afraid of her telling me on what day it is to be sold.' Mystery, on that occasion, seemed preferable to unbearable fact.

In the end, however, the facts had to be faced. The Barretts' furniture was put in store and, on 22 August 1832, the boys played their last game of cricket on the Hope End lawn. The next day, most of the family and their servants crushed into two carriages and left for Sidmouth. Elizabeth never returned to Herefordshire.

Under its new owners, the Barretts' Hope End survived until the 1870s, when it changed hands once more. In 1873 it was pulled down and a third Hope End, a pseudo-Gothic mansion, was built higher up the slope. This, a less unorthodox country house with a battlemented tower, was devastated by fire in 1910. Losses included the mother-of-pearl doors, transferred from Elizabeth's old home to the newer building. The servants' wing, however, survived, and was turned into a smaller house.

The fire did not, of course, touch the old Barrett stables with their Oriental ornaments and their much older underlying fabric. But, between the wars, these too suffered under less spectacular but equally powerful forces of decay. Then, however, at a period when other buildings of historical interest were being demolished right across the country, they were rescued and restored. The Barretts' stables are now a hotel and a Grade II listed building. As happens more frequently than might be expected, the real survivor on the site is the oldest structure of all.

❧Horton Hall and Horton Old Hall

At Little Horton, a mile or so from the centre of Bradford, two houses once stood next to each other divided by a high wall. Both were built in the seventeenth century by the locally eminent family of Sharp. Both, three centuries later, achieved listed status, and were given the Royal Commission's asterisk denoting their position as buildings of 'outstanding importance'. And both, very shortly after receiving this accolade, vanished. In a sense, they were almost twin houses.

This kinship even pre-dated their existence. By tradition, the building swallowed up in the older of the two—Horton Old Hall—had belonged to John Sharp, a Royalist and a man of firm and indeed extravagant loyalties. As a sign of lifelong mourning, he let his beard grow unchecked from the day news came of Charles I's execution. He was also something of a grumbler: he recovered from a battle-axe wound received during the Civil War but, until his death at the very reasonable age of seventy, moaned that he would never now live to be an old man.

In contrast, John-the-Beard's neighbour in the predecessor of Horton Hall—his nephew, another John Sharp—was a strong Parliamentarian. While his uncle was fighting for the king, John the Puritan was acting as private secretary to General Fairfax. The tension between the two family homes must have been considerable, and it was then that the wall dividing the two is believed to have been built.

Neither John seemed to suffer unduly from either the Civil War or its aftermath, and both left a considerable inheritance to their children. John-the-Beard's eldest son, Isaac, employed some of his on rebuilding his father's old home. Starting shortly after the Restoration and continuing until about 1675, he produced a typically Yorkshire stone house, built on the plan of a U, with mullioned windows, a two-storey great hall and a severe appearance. The severe effect continued inside: over a bedroom fireplace, Isaac put a sombre reminder in bad Latin that the room's occupant was but mortal, doomed to dust.

Outside, the high wall stayed in place but, in spite of this, building fever spread to Isaac's neighbour and relative, the Reverend Thomas Sharp. Interestingly, it was this younger member of the Nonconformist Sharp line that created the more ornate building. Round the timbers of his old home, he too built a two-storey, U-shaped house of stone, but the result was embellished with a large square porch-tower.

180

87 Horton Hall in the 1930s

88 Horton Old Hall, plainer than its non-identical twin

89 Abraham Sharp the astronomer, reproduced from *The Life and Correspondence of Abraham Sharp* by William Cudworth (1889)

Thomas, who used Horton Hall both as a residence and as a place of Nonconformist worship, was famous enough in his own time and district. But he was to be outshone by the house's next owner but one, his younger brother Abraham. At the age of nineteen, Abraham Sharp left the north for London, where he met John Flamsteed, the Astronomer Royal, and became his assistant at the brand-new Observatory at Greenwich. In middle age, he came back to Horton, succeeded to his brother's property, enlarged the porch-tower to make his own observatory, and set up his working quarters. Among the other alterations he made was a sliding hatch between his study and the next room. At regular intervals during the day, a servant would tiptoe in with food and drink and place them in the hatch. Abraham, when and if hungry, would later slide the hatch open and sample the food left for him. Often, however, the servant took the meal away untouched.

While no resident of Horton Old Hall was a match in celebrity for the mathematician and astronomer next door, the older building's owners brought a different kind of distinction to their house by adding treasure upon treasure to its contents. By the late nineteenth century, these included a Hogarth self-portrait, a mass of medieval manuscripts and a bed in which Cromwell was said, rather dubiously, to have slept while on a visit to the Parliamentarian household on the other side of the wall. The house's great hall, with its magnificent oak panelling and first-floor gallery, contained family treasures of a more war-like nature: Isaac Sharp's armour, a cannon ball used during the siege of Bradford and the helmet that had saved the life of John-the-Beard. The owner of this array was Francis Sharp Powell who, as well as representing part of the West Riding in Parliament, also continued the family tradition of strong involvement in religious matters. Given his ancestry, he was naturally a churchman and, whereas the Reverend Thomas on the other side of the family had once called people to prayer in his own house, this descendant of the Royalist Sharps created places for worship on a far greater scale. He helped to promote the building of no less than nine Bradford churches, and built a tenth himself: All Saints' at Horton Green, topped with a spire 200ft high.

All Saints' is still there, but the two halls of Horton are not. The reason for their disappearance was the same: badly needed repairs were too expensive. In fact, it was the newer of the two buildings, with its beautiful wheel window, that went first, in 1965. Only two years later, Horton Old Hall followed it. Divided though they were by family tradition and the wall of enmity, their curiously twin-like relationship persisted to the end.

183

From Blenheim Palace to the Braemars and Prestons and even Krakatoas of suburbia, it is a commonplace for houses to be named after localities. Directly or indirectly, localities probably form the most common inspiration for house names with, in the case of the peerage, the owner's name providing the link. For the situation to be reversed—for a house to lend its name to a district—is rare, although it does happen in remote areas. Instances of a house lending its name to some natural feature, a mountain or river, are practically unheard-of. But at least one link of this sort does (or did) exist, connecting the biggest of the African lakes with a moderately sized late Georgian building in the English West Country. The man who forged the link was, as might be expected, one of the great nineteenth-century explorers, John Hanning Speke.

Speke's exploration of equatorial Africa started in 1856 when, on an expedition led by Sir Richard Burton, he set out with the intention of finding and surveying Lake Nyasa. *En route,* the party heard of another lake that John, with the geographical flair that was one of his most outstanding gifts, thought might give the answer to the biggest geographical puzzle of Africa—the source of the Nile. In the summer of 1858, just before the expedition turned back for the coast and home, the thirty-one-year-old Speke pushed north on his own to test his theory and, on 30 July, came in sight of a muddy creek. It was the southernmost point of an inland sea that local Arabs called the Ukerewe and that Speke himself, in honour of his queen, was to christen Lake Victoria Nyanza. And to the creek itself—the sight of which he remembered as the real moment when the Nile puzzle was resolved—he gave the name of the home near Ilminster which his family had occupied since the seventeenth century: Jordans.

The house which Speke thus commemorated would, in the mid-twentieth century, be given the Royal Commission's asterisk that denotes 'outstanding importance'. But, during Speke's lifetime, it appeared relatively ordinary. Built by his grandfather in 1796 to replace a seventeenth-century house, it was a simple white block, fronted with Portland stone. Its main glory was the hall, which had delicate vaulting and a staircase that curbed gracefully round the back of the wide corridor between the rooms and up out of sight. In Speke's own day this, like much of the house, would have been abristle with antlers, for Speke himself

90 Jordans in 1832, a painting by John Buckler. From the Pigott Collection at Taunton Castle

was a man of the gun in the full Victorian tradition and took his sport to almost obsessive lengths.

In fact, Speke was not born at Jordans. His schooldays, which he did not enjoy, were spent in Barnstaple and London, while his career as a professional soldier caused him to spend most of his adult life abroad. But, as indicated by his use of its name to mark the greatest moment in his career, it was Jordans that he regarded as home. And it was to Jordans that, after a further expedition to the lake in 1860-3, he returned to a hero's welcome as the world-famous discoverer of the source of the Nile. Afterwards, the welcomers celebrated with dinner and a firework party on the Jordans lawn beside the stream.

Although Speke was convinced that he had found the Nile's source reservoir, the survey he had made of the territory still had important gaps in it, and Burton, with whom Speke was now on the worst of terms, pointed them out mercilessly. In 1864, an appointment was made for them to debate their opposing views in public at a meeting of the British Association in Bath. But on 15 September, the day before the meeting, Speke shot himself by accident while engaging in his favourite sport, and

91 John Hanning Speke. Bust by L. Gardie, dated the year of Speke's death

died almost at once. On hearing the news at the gathering, Burton filled in by reading a paper on Dahomey; then he went home and wept. The great question of whether Speke had found the Nile source or not was not resolved until the next decade, when the even more famous explorer Henry Stanley showed that Speke had been right.

Somerset guidebooks of the period tend to fight curiously shy of mentioning Jordans and Speke's connection with it. Perhaps Speke was too controversial a figure to touch; the theory, in all likelihood mistaken, had quickly grown up that he had committed suicide. Perhaps local authors wished to spare the Speke family pain. For, of course, the family were still living at Jordans: Speke's father and mother, then Speke's elder brother, then Walter, son of Speke's youngest brother, born six years after Speke's death. When in 1944 Walter died, Jordans again passed sideways across the family line and was left in trust for a nine-year-old great-nephew, Peter, until he came of age (Peter's father had been killed in the war). What happened subsequently is a classic example of the difficulties facing both the owner of a historic house and, by extension, any agency hoping to preserve it.

In 1945, Peter's mother and her two young sons went to live in Canada. Jordans was meanwhile let for about ten years, then stood empty for a further two. In 1957, Mrs Speke returned and found the family home in a bad way. There was dry rot in almost every room, while the lead on the roof had gone missing: perhaps it had been donated to the war effort, perhaps it had simply been stolen. Peter, by this time in his early twenties and still in Canada, decided that the house he owned in England was too big and potentially too expensive for future use. In 1964, Jordans was demolished and, as Mrs Speke recalls, the brick-and-stone fabric 'all tumbled down with the first push from a bulldozer'.

Following a pattern that is common all over the country, Mrs Speke converted and moved into part of the former Jordans stable, while Peter Speke now lives in a Tudor farmhouse on the estate. The Spekes are therefore still in the Ilminster area and the address of Jordans still exists. But it is not the Jordans that John Hanning Speke commemorated in the name he gave to his first glimpse of the Nile source.

92 George I: was he reincarnated as the Kendal raven? Portrait from the studio of Godfrey Kneller

---

Ravens are ambiguous birds in British tradition. The Tower ravens excluded, they were generally thought to bring bad luck, illness and death. In Wales and the West Country, however, they had a different reputation: they were the homes of a king's spirit, usually King Arthur's. But, in the unlikely setting of an eighteenth-century villa in Isleworth, a raven was once reported to embody the soul of a much less romantic monarch— George I.

Since German George never mastered the English language, it is doubtful whether he ever heard of the tradition prevalent in some parts of his kingdom. The other principal in the case, whose English was no better, had probably never heard of it either. Our authority for the event is Horace Walpole, and it is possible that he may have allowed the Celtic superstition to fertilise the imagination that produced the romantic spine-chiller *The Castle of Otranto*. Whatever the facts of the matter, though, it was in Kendal House, Isleworth, that Walpole set the tale.

The house, which was built in 1723, took its name from its owner, the Countess Melusina von der Schulenburg. The countess was one of George's mistresses. On his accession, she came scurrying to Britain in his wake, and soon collected a handsome string of Irish and English titles: Baroness of Dundalk, Countess and Marchioness of Dungannon, Countess of Feversham, Duchess of Kendal. It was as the Duchess of Kendal that Walpole (then ten years old) met her: 'a very tall, lean, ill-favoured old lady' was how he described her over sixty years later in his *Reminiscences*.

Uninviting though she appeared, however, Melusina was sure enough of her position to use it for collecting more useful stuff than mere titles. Her hand was continually outstretched for bribes, small, medium or huge. She was, Sir Robert Walpole was often heard to comment, 'so venal a creature that she would have sold the king's honour for a shilling advance to the best bidder', and it was an exceedingly wealthy woman that, on the king's death, took herself off to count her blessings and gold in her modern villa at Isleworth.

It was, indeed, rumoured that this retired harpy would have been richer still if the king's will had been honoured rather than destroyed by his heir. She had, it was alleged, been left £40,000, a sum that was never paid to her. However, another reminder of her dead lover did reach her, or she believed it did.

92 Kendal House and grounds at the height of their fame as a pleasure garden

Hard-headed though Melusina was, there was a superstitious streak in her nature. At some point in their relationship, Horace Walpole reports, the king told her that, if spirits could return after death, his would certainly return to her. The lady of Kendal House, far from jettisoning the thought as so much nonsense, appears to have treasured the promise, and to have been predisposed to see its fulfilment in any chance occurrence that gave off the right atmosphere.

The chance occurrence duly came when a large black bird came blundering in through an open window at Kendal House and found itself unable to get out. And the Duchess of Kendal welcomed it with open arms. 'She was', the *Reminiscences* go on, 'persuaded it was the soul of her departed monarch so accoutred, and received and treated it with all the respect and tenderness of duty, till the royal bird or she took their last flight.'

Her own last flight came in 1743, when she was seventy-six. After her death, Kendal House continued its connection with wealth, although the means employed to bring money in were more honestly commercial than those used by the duchess in her prime: it was sold and turned into a pleasure establishment in the style of Vauxhall. In the house there was food and dancing; in the grounds, patrons could walk, admire the view, enjoy the shade cast by trees near the canal, and listen to music played in the octagon seen on the left of the illustration. This elegant building also had another purpose: according to a contemporary advertisement, it had both 'an upper and a lower gallery, where gentlemen and ladies may divert themselves with fishing, the canal being well stocked with tench, carp, and all sorts of fish in great plenty.' However, the boom in pleasure grounds did not last. By 1795, the pleasure parties, strollers and anglers had all gone. And so, after less than a century in existence, had the house.

For every style of British domestic architecture, there is at least one highly celebrated gap in the ranks; a house which once exemplified the style to perfection and that has now vanished. Colen Campbell's Palladian creation at Wanstead (page 261) is a case in point, and so, among the black-and-white houses of England's north western counties, is Kenyon Peel Hall of Little Hulton, Salford. Kenyon—one of two Peel Halls in the area—came down in the 1950s. There is nothing, comments John Harris in *The Destruction of the Country House*, that can replace a house that 'gave so much visual delight'.

Part of that delight stemmed from the contrast the building made with its surroundings. The area was transformed by the Industrial Revolution and, indeed, the hall at one point suffered considerably when coal was mined beneath its very foundations. Part, too, came from the delicacy and sheer prettiness of the timbering: the uprights and diagonals and four-pointed stars that, when looked at for a second time, transformed themselves into circles.

A pleasure not shared by more recent observers was the mellow effect produced by the weathered façade and the grey stone tiles on the roof. When, in the wake of the settlement caused by mining, the hall was restored in the 1880s, the old tiles, gapped and uneven, were by necessity one of the casualties. Newly roofed with blue slate, the building was refurbished to produce what the *Victoria County History* condemned in 1911 as hard and glossy glitter in place of 'picturesque decay'.

Picturesque or not, the decayed Kenyon certainly needed rescuing, and the operation allowed admirers another seventy years to enjoy what was undoubtedly its main source of appeal: the overall harmony produced by its proportions, its collection of gables, its decorated walls topped by plain roofs and the satisfying way it faced squarely on to its symmetrically planned court. Linked with this satisfaction was an element of surprise: visitors to Kenyon were not admitted straight away to a full sight of its black-and-white splendour, for a high wall separated the house from the road. To enter, the visitor turned in through a carriage gateway, skirted an outer courtyard overlooked by stables (once a farmhouse) and turned right under the tunnelled arch of a stone gatehouse. Only when he emerged from the tunnel's gloom did the black-and-white vision spring before him. On a sunny day the effect would have been dazzling.

In spite of its name, Kenyon was the creation of one George Rigby, who took a sixteenth-century building and, in the early years of the seventeenth century, refashioned it. But its role as the hall of the Rigbys was short. In 1657, George's heiress, his daughter Alice, married the governor of the Isle of Man, Roger Kenyon. The hall passed to the Kenyon family and gained its permanent name. The name, however, turned out to be more enduring than the house, whose history during the last years of its existence was a melancholy one of raised and finally shattered hopes.

In fact, the building lost its claim to be the main seat of the Kenyons just as quickly as it severed its connection with the Rigbys. Roger's son, another George, moved away to Salford and later Kenyons (who included the first Baron Kenyon, Lord Chief Justice) lived in the Welsh border country. By the beginning of the twentieth century, the hall was occupied by a caretaker who operated a small market garden. After his death and until World War II, the house stood empty. Occupancy was resumed when a Salford family, which had suffered from bombing, came on a visit to Little Hulton, saw the hall, liked it, and rented it from the Kenyons. They made repairs, held archery parties in the outer court between the old farmhouse and the gatehouse and then, in their turn, moved away.

Against a background of growing local concern about Kenyon Peel Hall's future, owner and local authority representatives met to discuss its possible future use. A grant for repairs was forthcoming and a charity showed interest in using the hall as a residential home. All seemed set fair until the dismal discovery was made that the building, far from being repair-worthy, was in too bad a state for anything except demolition. Even its greatest admirers acknowledged that it had to go and, in 1958, its zigzag beauty vanished from the Little Hulton landscape.

94 Kenyon Peel Hall before restoration, shored up against mining subsidence in the second half of the nineteenth century

❧*Llanthomas*

A little to the north of Llanigon Church in south-east Powys, a driveway leads off the road and runs across a strip of parkland. Round the corner, there are two more: one goes to a farm, the other to a bungalow. Together with some rhododendrons from an ancient shrubbery, they are the last obvious remains of a house made perennially famous by a modest country clergyman in his thirties, Francis Kilvert. Until its demolition in the middle of this century, the three drives all led to Llanthomas, home for most of her life of Daisy Thomas and scene of the unspoken and unfulfilled attachment between herself and the curate of Clyro across the River Wye.

Kilvert's side of the romance—its head-over-heels beginning, the check speedily applied by circumstances and Daisy's father, and its lingering end —is described in moving detail in his own *Diary*; for Daisy's feelings, we have again to rely on Kilvert's own report. But his powers as an observer were outstanding, and from his account of her chatter, hesitations, fragile hints and tears, it is possible to guess the extent of her own involvement and its effect on her. Kilvert, true to his engagingly susceptible nature, bounced back—a recovery assisted by the considerable mobility enjoined on him by his social and professional life. But Daisy's feelings, suppressed though they were, seemed to outlast his in intensity, and it is this that turns the affair from the merely pitiful into the harrowing. Nor was she ever to know release from the restrictions her spinsterhood imposed on her. None of the five Thomas girls married; Daisy lived and died a Miss Thomas of Llanthomas.

The Thomas family came to Llanigon in the 1850s when Daisy's father became the vicar there. The family was a big one, so the house, generally thought to have been built twenty years earlier or more, was enlarged. When finished, it presented two distinct styles of architecture, possibly even three. At one end were the high, flagstoned kitchen and storerooms. These gave on to a long passage, also flagged, that ran through the central part of the house and ended in the new, much taller block with its handsome porch. Standing between the porch's pillars, Daisy would have been facing south—across a lawn, a stream and the still-existing strip of parkland—to the rising ground on which stood Llanigon Church. Beyond it, the ground rose much higher still to the Twmpa in the Black Mountains. To the left, the foreground was punctuated by two cedars.

95 Llanthomas, undated but probably early in the twentieth century

Round the side of the house to her right were the stables with, beyond them, a farm belonging to the property.

As an elderly woman, Daisy tended to withdraw from the newer end of the house to the old one, especially to the bay-windowed parlour which the sisters used as a kind of 'aunts' enclave'. She and, later, the rest of the family gradually deserted the official drawing-room, also with a bay window, in the new block. In the words of a visitor to the house a few years after her death in 1928, this room was 'almost like a museum': enormously high ceilinged, decorated in red, and furnished with, among other things, a spinet, a quantity of small tables and at least three sofas with silk cushions. On the walls hung family portraits and paintings by one of Daisy's sisters, Edith.

While Kilvert gives few details of the Llanthomas furniture, it seems reasonable to assume that this room, so at odds with contemporary 1930s taste, contained several items that would have been familiar to him. He was certainly familiar with Edith's paintings, for he had a high opinion of her 'beautiful drawings of wild flowers and fungi'. The tennis court outside the windows would have been new to him, but he would have appreciated the reason for its position: in his day, sixty years before, family and guests had played croquet there, watched by a spruce Daisy in black velvet jacket and blue ribbons.

The *Diary* starts in 1870 when Kilvert had been at Clyro for five years. He knew the family at Llanthomas as a matter of course; both he and they were members of the area's ruling caste, although, as a mere curate, he had far less financial power than they did. In his accounts of the local social round, the Thomases of Llanthomas come and go, with Daisy

194

appearing under her alias of 'Fanny'. (Frances was, in fact, her given name.) But then, on 8 September 1871, everything altered. Kilvert walked over to Llanthomas to spend the afternoon and evening. In the afternoon, the party—a fairly large one—split up to play croquet or practise archery; later, there was dancing. At supper, Kilvert sat next to Daisy 'at the bottom of the side table in the window'. (The dining-room, also bay-windowed, was round the corner of the house.)

'Today', he wrote afterwards, 'I fell in love with Fanny Thomas . . .. How little I knew what was in store for me when I came to Llan Thomas [*sic*] this afternoon.'

Five frantic days later he was back, with his mind made up, and confessed his feelings to Daisy's father. But Mr Thomas, though kind, was also decided: Daisy, at nineteen, was so young; Kilvert was so poor; an engagement was for the time being out of the question. Kilvert could certainly continue to visit the family, but he was not on any account to show his true feelings. The interview, which left Kilvert 'deeply humiliated, low in spirit and sick at heart', took place outdoors, probably in the neighbourhood of the old shrubbery. A path ran past it from the house to a large walled garden and, although the *Diary* is ambiguous, this area could well be the place which, in Kilvert's words, 'is inextricably entwined in my remembrance with the conversation and the circumstances'.

96 The Thomas family on their doorstep. Daisy is standing in the centre, in front of the door

Dispirited though he was, the suitor again returned to Llanthomas in a few days and suffered agonies when Daisy did not join the croquet party on the lawn. At last she did, and Kilvert fell victim afresh to her gentleness and charm (the outfit with the black jacket was dashingly set off by a feathered hat). Under the eye of her mother, the pair wandered happily round the garden, Daisy picking flowers for the attentive curate. Kilvert by now was in a total fever of 'she loves me, she loves me not'. Did she feel for him? Or was she pleasant to him just because she was pleasant to everybody? Two days later, he began to get an answer. He met Daisy at another croquet party, at Hay Castle, and noted that her manner had changed. She was quieter, shyer. Kilvert wondered if she was acting on directions received. Then he had an answer of another sort: a letter from Daisy's father, telling him to give up all hope. With considerable insight, the unhappy lover acknowledged that time and separation might alter feelings 'which at present appeared to be unalterable'.

For some time, his feelings did indeed appear unalterable. Meanwhile, Daisy recovered her poise; in fact, she started taking the initiative. In November, she urged him to come to Llanthomas '*very soon*'. In February 1872, when she met Kilvert at a concert in Hay, she was even more specific. 'It's a long time since you have been over to Llan Thomas', she told him. 'I suppose you have been very busy. If you come over you will find some of us at home. We don't usually go out till half past three.' On this occasion, to Kilvert's disappointment, the seats next to her were taken, and the pair were separated. But when he visited Llanthomas in March, he had his reward: a long conversation with Daisy, camouflaged by the chatter of a stream of other visitors. When they met at a dance a few weeks later, they talked harder than ever, but then Daisy had to retreat; her father came on them as they were sitting out and, as soon as she heard his voice, she leapt up 'in a slight and pretty confusion'. Thereafter, Kilvert was strangled by his own politeness. He longed to dance with her again, but was afraid of getting her into trouble. By this time, he had plans in hand for leaving Clyro and, wretched though he was over his hopeless love, he jibbed at the idea of approaching Mr Thomas again and repeating his experience of the Llanthomas garden.

From now on, it is Daisy's emotions that move into the foreground. For the next four years, Kilvert worked as his father's curate in Wiltshire, but he did not sever his links with Clyro and his friends in the area. In March 1873, for example, he stayed the night at Llanthomas, and Daisy showered him with attentions. The pair spent the evening playing cards in the drawing-room: Kilvert shaded his eyes against the light, and Daisy

jumped up to fetch a lampshade; Kilvert coughed, and Daisy anxiously asked if his cough hurt. The diarist noted her kindness in some detail—but the raptures of earlier entries are absent. Again, almost exactly a year later, Kilvert met Daisy by accident on a station. 'There was', he reported, 'a half sweet, half sad look, a little reproachful in the beautiful kind eyes as she said in a low voice, "I have been looking out for you such a long time." Poor child, my poor child.' Soon comes the most harrowing entry of all:

> I walked over to Llanthomas to luncheon with Captain John Thomas. Howarth Greenly was there at luncheon and they played quoits after lunch while I walked to the gardens with Charlotte and Fanny . . .. My poor, poor Daisy. When we parted the tears came into her eyes. She turned her face away. I saw the anguish of her soul. What could I do?

What, indeed? Daisy, surrounded by her sociable family, swallowed her tears; Kilvert went back to Wiltshire. In July, there was one last flicker of the flame: he was suddenly haunted by the memory of Daisy, especially

197

98 Daisy, again in the centre, in old age. In the background is the Llanthomas family coach

of their evening card game in 1873. But, in August, his recovery was complete. 'Today', he wrote on 11 August, 'I fell in love at first sight with sweet Kathleen Mavourneen.'

Only a portion of Kilvert's original diary survives, so we do not know how often Kilvert and Daisy may have seen each other again. But the diarist does note in detail one further visit to Llanthomas. He arrived on a sunny April day in 1876 to find the young members of the family, as always, playing croquet on the lawn before the house. In the drawing-room he met Daisy herself, 'shy, confused and blushing painfully, but looking very nice and well.' At the end of the visit, Daisy and Edith walked half a mile down the road with him. After parting, Daisy turned back to give a last look and a message that does not sound over-genuine: 'Please give my best love to your sister.'

That year, Kilvert secured a living of his own. In 1879, he married an Elizabeth Rowland and, tragically, died very shortly afterwards. Daisy went on living at Llanthomas, grew older, became an aunt and withdrew to the Aunts' Parlour. She died in 1928 at the age of seventy-six. Llanthomas continued as a family house, and Daisy's great-nephews played tennis on the former croquet lawn. During World War II, the house was occupied by a girls' school. After it, in 1950, both house and farm were sold. The farm survived, but the house finally went to a demolition firm.

In the churchyard up the road, Daisy, Edith and their sister Charlotte share the same grave, while their parents are buried nearby.

In a letter to Lady Hamilton, Horatio Nelson once wrote: 'Whilst I serve, I will serve well, and closely; when I want rest, I will go to Merton.' He served, in all, for over thirty years; he owned Merton Place, his house in what was then rural Surrey, for only four, and lived there for considerably less. But in spite of that, his name is as closely associated locally with this south London suburb as it is with the even more rural area in which he was born and spent his childhood. In Norfolk, pubs called The Nelson, The Lord Nelson and The Hero are thick on the ground; Merton has its Victory and its Nelson Arms. It also has a Victory Road, a Nelson Road, a Hamilton Road, a Trafalgar Road, a Nelson Grove Road and a Nelson's Fields. But the area's most important monument to Nelson—the home that his Emma called 'Paradise Merton' and that stood between Merton High Street and today's Nelson Grove Road—vanished within forty years of his death, initially pushed towards destruction by the improvidence of Emma herself.

Although the house was Nelson's, her involvement was greater right from the start. She found it, organised its purchase, prepared it for her lover and altered it, Nelson providing encouragement and directions from a distance. Given her remarkable temperament, it was also inevitable that sooner or later she should herself be turned out of Paradise. What happened afterwards casts an interesting light on a society that put a high value on keepsakes but an even higher one on real estate.

Nelson's connection with Merton had its roots in the famous complications of his private life. In 1801, his estrangement from his wife became to all intents and purposes complete. He was totally in love with Lady Hamilton, who had borne his daughter, Horatia, early that year. Sir William Hamilton, a cousin of the owner of Hamilton Palace, was mocked for London's most famous cuckold, but he blandly and even good-humouredly refused to take the pose of a jealous husband. What Nelson now needed was a home to which he could 'invite' the Hamiltons, and in which they could all lead as normal a life as was possible under the circumstances.

In August, Emma found one: a century-old brick building, rather small and priced at about £9,000. By contemporary standards, it was anything but grand: a surveyor hired by Nelson's solicitor pointed out that its situation was lamentable, that it lacked stables and kitchen garden, that it

199

99 Viscount Nelson, victor of the Nile and owner of Merton Place

was damp and that another £2,000 would have to be spent before the place could be brought into comfortable working order. However, Nelson was adamant. He raised enough money to meet the cost (some had to be loaned by friends) and fretted about the lawyer's slowness. On 6 October, he wrote to Emma from the *Amazon* as follows:

> Am very angry with Mr. Haslewood for not having got you into possession of Merton, for I was in hopes you would have arranged everything before Sir William came home . . . .. You are to be, recollect, Lady Paramount of all the territories and waters of Merton, and we are all to be your guests, and obey all lawful commands. What have you done about the turnip field, duck field, &c? Am I to have them? I wish I could get up for four or five days. I would have roused the lawyers about.

Later in the month, however, the Hamiltons moved in. Sir William, an ardent fisherman, cheerfully endorsed Nelson's plan of stocking the 'waters' (part of the Wandle) with fish, while Emma and her mother rushed round making arrangements for hens and pigs. 'You are in *luck*', Sir William wrote to Nelson on 16 October, 'for in my conscience, I verily believe that a place so suitable to your views could not have been found, and at so cheap a rate; for if you stay away three days longer, I do not think you can have any wish but you will find it completed here.'

200

In the early morning of 23 October, Nelson himself arrived, drawn in his post-chaise under a triumphal arch put up by the people of Merton and on through the gates that stood on the Merton High Street site of today's Nelson Arms. The building in front of which the chaise drew up was indeed not over-spacious for a *ménage* that naturally included servants: Jack Russell, in his *Nelson and the Hamiltons*, puts the number of bedrooms at no higher than eight, while the original surveyor's report suggested that only one of these could in any way be called a master bedroom. But with its portico and rows of white-painted sash windows overlooking the canal (Emma's name for this was the 'Nile'), the house had a certain trim style. And at all events it was to be large enough for the time being. Here, for the better part of the next nineteen months, Nelson and Emma were to live with immense delight. Sir William was to go on putting up with the situation as best he could, and friends and relatives were to descend in quantities to stay for shorter or longer periods of time. An important guest was little Horatia, who was being brought up *incognita* by a Mrs Gibson of Marylebone. Others were Nelson's nephews and nieces; the Victor of the Nile was extremely fond of children. He was also interested in gardening, anxious to support local tradesmen and an attender at services in the local church.

But for all that these were the typical quiet concerns of a country gentleman, his fame and Emma's gusto combined to turn the atmosphere at Merton Place into something far from typical of life in the average quiet country house. No visitor, for example, could escape the fact that Merton was a hero's home: the place was so stuffed with Nelson mementoes that it practically resembled a shrine. The constant entertaining—twelve at table, or fourteen, or nineteen—put a strain on the less than generous space available, and taxed both Nelson's and Sir William's resources. (It had been agreed that the two men would share the running expenses of the establishment.) And the parties themselves sound jolly to the point of rowdiness. On one occasion, a friend of Nelson's young niece Charlotte was sick before the whole company, while an older female guest got drunk; Emma, however, took both incidents in her stride, and even declared the evening a success. Sir William, who was now in his seventies, wanted merely to fish, to potter up to London and to enjoy Nelson's friendship, and became progressively more upset by all the turmoil. In 1802, his concern found expression in a pathetic letter to his wife that, in courteously restrained language, described his hopes, his distress and a possible solution: separation. Emma must have made amends, for no separation took place. However, in February the following year, he became ill, and in April he died at his own house in Piccadilly, with the two people he loved best beside him.

The collective life of the *tria juncta in uno*, as the three had nicknamed themselves, came to its long-foreseen end, but even if Sir William had rallied the trio would in any case soon have been separated. By the end of May, Nelson was back at sea, Commander-in-Chief of the Mediterranean. Between then and August 1805, he blockaded Toulon and chased the French admiral Villeneuve across the Atlantic to the West Indies and back to Europe. Emma, who in 1804 gave birth to Horatia's short-lived younger sister, spent much of the time visiting, socialising in London and Merton and overseeing massive alterations to the Surrey house. All manner of projects were underway: the dining-room was to be enlarged, the main entrance transferred to the north side of the house, a new drawing-room created and the grounds added to and improved. Nelson, on board the *Victory* off Toulon, wrote in March 1804 to the Lady of Merton with warnings to save where she could: a 'common white gate' would do for the time being at the entrance, and the barn could be turned into a temporary coach-house for the coming winter. Another warning concerned Horatia, now three and soon to take up permanent residence at his home: 'I beg, as my dear Horatia is to be at Merton, that a strong netting, about three feet high, may be placed round the Nile, that the

100 Merton Place, as refashioned by Lady Hamilton and Nelson. Sketch by Thomas Baxter

little thing may not tumble in; and, then, you may have ducks again it it.' The Commander-in-Chief added that he forgot 'at what place we saw the netting; and either Mr. Perry, or Mr. Goldsmid [both local residents] told us where it was to be brought. I shall be very anxious until I know this is done . . ..' And indeed he was; on 30 May he was returning to the same subject, this time with particular reference to the Nile's bridges:

> Every thing you tell me about my dear Horatia charms me. I think I see her, hear her, and admire her, but she is like her dear, dear mother. I wish I could but be at dear Merton, to assist in making the alterations. I think I should have persuaded you to have kept the pike and a clear stream, and to have put all the carp, tench, and fish who muddy the water into the pond. But as you like, I am content. Only take care that my darling does not fall in and get drowned. I begged you to get the little netting along the edge; and particularly on the bridges.

In August 1805, he was at last in a position to check Emma's safety precautions for himself. After the 'Long Chase', he went back to Merton on leave, arriving there on 20 August. In all, he spent only twenty-five days there before setting out on the route that took him towards Trafalgar, and he spent them in a frantic rush: conferences in London, dinners at home with the usual crowd of friends and family, attendance at church, a visit by royal invitation to the Prince of Wales. His own visitors included William Beckford of Fonthill, who treated the party to music on the harpsichord, and one of his own officers, Captain Keats, whom he took

101 Nelson's Emma: 'Lady Paramount of all the territories and waters of Merton'

to the summer-house in the garden nicknamed 'the Poop' and there outlined how he planned to startle the enemy into battle. (The Poop was another creation of Emma's hero-worship; it was in the northern part of the grounds which, somewhat inconveniently, lay on the other side of the High Street from the house. To get there, Nelson had first to go underground, through the brick tunnel that linked the two parts of the estate.)

Early on 2 September, the news came to Merton that Villeneuve had been located in Cadiz. On the evening of 13 September, Lord Nelson prayed briefly beside the bed of the sleeping Horatia, said goodbye to Emma, climbed into his carriage and set off for Portsmouth. Together with its fellow written just before Trafalgar, the prayer he wrote in his diary during the journey is probably one of the most famous in the English language to be composed by a layman:

> Friday night, at half-past ten, drove from dear, dear Merton, where I left all which I hold dear in this world, to go to serve my King and country. May the great God whom I adore, enable me to fulfil the expectations of my country, and if it is His good pleasure that I should return, my thanks will never cease being offered up to the throne of His mercy. If it is His good Providence to cut short my days upon earth, I bow with the greatest submission, relying that He will protect those so dear to me, that I may leave behind. His will be done. Amen, Amen, Amen.

Early in November, the news came back to Merton that he was dead.

The house became Emma's, and Emma, under the terms of the codicil signed on board the *Victory*, became Nelson's legacy to the country. The country, however, failed her and Nelson, while her enthusiasm for both things and people remained generous to a fault. Both Sir William and Nelson himself had left her money, but it was not enough. She got into debt, and the temporary solution found to her difficulties included the sale of 'dear Merton'. In 1809, priced at £12,930, it became the property of neighbour Abraham Goldsmid. Emma moved into London lodgings and then to France where, a poverty-stricken alcoholic, she died in 1815.

Mr Goldsmid had, in fact, predeceased her. He too began to have acute money difficulties and committed suicide in 1810. Merton Place—the enlarged Merton with its two drawing-rooms, five master bedrooms (each with a water closet and dressing-room attached), ample servants' quarters, dairy, icehouse, subterranean walk and the Poop—came on to the market again in the year of Emma's death. In 1823, the whole estate was sold, the sale being advertised over the ominous legend: 'The whole will be divided, to meet the public convenience, into lots adequate for detached villas.' By the 1860s, nothing was left. The house vanished in about 1840, and, under the pressure of Victorian land-hunger, the grounds of Paradise Merton were replaced by a rapidly growing settlement served by the railway. It had, at least, been a shrine to its owner during his lifetime—a piece of good fortune greater than that enjoyed by many heroes.

Not surprisingly, the site occupied by the Old Royal Observatory at Greenwich, one of the most commanding in the whole of London, has been occupied by a building of one sort or another since the fifteenth century and possibly even longer. The function of each building has been determined by the height of the ground on which it stood and by the advantages this conferred—military strength, a clear and healthy atmosphere, isolation or, quite simply, a splendid view. In addition to its role in the furtherance of science, the same site has offered a home to minor royalty, a discreet haven to royal mistresses, a working base to gamekeepers and a prison to erring aristocrats. The building that, from the fifteenth to the seventeenth centuries, sheltered these various elements of society was a structure known at different times as Duke Humphrey's Tower, Greenwich Castle and Mirefleur.

The Duke Humphrey who built it in 1433—Duke Humphrey of Gloucester, a brother of King Henry V—enclosed Greenwich Park as well and built the much larger (and also lost) Bella Court, later Greenwich Palace, near the river. At first, his tower was a tower only and no more. But during the next century, Henry VIII enlarged it to make a suitable home, favoured by clean breezes, for branches of his family and for his friends. The latter included an unnamed 'fayre lady whom the King loved' who, from her windows looking up river, could watch her benefactor's progress downstream to his birthplace of Greenwich Palace below.

On one such journey, the king was moved by the sight of Mirefleur's battlements, chimneys and two towers to break into poetry. After improvising on the theme of 'there lieth a flowre that hath my hart', he urged his standard-bearer, Sir Andrew Flamock, to finish the verse. But Flamock rashly allowed his enthusiasm to run away with his wits: the forecast he gave of the next hour's events at Mirefleur was so lively that the king, touchy where his own interests were concerned, brusquely told him to keep quiet.

Later in the sixteenth century, Mirefleur was briefly occupied by another object of royal affections, but under circumstances that were much less cheerful. In 1578, Robert Dudley, the widowed Earl of Leicester and

102 (*opposite*) Sometime prisoner at Mirefleur: Robert Dudley, Earl of Leicester. Portrait by an unknown artist

103 Greenwich at the beginning of the seventeenth century. Mirefleur (on the left) dominates the skyline

long-standing favourite of Elizabeth I, secretly married again and Elizabeth, when she finally heard about it, was outraged. She decided to send the faithless earl to the Tower, but after the damaging consequences of this decision were pointed out to her, Leicester was hustled off instead to Mirefleur with a hastily assumed diplomatic illness.

In the seventeenth century, Mirefleur received a further refurbishing at the hands of a new resident, the Earl of Northampton, Lord Privy Seal. Soon, however, it reverted to a rougher role. At the opening of the Civil War, Parliament saw the place's military possibilities and hastened to secure it. In the year of King Charles's execution, the property was being secured in a rather different way: Mirefleur, with its commanding outlook, was given over to soldiers of Cromwell's army, under orders to guard the Greenwich Park deer from poachers.

At the Restoration, the building entered the last phase of its existence. Its position fitted it for other functions besides a fort and a pleasure house, and it was Mirefleur's site that, on the counsel of Sir Christopher Wren, was chosen by Charles II as the location for his new Observatory. Mirefleur came down, and in 1675 the Royal Observatory went up, partly built with materials salvaged from the earlier structure. From then until twentieth-century urban pollution finally negated the site's advantages, its occupants would in the main look not downwards to the river but towards the sky.

❧ Montagu House

Even in the eyes of his own society, James Brydges of Canons (see page 86) was no saint. But, compared with his near-contemporary, the first Duke of Montagu, he appears a positive pillar of rectitude. Chandos, in the view of Swift and everyone else, was a fraud; Montagu was an out-and-out knave. Both displayed their wealth and power by building palaces for themselves (Montagu built two). But Chandos' building works and life-style were financed by his own efforts, dubiously moral though these were; a considerable part of Montagu's finances came from his luckless wives, for the second of whom the Duke's house in London became no less than a private lunatic asylum. It was the oddest twist of circumstance that turned this monument to a double-crossing rogue into one of Britain's most famous institutions.

Ralph Montagu, son of a Northamptonshire baron, came into public view shortly after the Restoration. Again unlike Chandos, Montagu wooed and wenched his way into high office and became ambassador to the court of Louis XIV. Purchase of another post—that of Master of the Great Wardrobe—depleted his finances to the tune of £14,000, but he speedily recovered them by successfully paying court to Elizabeth Wriothesley. Elizabeth—good-looking, worth an annual £6,000, daughter of one earl and widow of another—weighed Ralph's ardours against the advice of her family and married him in 1673. Within the year, they were scarcely on speaking terms.

However, he had her money, and he used part of it on building a magnificent establishment in Bloomsbury. It was, of course, visited by John Evelyn, who found it a 'stately and ample palace' and was extremely struck by Verrio's frescoes showing the funeral of Dido and the labours of Hercules. About the exterior, Evelyn commented:

The garden is large, and in good air, but the fronts of the house not answerable to the inside. The court at entry, and wings for offices seem too near the street, and that so very narrow and meanly built, that the corridor is not in proportion to the rest, to hide the court from being overlooked by neighbours; all which might have been prevented, had they placed the house further into the ground, of which there was enough to spare. But on the whole it is a fine palace, built after the French pavilion-way, by Mr. [Robert] Hooke, the Curator of the Royal Society.

Evelyn also reported the house's end after only eight years in existence. The winter of 1685-6, he recalled, had been so wet and mild as had 'scarce been seen in man's memory'; on 19 January, a servant was set to air some damp hangings before a fire, and the result was a blaze that destroyed the house completely and cost Montagu £40,000. Undeterred, however, he built another one, in which the French influence was equally marked.

Montagu House II, like its predecessor, gave on to Great Russell Street and, again like its predecessor, had a somewhat private air about it. The main view given to the passing public was that of a high wall, broken by a gatehouse and terminating at each end in a square pavilion. Only from inside could the grandeur of the whole complex be appreciated: the pavilions were the ends of two long wings, extending 150ft from a red-brick mansion with a dome in the centre and a broad flight of steps leading up to the main entrance. (Except at roof level, the mansion's general outline was not unlike that of Clarendon House, demolished during the same decade.) Behind and to one side of the house was an immense garden, also laid out with French formality. Within, classical mythology again ran riot across ceilings and walls, causing visitors to look twice for where the doors were.

The building was probably finished at about the time that its owner was engaged on one of his most successful changes of allegiance: from a

104 The British Museum as it used to be: the forecourt of Montagu House, drawn by John Buckler in the early nineteenth century. Great Russell Street lies on the other side of the colonnaded wall

105 Instrument of his father's ultimate advancement: John, second
Duke of Montagu. Portrait by Godfrey Kneller

fervent (and even crawling) courtier of James II to staunch supporter of
William III. In 1689, he was rewarded by being made an earl. Then,
channelling his energies in another direction, the recently widowed peer
crowned his success by netting a second enormously rich wife.

We have met the object of his attentions before, again in connection
with Clarendon House. She was the Duchess of Albemarle, widow of the
duke who had so improbably made a success of his treasure hunt in the
Caribbean. Her fortune was even greater than that of Montagu's first
wife, but there were two grave disadvantages attached. Duchess Elizabeth
was insane and had announced that she would marry into nothing less
than royalty. Characteristically, Montagu made light of both difficulties;
indeed, he even used the one to cancel out the other. He presented
himself as the Emperor of China and the poor crazed duchess believed

212

him. They were married in 1692 and, from then until the duke's death seventeen years later, Elizabeth kept state with her fantasies in the mansion in Bloomsbury—'served', as Horace Walpole reported much later, 'on the knee, taking her maids for ladies of the bedchamber'.

By the time she became a widow, she was a duchess again. Montagu was refused a dukedom by William, but extracted one from Queen Anne, mainly for having had the good judgement to marry his son John to the daughter of Anne's favourite, the Duchess of Marlborough. After Montagu's death, his mad wife moved her imaginary court to Clerkenwell and continued to reign there. But even though Montagu House was now available, her stepson moved away and built a house of his own in Whitehall. Shortly after his death in 1749, his heirs—both women—sold the Bloomsbury white elephant to the government. It became the first home of the British Museum.

The museum had its beginnings in the proposed sale to the country of the natural history and art collection of Sir Hans Sloane, the erudite Chelsea physician whose names are remembered in Hans Place and Sloane Square. The legacy also included Sir Hans's library and collection of manuscripts. The government accepted and, on 15 January 1759, the new acquisition was opened to the public. The museum was much admired, even though, in its earliest days, visitors to Montagu House had to apply in writing for admission, and were whisked on a fast and completely silent tour through the three museum departments. The apply-in-advance system was later abolished and the public—the 'studious and curious' for whom the exhibition was intended—responded in gratifying manner.

Inevitably, the building they visited began to change. At the head of the main staircase, a group of stuffed giraffes and a rhinoceros contrasted oddly with the frescoes showing the festivals of Bacchus. A Palladian building was put up in the garden to house a new Department of Antiquities; a flimsy shed sheltered the Elgin Marbles (later moved into more permanent quarters). The presentation in 1823 of George III's library by his son precipitated a crisis and, by 1828, Ralph Montagu's town house was being added to in a new and much more purposeful manner. Down the east side of the garden, a whole new wing went up. Others followed, enclosing a square, and, as they were built, so the old Montagu House and its additions came down. Last to go, in about 1850, was the gatehouse. Today, if the omnipresent visitors to Bloomsbury should ask for a Montagu, or Montague, House, the chances are they would be directed to a publisher, round the corner in Russell Square.

213

Every culture has one or more Camelots: palaces or citadels that embody the aspirations and achievements of contemporary society. Some, like Versailles, the Kremlin, the Forbidden City, survive. Others, like the 'real' Camelot itself, remain places of legend until the archaeologist's trowel starts to disclose clues about their nature and whereabouts. The boundary between the two groups is not, of course, fixed. Real places can easily become myths; myths can, with more difficulty, be re-examined in terms of reality. In the nineteenth century, for example, the archaeologist Heinrich Schliemann dug down through the mound of Hissarlik and found no less than nine different cities of Troy. By about the same time, the site of another Camelot—a newer, smaller, English one, which had in its day been famous across Europe—had sunk into an obscurity so deep that few even bothered to wonder about it. This was Nonsuch, the great, glistening Surrey palace of the Tudors, built by Henry VIII in a deliberate attempt to wipe the eye of his royal colleague and rival, Francis I of France.

For a long while after Nonsuch Palace became one of Britain's greatest lost houses, its remains were few indeed: folk memories, an unevenness in the terrain, the name Nonsuch itself. Nonsuch Park—at 255 acres, a mere fragment of the park that once surrounded Henry's palace—still exists and lies to the north east of Ewell. The site of the palace itself straddles an avenue through the park, and this was the fact that became such a closely (if involuntarily) guarded secret. The secrecy, which started to gather in the eighteenth century, was only dispelled for good when, in the twentieth, Nonsuch became the focus of an archaeological inquiry that in the words of one of its organisers 'was to be the largest operation of its kind ever undertaken in a single year in this country'.

Like the stories of all the other Camelots that have drifted into legend and have been hauled out again, that of Nonsuch Palace falls naturally into three parts: its life, its death and its rebirth. The excavation of the palace site in 1959 provides the climax to the whole. Earlier that year, the organiser just quoted, John Dent, had become honorary treasurer to the Nonsuch Palace Excavation Committee. But in a sense the rebirth of the palace had started over twenty years before, when sewer-trenches were being dug through the site. A local historian, Cloudesley Willis, noticed in them foundations of a large building. Later, when the war came and more trenches were dug through the park to prevent gliders landing,

HENRICVS VIII REX
ANGLIE ﹐

106 Henry VIII, creator of Nonsuch. Portrait after Hans Holbein

Willis spotted further masonry and a large drain. His observations could then be added to crucial information from a much earlier source: a survey of the palace, with measurements, made in the seventeenth century by a Parliamentary Commission. Other pointers included three maps, dating from the seventeenth and eighteenth centuries, and the evidence of two eighteenth-century writers who said that the site was close to a farm (once called the 'Cherry-garden', later 'Cherry Orchard', now Cherry Orchard Nurseries). With Willis and the survey as principal guides a pre-excavation plan of the palace was drawn up in 1958. The Nonsuch Palace Excavation Committee came into being the following year, and with help from the Ministry of Works, local sources (including the Ewell residents who lent pillows for the site dormitory) and 500 volunteers, Nonsuch itself was restored from legend to real life that summer.

For Dent himself, the last few weeks before the first sod was cut became increasingly tense. As he describes in *The Quest for Nonsuch*, his account of both the dig and the palace's history, he had written a visitor's guide to the site and had made some 'fairly dogmatic statements' about where Nonsuch really stood. By the evening of 6 July, however, his anxiety was at an end: 'I had assumed', he said, 'that the modern roadway ran through the centre of the site, and it was with some relief that I saw, on the first day, evidence that the roadway was in fact only a few feet off-centre.'

In all, over 60,000 visitors witnessed the palace's reappearance. Those that came in September, when the dig was nearing its end, were in a position to see much more than the position of the building in relation to the road. Spread out in front of them were the remains of the whole structure—foundations, sewers and a large wine-cellar with a cobbled floor and holes in the walls to show where the wine-racks had been. There were lavatory-pits, a well in the former kitchen and the surround of a cistern that fed the palace's famous courtyard fountain. There were even vestiges of a church; to build Nonsuch, Henry had razed the entire village of Cuddington, church included. For the first time since the eighteenth century, when the last remnants of the palace faded from view, it was now possible for onlookers to bridge the gap between surviving accounts and pictures of the building and its physical self.

The best-known representation of Nonsuch—the drawing made in 1568 by Hoefnagel—all but disguises a key fact about the palace: its depth. Seen from above, Nonsuch would have looked like two adjoining squares or a figure 8 with square corners. The southern front shown in the drawing made up the base of the 8; behind it lay a courtyard known as the

107 Nonsuch Palace, drawn by Joris Hoefnagel in 1568

Inner Court, on the first floor of which were the rooms used by royalty. The buildings on the furthermost side of the court—the crossbar of the 8—can just be seen. Their main feature was a tower with an (inaccurately drawn) cupola marking a gatehouse. Beyond this was a second court, with a kitchen block (half-concealed by bushes in the picture) leading off it to the right. A second gatehouse lay directly beyond the clock tower and formed the palace's main entrance. So Hoefnagel's view of Nonsuch, imposing though it looks, is quite literally only half the story; the palace was, in fact, almost twice as deep as it was broad.

Another aspect of the palace that Hoefnagel's drawing disguises is the garden. In spite of the riotous invention of its towers and spires, the mansion as shown by the artist still has a curiously blank, forbidding look—like a madly ornate prison. This is because both the ground floor of the south front and the Privy Garden that lay before and round it are hidden by the uncompromising line of the garden wall that stretches across the picture. An engraving made in 1610 by the cartographer Speed shows a formal knot garden of the type much admired in the sixteenth century: large, geometrically shaped beds broken into squares and triangles by low hedges and separated by paths. There were also a maze, statues and fountains, one of which represented a nymph whose interior plumbing was arranged so that water flowed from her breasts. She was, the Parliamentary Commissioners were to note, surrounded by a little grove of six 'Lelack' trees, or lilacs.

Fountain and lelacks were later additions to the list of appointments. The main, the most outstanding characteristic of the building was there from the start: the decoration of the walls of the Inner Court. Much of the timberwork here was covered with panels of slate, carved and frequently gilded—the point was, as John Evelyn explained over a century later, that the panels acted 'like a coat of armour' and preserved the wood from rotting. Between them were fixed row upon row of moulded plaster panels, all in eye-searing white. 'I much admired', Evelyn went on 'how they had lasted so well and entire since the time of Henry VIII., exposed as they are to the air; and pity it is they are not taken out and preserved in some dry place; a gallery would become them. There are some mezzo-relievos as big as the life; the story is of the Heathen Gods, emblems, compartments, &c.' It is now thought that Evelyn had slightly exaggerated the size. But he was right about the period: the pagan deities, the soldiers, animals and angels that paraded round the walls were going up only three years after construction started in 1538.

Although it was Henry who, with the help of craftsmen from England, France, Germany and Italy, had brought the whole splendid vision into existence, the palace has more historical associations with Elizabeth than with her father. As far as is known, indeed, Henry seldom used it. After his death, Surrey's newest ornament passed through a somewhat scrambled phase of existence during which it served mainly as a source of venison for aristocratic larders. (Its main role, as indicated by the park surrounding it, was that of a hunting lodge.) It also narrowly escaped being pulled down and sold off for what the materials would fetch. Tudor Mary, seriously concerned at the drain on resources that the palace represented, considered taking the obvious—and profitable—way out. However, she ended by exchanging the mansion for several properties owned by one of her leading noblemen, the Earl of Arundel. It was Arundel and his son-in-law, Lord Lumley, who added the final refinements to Nonsuch and its gardens, and it was Arundel who, willy-nilly, introduced the palace to the woman who would be its most famous owner.

The young Queen Elizabeth first visited Nonsuch in the course of a royal progress in the summer of 1559. The widowed Arundel, who was regarded by many as a possible husband for her, naturally extended himself. His royal guest stayed a week and was entertained with banquets, dramatic spectacles, music and the chase. She returned again and again. Lumley, who inherited Nonsuch after Arundel's death, perforce became used to the sight depicted by Hoefnagel of the queen's coach lumbering into view, accompanied by men-at-arms, outriders, courtiers and an interminable train of servants and baggage carts.

Lumley, whose cares as a host were only part of a range of money worries, ended by giving Nonsuch to Elizabeth in settlement of his debts to the Crown. She took it over in 1592 and, within a few years, the palace had the reputation of being her favourite. All through the last decade of the century, the baggage trains heralding her arrival trundled up to the gate of the Outward Court, bringing in their wake the armies of royal personnel. Elizabeth, when she herself arrived, would progress under the clock tower of the inner gatehouse to the sparkling Inner Court, where she would turn right, enter the court's western side (hidden behind the left-hand tower in Hoefnagel's picture) and climb a stately staircase to her apartments on the first floor. Most important of these, and almost the first, was the audience chamber or Presence Room, with its canopied chair and magnificent wall-hangings. Nearer the south front of the

108 Queen Elizabeth I in old age.
Unfinished miniature by Isaac Oliver

building was, among others, the privy chamber, used as a royal dining-room. Some doubt hangs over the position of the royal bedchamber, but the indications are, Dent suggests, that it was round the corner of the building, in the south wing, looking over the knot garden. If it was, then some of the windows just visible in the picture lit one of the most re-markable scenes in the history of both the palace and of Elizabeth herself: the confrontation between the elderly queen, still in a state of undress, and her breathless, mud-spattered and doomed favourite, the thirty-two-year-old Earl of Essex.

Robert Devereux, the second earl of his line, had good looks, charm and dash, and Elizabeth was only one of a multitude who fell under his spell. However, his personal gifts were counterbalanced by a fatal tendency to forget on which side his bread was buttered. His career as a leading courtier and soldier reached its conclusion when, in March 1599, Elizabeth sent him to quell a revolt in Ireland. He did not quell it, however; instead, he declared a truce with the rebel leader and then came rushing back to England to tell his story first. Muddy to the eyebrows, he arrived at Nonsuch at ten in the morning of 28 September, tore through the outer apartments, round the corner of the building, and into Elizabeth's bedroom. Here a traumatic shock awaited him.

Just as Nonsuch provided a gilded, glittering housing for Majesty, so did Elizabeth's paints, velvets and brocades act as housing and protection for the now ageing and less-than-dazzling queen. Apart from her attendants, no one had seen her without them—until Essex came dashing in. As an on-the-spot chronicler, Rowland Whyte, noted the next day, the Earl 'staid not till he came to the Queen's bed-chamber, where he found the Queen newly up, the hair about her face'. The face itself would have been like the one shown in Isaac Oliver's unfinished miniature: hollow eyelids, shadows under the eyes, lines at the corners of tight-lipped mouth.

The Queen's disarray was, of course, matched to some extent by Essex's own: 'Tis much to be wondered at here,' Whyte continued in his letter to Sir Robert Sidney, 'that he went so boldly to Her Majesty's presence, she not being ready, and he so full of dirt and mire that his very face was full of it.' Perhaps it was the queen's awareness of this fact that kept the storm from breaking over the earl right away. Indeed, a short and apparently friendly interview was followed by another, just as friendly, as soon as the pair had made themselves fit to be seen. By midnight, though, Essex was a prisoner in his own room and, the next day, was made to stand through a three-hour interrogation on charges that included his presumptuous dash into his sovereign's bedchamber. In October, he left Nonsuch for a ten-month spell of house arrest in London; the queen eventually released him but, imprudent to the last, he tried to mend his fallen fortunes by staging a *coup de'état*. The plan misfired lamentably, and Essex went to the scaffold in 1601.

Two years later, Elizabeth herself died, and Nonsuch passed to the Stuarts. Before the Civil War, the palace continued to enjoy royal favour; after it, the glory had gone. The Parliamentarians sent their surveyors in 1650 to report on the building's value and received a highly favourable answer. The palace then moved briskly from the hands of one army officer to another. When it came back to the royal family after the Restoration, it was in a state of some disrepair: 'We . . . altogether believe it to have been a very noble house', wrote Pepys, who recorded a Sunday visit paid to the

109 (*left*) Anti-hero of the scene in the Nonsuch bedroom: Robert Devereux, second Earl of Essex. Portrait after M. Gheeraerts the Younger. 110 (*right*) Samuel Pepys the diarist. Other lost houses he visited included Clarendon and Sayes Court, John Evelyn's home. Portrait by J. Hayls

district in 1663 and who, like any tourist at any time, peered through the gates to see as much as he could of the court beyond. In the Plague year of 1665, he made further visits, for Nonsuch became the temporary offices of the Exchequer during the emergency. It was also during this period that Evelyn noted the famous plaster panels. As one would expect of the author of *Sylva*, Evelyn also remarked on the 'rows of fair elms' planted in the grounds. 'But', he went on, 'the rest of these goodly trees, both of this and of Worcester Park adjoining, were felled by those destructive and avaricious rebels in the late war, which defaced one of the stateliest seats his Majesty had.'

Within a few months, another emergency struck: the Great Fire of London. Back went the Exchequer to the Palace and this, linked with the 'change and decay' tone of both diarists, is an indication of the palace's new status. Far from being a favourite royal residence, it was turning into a mere outpost of government, a temporary office block, as it were, and one that needed extensive repairs. Repairs were carried out, but soon Nonsuch suffered its final change of ownership. In 1671, Charles II gave it in trust to one of the most celebrated of his mistresses: the noted beauty and spendthrift Barbara Villiers, Countess of Castlemaine. And Barbara, who was always short of money, eleven years later started to take

the step considered by Mary Tudor over a century before. By degrees, Nonsuch started to come down. First to go was the Inner Court, with its magnificent plasterwork. As the excavation in 1959 revealed, much of this remained on the site, smashed to fragments and used to fill in holes and hollows left by the demolishers. The presence of these fragments, writes Dent,

> more than anything else, drove home a full realisation of the ruthlessness and wantonness of those who pulled down the Palace; for, whatever we may think of the building as a whole, the Nonsuch stuccoes were unique and priceless treasures, as works of art, as a colossal three-tiered decorative scheme covering at least 900ft of wall, and as the most important and striking component in the adornment of the first English building to be decorated largely in the Renaissance manner.

By the middle of the eighteenth century, little visible was left of Nonsuch but the foundations; by the end of it, even these had vanished from sight, and the great Nonsuch mystery had started to gather. Compared with that surrounding the site of Troy, it was short-lived; it was still, however, potent enough to draw a huge throng of fascinated witnesses to its demise in the summer sunshine of a Surrey park.

❧ Northumberland House

When the Strand was a riverside highway between Westminster and London, it presented a spectacle of ribbon development at its most prestigious. One of the great mansions built along its length was Old Somerset House, described on page 229. Others included Essex House, named for Elizabeth's Essex; Arundel House, the London home of the Arundels, and not to be confused with the one at Highgate; Worcester House, used by the Earl of Clarendon as a London base while his own Piccadilly house was going up; Salisbury House, built by Lord Burghley's son; York House, where Essex was imprisoned after the debacle at Nonsuch; and Northumberland House, boldly topped during the later part of its career with the cheerful Percy lion.

Some of these were purpose built for their aristocratic owners; others were palaces that had once belonged to princes of the Church. Some changed their names frequently; others stuck to their original ones through thick and thin. All have now gone, with York House leaving in its place a clutch of streets that recalled every component of the name of the man who sold it off for building materials: *George* Street (later York Buildings), *Villiers* Street, *Duke* Street, *Of* Alley (now York Place) and *Buckingham* Street. The last house to go, in 1874, was the most westerly of the string, Northumberland House. Its demolition, for which its owner was paid about £2 million in compensation, allowed Northumberland Avenue to be driven from Trafalgar Square to the Embankment.

Unlike York, its great neighbour to the east and sometime residence of the archbishops of York, Northumberland House did not start as an ecclesiastical palace. The first building on the site was, however, a convent which was later turned into a house. It would be surprising if the Earl of Northampton did not follow the time-honoured practice of recycling its materials when he pulled the old building down and, about 1605, put up a palace in keeping with what he felt was his due. The new house, which was built around three sides and backed on to a garden and the river, was judged suitably magnificent, but the earl did not live long enough for his name to become permanently fixed to it. Within ten years, it was being called after his heir, the Earl of Suffolk, and it took a further change of ownership—via the marriage of the earl's granddaughter in 1642—to bring it to the Percys.

The bridegroom, the tenth Earl of Northumberland, was a leading

112 The garden front of Northumberland House in the 1760s. The Percy lion has been in place on the street side of the building for some years; the two towers that dominated the south front have been removed

statesman and a connoisseur of the fine and applied arts. He completed the building by adding the missing side facing on to the river (the result had a massive turret at each corner of the house and looked not unlike the Tower of London), and he laid the foundation of one of the mansion's main claims to fame: its picture gallery. Evelyn visited it in June 1658 and left a short but dizzying catalogue of its contents:

> I went to see the Earl of Northumberland's pictures, whereof that of the Venetian Senators was one of the best of Titian's, and another of Andrea del Sarto, viz. a Madonna, Christ, St. John, and an Old Woman, a St. Catharine of Da Vinci, with divers portraits of Van-dyke; a Nativity of Georgioni [*sic*], the last of our blessed Kings (Charles I.) and the Duke of York, by Lely; a Rosary by the famous Jesuits of Brussels, and several more.

Evelyn continued by indicating the time-lag between the change of a mansion's ownership and its change of name: he called the building Suffolk House and, with his usual eye for errors of taste, added that the new garden front was 'tolerable, were it not drowned by a too massy and clumsy pair of stairs in stone, without any neat invention'.

Stairs and all, the house nearly went through yet another change of name before the Northumberland label fairly stuck. A lack of male heirs to the earldom took the building, via the marriage of another heiress, into the hands of the sixth Duke of Somerset, nicknamed the 'Proud'. (What

224

the heiress herself, Lady Elizabeth Percy, thought of the match is an open question. Edward Walford, writing in *Old and New London*, told how the duke once scolded a later wife when she took the liberty of kissing him; the august Lady Elizabeth, the poor woman was informed, would never have dreamt of initiating such intimacies.) However, the next Somerset was created Earl of Northumberland anew and his successor—a son-in-law who had started as a baronet called Smithson—pleaded his case for honourable recognition so well that he ended up, not just as an earl, but a duke: Hugh Percy (*né* Smithson), first Duke of Northumberland.

Among the vast possessions that came to him by marriage was, of course, a Strand mansion that matched his pretensions. His father-in-law had indicated its permanent status as the Percys' town house by putting up the famous lion in 1749, the year before he died. Hugh Percy, the first duke, took over, enlarged the building and, more important, bred a line of direct male heirs that took the new dukedom well into the next century. He also showed himself quite capable of carrying on the tradition of taste and discrimination developed by previous occupants of Northumberland House. Almost at once, he got rid of the two forbidding

113 Hugh Percy, first Duke of Northumberland. Portrait by J. Tassie

towers that overlooked the river (and later scaled down the two at the front); he continued to increase the picture collection and, in a princely gesture, went so far as to invite the general public to walk round. Another, more specific, invitation went to the distinguished if rackety man of letters, Oliver Goldsmith. Poor Goldsmith was a master of the written word, but hopeless at conversation. He chattered, babbled, lost the thread. He found himself at his most profuse when, on his visit to Northumberland House, he came face to face with a magnificent personage who could only be his ducal host. Goldsmith laboured on to the end of his speech of thanks and then, to his dismay, was told that the magnificent personage was the duke's valet.

Goldsmith might not have known the duke at first sight, but he was on considerably better acquaintance with another of the inhabitants of Northumberland House: Thomas Percy, the duke's chaplain and later Bishop of Dromore. This Percy was a man of considerable erudition and his fame has easily outlasted that of his noble patron. Like Pepys before him, he collected ancient verse and, in 1765, published his collection under the title *Reliques of Ancient English Poetry*. Its contents included such well-known ballads as *Sir Patrick Spence* and *The Bonny Earl of Murray*, and, naturally, much celebration of the Percy family in general. Some of it was 'made' poetry rather than products of the oral (and anonymous) tradition that had produced the great ballads. But in spite of this (and in spite of his

114 The public face of Northumberland House in 1830. Note the adjoining warehouse

115 The beginning of the end; the Percy lion is ceremonially removed in 1874

tendency to alter texts) Percy is still regarded today as one of the great ballad collectors, while his earlier reputation among the writers of the Romantic movement was enormous. Earlier still, the first Duke of Northumberland had recognised an asset when he heard of one, and brought the learned celebrator of the Percys' history into his London household.

In fact, the arrangement nearly turned out disastrously for Thomas Percy for, in 1780, the house was ravaged by fire, and the chaplain's rooms were destroyed. But most of his unique library was found to be untouched, and his patron lost no time in replacing the Strand front of the mansion that the flames had destroyed.

From the early nineteenth century, that front was, for a long while, all that Londoners were really able to see of the building. Under the first duke's descendants, Northumberland House gave up its role as a public picture gallery and went into purdah. In 1848, the essayist Leigh Hunt wrote that, 'though the house still exists, the public see little of it. All they behold, indeed, is the screen or advanced guard, which is no very fine sight, and only serves to narrow the way. Of the quadrangle inside the public know nothing; and thousands pass every day without suspecting that there is such a thing as a tree on the premises.' This curtain resulted from more than the ducal family's desire for privacy; it seemed to represent a conscious withdrawal from the sort of area that the westernmost end of the Strand had become. The neighbourhood had gone downhill considerably from the days when Northampton, Somerset and the first Duke of Northumberland had lived there in state. The house and its great secret garden were now cooped up among shops and Thames-side coal depots.

In the exhibition year of 1851, the public was again allowed to enter the building and admire the pictures, but the house's likely future was by then becoming increasingly apparent. Mayfair and the newly developed Belgravia were now the centres of aristocratic and fashionable circles; Northumberland House was a dinosaur among buildings, an unwieldy representative of a past age. The Metropolitan Board of Works had its eye on the space that this anachronism took up and, in the 1870s, made the sixth duke an offer. The duke accepted and, in 1874, sold his London house to the Board for just under £500,000. The lion was ceremonially removed and reinstalled at Syon House in Isleworth, and Northumberland House was dismantled, sold off in lots and razed. The dullest street in all central London seems a poor, if functional, exchange.

From its earliest days, the first Somerset House in the Strand was a place of controversy. Indeed, the controversy started before the walls were fairly up. The Duke of Somerset, brother-in-law of Henry VIII and future protector of England, tore down a wide range of buildings to clear a site for his new house, and among them was the first Strand church of St Mary. The parishioners could, of course, do nothing to prevent the loss, but the duke had promised to build them another church, and they crossly waited for him to do so. They waited in vain. Somerset, far from building a new St Mary's, pulled down still more ecclesiastical buildings (among them the chapel over the Old St Paul's charnel house) and used the materials to start his fine new home on the bank of the Thames.

The parishioners took themselves off to St Clement's and Somerset went on with his building project, which he had started in 1546. The next year, Henry VIII died, leaving Edward VI on the throne and Somerset within reach of all but total power. As protector, he became the most important man in England, but his glory did not last. In 1551, he was charged with treason and sent to the Tower. It was his second term of imprisonment there, but while the first had ended in his release, this one did not. On 22 January 1552, he was executed on Tower Hill and his house, still in an incomplete state, passed to the Crown.

Thereafter, it became a house of women. Edward's sister, Elizabeth—herself a controversial figure in Mary Tudor's time—stayed there. James VI's wife, Anne of Denmark, made it her own (at which point the building was renamed Denmark House). And after Anne came another royal consort, the French-born Henrietta Maria. When she came to England in 1625 as the wife of Charles I, Henrietta brought with her a huge train of fellow-nationals—priests, ladies-in-waiting and servants. Their presence had been agreed in the queen's marriage settlement, but their numbers (over 400) and their enthusiastically displayed Roman Catholicism were a constant thorn in the British Establishment's side. Breaking point was reached when the Queen's priests set her as a public penance to walk to Tyburn. Charles, deciding to call a complete halt, had the whole company hustled under house arrest to Somerset House and there told them that, agreements notwithstanding, they must go.

'The deportment of some amongst you hath been very inoffensive to me,' he said, 'but others again have so dallied with my patience, and so

116 Old Somerset House in its earliest guise, c.1570

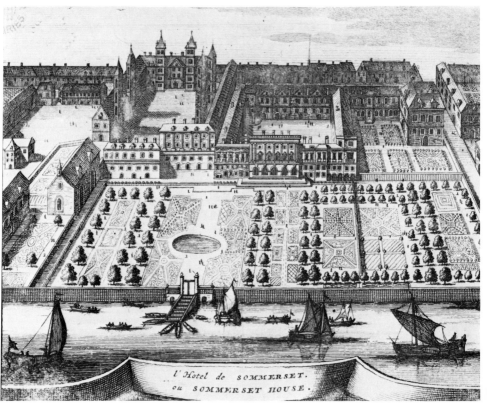

117 Old Somerset House as it was later developed

l'Hotel de SOMMERSET.
ou SOMMERSET HOUSE.

highly affronted me, as I cannot, and will not, longer endure it.' The fuss, unsurprisingly, was tremendous: the foreigners, who were informed that they were expected to leave within twenty-four hours, protested that they owed money in London; that they were themselves owed money; that the whole thing could not be done. Their departure was postponed for a while, and they took full advantage of this breathing space. Those with heads for figures cooked the queen's books to the tune of £10,000—all of it, they said, bills they had run up on her behalf. Others took a more direct way of enriching themselves: they rifled the queen's cupboards and jewel boxes so thoroughly that she was reportedly left with nothing to wear but what she stood up in.

Charles, out of all patience, told his favourite, the Duke of Buckingham, that he must get them out of London in any way he could: peacefully, if possible, but 'otherways force them away, dryving them away lyke so manie wilde beastes, until ye have shipped them, and so the devil goe with them'. And in the end, with the yeomen of the guard standing over them as a reminder of where power lay, they went.

The house, however, continued to be a target for public criticism. Catholic Henrietta was still allowed full liberty of religious practice, and the new chapel she had built on the Somerset House tennis-court, to a design by Inigo Jones, was always crowded with her English co-religionists. Masses were celebrated all morning, special instruction was held three days a week in both French and English and the number of converts grew apace. It was one more grievance to add to the many against the royal house and, at the beginning of the Civil War, Henrietta's chapel was torn apart by a troop of armed men. A Rubens that had decorated it was hurled into the river, while the queen's Capuchin priests were put under arrest. In 1644, the queen fled to France, and stayed there until the Restoration.

During her absence, the palace stood idle, except for two months when it was used for Cromwell's lying-in-state. (It was not, in fact, his body that received the populace's last respects, but a model.) When Henrietta returned, however, she made up for lost time, set the chapel to rights and, in the first three of the five years she spent in England before leaving again for France in 1665, authorised building works to the value of £23,000. New stables were created; so were new state rooms facing the garden with Henrietta's own presence chamber over the arcade in the centre of the illustration. Pepys much admired its furnishings. He also noted a piquant gathering there consisting of Henrietta, her son Charles II, her barren daughter-in-law Catherine of Braganza, Barbara Villiers (Countess of

118 (*left*) Charles I, the harried husband. Portrait after Anthony van Dyck and 119 (*right*) Queen Henrietta Maria. Portrait after Anthony van Dyck

Castlemaine and lady of the bedchamber to Catherine), and one of Charles' bastards, the fifteen-year-old Mr Croft. (In spite of his youth the latter appeared to be extremely interested in the Countess.)

When Charles died, his widow in her turn moved into Somerset House, which had by now reached its fullest size. But as a royal residence, it did not last much longer. Catherine, who did not return to her native Portugal until some years after the fall of the Stuarts, was in fact the last queen to use it. Afterwards, although it continued as the property of British queens, it was employed sometimes as a residence for visiting notables and sometimes as an overflow department for royal pictures. All the time, the structure gradually grew more and more dilapidated.

The end came in the 1770s when Queen Charlotte indicated that she preferred Buckingham House, where she was then living, to the palace on the Strand. An Act of Parliament was passed that effected the exchange, and the demolition of the building started in 1776. Its replacement housed many organisations—among them the Royal Society, King's College and, on a less elevated plane, the Inland Revenue.

❧Osborne House

In 1560, during the reign of Elizabeth I, a gentleman with the ancient Isle of Wight name of Lovybond bought a property on the north-east coast of the island called Osborne. With it he may have bought the first Osborne House; if not, he built it himself. A later Lovybond, called Thomas, also had building fever. According to a seventeenth-century account, he 'bwylt ye newe house at Osberon, which his soun solde to Captayne Maun, and hath been ye ruine of that howse; soome bwyldeth and some destroyeth.' With these moralistic remarks, a name that in the end became world-famous first entered the records of houses built, rebuilt, lost and recreated.

The most junior of the Lovybonds might have been notorious locally, but he was soon outshone by the gallant captain who bought his house. Eustace Maun, or Mann, had a prudent but forgetful nature. When the Civil War came, he decided to hide as much of his fortune as was portable against future emergencies. The tradition is that he buried it in the grounds of his house—the alleged spot was later called Money Copse—and then forgot where he had put it. When the Restoration came he sensibly

120 The Blachford house at Osborne, soon after Queen Victoria bought it

121 Queen Victoria, shortly before the purchase of Osborne House. Portrait by A. Penley

applied for, and received, a grant of all treasure trove found at Osborne, but his valuables stayed obstinately hidden.

In spite of this mishap, however, the Manns prospered at Osborne and eventually handed it over, via an eighteenth-century heiress, to a Hampshire family called Blachford. One of them, Robert Pope Blachford, complied with the spirit of the times by pulling down the old-fashioned Osborne II and erecting in its place a three-storeyed Georgian mansion that, like its predecessors on the site, enjoyed a superb view over the

Solent. The position had, in fact, considerably more to commend it than the house itself. As the *Illustrated London News* commented in the following century:

> Osborne is beautifully situated in the neighbourhood of East Cowes, one of the best points in 'the Island'. The mansion is placed in a fine park, well stocked with noble timber, and adjoining eastward the grounds of Norris Castle . . .. Very little of [the building] is seen from the high road; but in sailing along the coast, the house appears to be a handsome square edifice, seated at the head of an ample lawn, which slopes gently to a valley open to the sea-beach. The whole park, strictly private, extends down to the sea, with good landing places.

This park, the *Illustrated London News* added, stretched over 346 acres, but the house, in contrast, was not particularly spacious. 'The mansion has on the ground floor a drawing-room, dining-room and library, with two ante-rooms and halls', the paper commented. 'The first and second floors contain sixteen bed and dressing-rooms—very inadequate accommodation for a royal suite.'

The suite was, of course, that belonging to Osborne III's most celebrated resident, Queen Victoria, who bought the house from the Blachfords in 1845. Victoria had known the Isle of Wight since 1831 when, as a twelve-year-old, she had gone there for a holiday with her mother. On this occasion and a second one two years later, the Duchess of Kent and her daughter had stayed in neighbouring Norris Castle, and it was of the Castle and its neighbour that Victoria thought when, as a queen, she wanted to buy a house of her own.

By the time she was twenty-four, Victoria had a husband, three children, and an increasingly intense desire for some space and privacy in which the whole family could be themselves. Windsor and the Brighton Pavilion were too open to the public; Buckingham Palace was too uncomfortable and too small. In October 1843, the queen noted that she and Albert had begun to consider the idea of house-hunting in the Isle of Wight.

The royal couple ended by choosing Osborne rather than Norris. They leased the house for a year to see how things went. The queen was charmed by what she saw (although she admitted that the rooms were on the small side), while Albert was full of plans for improving both the building and the estate. Both of them made light of the alterations likely to be needed, but the *ILN*'s damping comment that 'considerable alterations must be made' was echoed in essence by the expert the pair called in before committing themselves to purchase: the builder Thomas Cubitt.

122 Osborne, old (left) and new; a print dated 1 October 1846

Cubitt was definite about Osborne III's future. There was no possible way, he advised the prospective buyers, of altering the house into something equipped to take both their growing family and their entourage. It would have to come down, and a new one built in its place. But Victoria and Albert were not put off. After some haggling with the house's owner, Lady Isabella Blachford, over the fixtures and fittings, the sale finally went through on 1 May 1845. At last, at a price of £26,000, Victoria had a place that she could call her own.

Alterations to the existing Osborne were put in train immediately, while arrangements for building the new house went ahead with equal speed. At 10.00am on 23 June, the Queen, her husband, the Princess Royal and the Prince of Wales all trooped out into the grounds where the deer grazed north of the house, and there laid the foundation stone for Osborne IV. Cubitt, meanwhile, was facing a formidable task. 'In the course of four or five years,' comments his biographer, Hermione Hobhouse, 'one large and very substantial mansion had to be built, a very large house had to be demolished, and extensive improvements to the grounds made; none of this was to prohibit fairly frequent visits by the Queen and the Royal Family, together with the Household, and important visitors, including foreign royalty.' The builder proceeded in stages. The progress he had made within sixteen months is shown in the illustration, in which the Pavilion block of the new house dwarfs the Blachford building. The Household Wing, which lay behind the Blachfords' Osborne, was started just before the print was engraved. Last to go up was the main block, to build which Osborne III had to come down completely. Seldom can a house have been consigned to the dustbin with so much care and tact. It was an approach that Cubitt adopted again when he built his own country home near Dorking.

Delighted as Victoria and her husband were with the Pavilion into which they had moved in September 1846, the Queen was saddened to lose the old house. In December 1847, she walked through its rooms for the last time and noted that the snug and happy atmosphere which had first attracted her was still present. Various reminders of Osborne III, though, were kept: its fire-baskets reappeared in Osborne IV and the Blachfords' front porch was found a new home in a garden wall. And a reminder of an earlier Osborne still was also preserved in the new building's cellars. Their thick limestone walls had probably belonged to the Lovybond house, although it has been suggested that they date back as far as the shadowy Osborne I: the *old* house at 'Osberon', first of a sequence that, from ordinary enough beginnings, ended as home of a queen and death-place of a queen-empress.

❧Peterborough House

In the middle of the Civil War, a Fulham gardener took a gamble for posterity by growing a unique sapling in the grounds of a house whose future was anything but sure. The house—the Villa Carey at Parson's Green—belonged to a loyalist who was soon to follow Charles II into exile; in his absence, Parliament ordered that his home should be sold. The sapling was believed to be the first tulip tree ever raised in England. The tree survived and lived to become the glory of the neighbourhood; the Commonwealth did not. After the Restoration, the house and its grounds came back to their rightful owners: John Mordaunt, brother of the Earl of Peterborough, and his wife Elizabeth, *née* Carey.

Elizabeth had brought her husband more than a home and a botanical curiosity. Her husband, also a fervent loyalist, had been thrown into the Tower during the Protectorate and put on trial for his activities. But his wife—according to the Earl of Clarendon, a young woman of 'notable vivacity of wit and humour'—helped a key witness to abscond. As a result,

123 Peterborough House and grounds

her husband's judges were divided and their president somewhat scep-
tically gave him the benefit of the doubt. After a further spell in the Tower
(Cromwell, enraged at the trial's extraordinary outcome, had him temporarily imprisoned again), John threw himself back into further efforts
for the loyalist cause, and reaped the reward of a barony.

The enterprising Mordaunts passed their Fulham home on to their
even more enterprising son Charles who, as the third Earl of Peterborough,
was to earn the nickname 'the great'. Charles led an energetic career as a
soldier and international man of affairs. Jonathan Swift summed up the
Mordaunt style in his lines to 'the Earl of Peterborough, who Commanded the British Forces in Spain':

> Mordanto fills the trump of fame,
> The Christian worlds his deeds proclaim,
> And prints are crowded with his name.
>
> In journies he outrides the post,
> Sits up till midnight with his host,
> Talks politicks, and gives the toast.
>
> Knows every prince in Europe's face,
> Flies like a squib from place to place,
> And travels not, but runs a race . . ..
>
> Mordanto gallops on alone,
> The roads are with his followers strown,
> This breaks a girth, and that a bone;
>
> His body active as his mind,
> Returning sound in limb and wind,
> Except some leather lost behind.

The house inherited by this hustling aristocrat—who once professed
that he had seen more kings and more postilions than any other man in
Europe—was one that allowed him to live in the style that was his due.
Described in the eighteenth century as a 'very large square regular pile
of brick', it had been rebuilt by the earl's grandfather with an 'abundance
of extraordinary good rooms with fine paintings'. A gallery ran round the
roof, enabling Mordanto to admire both the famous tulip tree (now nearly
80ft high) and his whole garden of 20 acres. However, he was notoriously
and chronically hard-up—the family wealth, unlike the title, had been left
to a cousin—and, during the early years of the eighteenth century, the
grounds started to lose their elegance. 'Their beauty', the antiquarian John
Bowack wrote in 1706, 'is in great measure decayed; and the large
cypress shades, and pleasant wildernesses, with fountains, statues, &c.,

have been very entertaining.' The decay was none the less reversed during a later upturn in the earl's fortunes, for in 1711 Swift commented that 'it is the finest garden I have ever seen about this town, and abundance of hot walls for grapes, where they are in great plenty, and ripening fast.'

Swift was by no means the only noted frequenter of the erstwhile Villa Carey, now called Peterborough House. The philosopher John Locke went there for his health; Pope, too, was a welcome visitor. Another guest, oddly enough, appears to have been the earl's wife. The second countess (the first died in 1709; it had been one of their daughters who had turned the second Duke of Gordon's children to Protestantism) had been born Anastasia Robinson and, when the earl met her, she was an opera singer. Anastasia appears to have been charming rather than beautiful; she was also highly talented and reasonably virtuous. She looked after her elderly father till he died and, when the earl made the inevitable proposal, she seems to have held out for marriage, and won. Although her suitor imposed a condition of his own—he refused to acknowledge her as his wife—the alliance was an open secret, especially after the ageing but still

124 'Knows every prince in Europe's face': Charles Mordaunt, Earl of Peterborough. Portrait after Godfrey Kneller

CHARLES
Earl of Peterborough &.

125 Anastasia Robinson, Peterborough's secret wife. Portrait after Godfrey Kneller

brisk Mordanto took his whip to another singer who had offended her.

When she retired from the stage, she and her mother—according to one report—moved into a nearby house the earl had taken for them. According to another, she ruled over the earl's table but never lived under the same roof as her husband. Their scruples later faded when Peterborough fell sick and at last, in 1735, he acclaimed his tactful and self-effacing wife as his countess. He died shortly afterwards, whereupon his widow regrettably deprived posterity of some lively reading by loyally burning his secret memoirs.

By the end of the century, the once-splendid house on the south-east side of Parson's Green was being replaced by a new building, and much of the magnificent garden had been let off to a market-gardener. The almost legendary tulip tree had gone as well; twenty-one years after its illustrious owner died, it died too, of simple decay.

241

❧ Sayes Court

Beyond Dacca Street in Deptford in the London Borough of Greenwich is a park called Sayes Court. To the west is Grove Street and to the north lies the Old Foreign Cattle Market, once the royal dockyard and now used by wharfage companies. In the area contained by these two streets and the market, a minor civil servant once kept bees, planted myrtles and cypresses, played host to royalty, was burgled three times, wrote poems, read them aloud to the diarist Samuel Pepys and kept a diary himself. He was, of course, John Evelyn, who has already featured prominently in this book. Among the lost houses described in his *Diary* is his own, Sayes Court. Interestingly, it survived much longer than many greater buildings whose appointments he admired and whose disappearance he mourned.

Evelyn settled permanently in Sayes Court in 1652, three years after the execution of Charles I. A royalist, though a discreet one, he had been abroad for much of the Civil War and its immediate aftermath; now he wanted to come home. His king, the exiled Charles II, had commissioned him to do some gentle undercover work for the royalist cause, but this was not the only reason for his return.

Until the old king's death, Sayes Court had been held on a Crown lease by Evelyn's father-in-law, Sir Richard Browne. It had since been seized by the state and, the diarist noted, was 'very much suffering for want of some friend to rescue it out of the power of the usurpers'. So although he was profoundly depressed by the national state of affairs, Evelyn was hoping to liberate the family property. In addition to this, he had a young wife and, all in all, was drawn to the idea of settling 'henceforth in England, having now run about the world, most part out of my own country, near 10 years'.

The property he eventually redeemed consisted of a battered two-storey house with cellars, stables and courtyard. Downstairs, according to a survey made in 1651, was a hall, parlour, kitchen, buttery, larder (with dairy attached) and one extra room. Upstairs were eight more rooms and various closets and garrets.

The house stood on 2½ acres of land, an area which was to prove much too small for its new owner, whose interest in gardens and gardening was passionate. Within less than a year, he had added 100 acres to his grounds and had started to plant it. His new orchard went in three days before he took formal possession of the house it was to serve.

126 John Evelyn the diarist, soon to settle at Sayes Court. Engraving by R. Nanteuil

127 A house reduced to its essentials: Sayes Court, sketched in the 1830s from an original drawn by Evelyn himself

128 A visitor to Evelyn's 'poor habitation': James II, formerly the Duke of York. Portrait by Godfrey Kneller

129 Another visitor to Sayes Court: Charles II. Portrait after Peter Lely

The Evelyns lived at Sayes Court for forty-two years. In that time, the diarist turned the 100 acre field into one of the most celebrated domains in England: a 'most beautiful place', as Pepys called it. He also restored the house itself. An undated memorandum found among his papers indicates the sweeping nature of the two operations and, in a muted but unmistakable way, indicates which Evelyn preferred. The note of weariness at the end is conspicuous.

The hithermost Grove I planted about	1656
The other beyond it	1660
The lower Grove	1662
The holly hedge, even with the Mount hedge below	1670

I planted every hedge & tree not onley in the garden, groves &c. but about all the fields & house since 1653, except those large, old & hollow elms in the stable court & next the sewer; for it was before, all one pasture field to the very garden of the house, wch was but small; from which time also I repaired the ruined house, & built the whole of the kitchen, the chapel, buttry, my study, above & below, cellars & all the outhouses & walls, still-house, orangerie & made the gardens &c. to my great cost, & better had I don to have pulled all down at first, but it was don at several times.

However, major works of this kind took up only part of Evelyn's attention. He wrote on current affairs, fashion, smoke abatement in London, medals and—naturally—on plants and gardens. (During his own lifetime, his most famous work was probably *Sylva, or a Discourse of Forest Trees*.) He helped to form the Royal Society and was one of its earliest members. After the monarchy was restored in 1660, he went to Court and, as the *Diary* shows, frequented the houses of some of the greatest figures of the day. He held various official posts, he discovered Grinling Gibbons and introduced him to the king, and he experimented with the latest art form of the day, the mezzotint (in which he was instructed by Prince Rupert of the Rhine). And he had nine children, of whom only one lived longer than her mother and father.

Sayes Court formed the background for much of this activity. Thus:

My son, John Stansfield, was born, being my second child . . .. Christened by Mr. Owen in my library at Sayes Court, where he afterwards churched my wife.

My Lord Brereton and others dined at my house, where I showed them proof of my new fuel, which was very glowing, and without smoke, or ill smell. [It was a mixture of charcoal dust and earth.]

Having notice of the Duke of York's intention to visit my poor habitation and garden this day, I returned, when he was pleased to do me that honour of his own accord.

The Duke's brother, Charles II himself, was also a visitor.

Oddly, Evelyn was less than forthcoming about the house and garden he had created. In the *Diary*, other people's houses and acres receive fascinated and highly informed attention. Sayes Court, however, tends to be summed up in such curt entries as, 'I planted all the out limits of the garden and long walks with holly'. Successes, apart from success in attracting visitors, go unrecorded, but disasters in contrast are given slightly fuller treatment. During the big freeze of 1683/4, the diarist commented

> I went to Sayes Court to see how the frost had dealt with my garden, where I found many of the greens and rare plants utterly destroyed. The oranges and myrtles very sick, the rosemary and laurels dead to all appearance, but the cypress likely to endure it.

The ravages of winter, however, were nothing compared with a disaster that struck Sayes Court fourteen years later. By this time, Evelyn and his wife had moved to Surrey, and the Deptford house had been let to Vice-Admiral Benbow, 'with condition to keep up the garden'. It was a vain hope.

Benbow, no respecter of property himself, sublet Sayes Court to a foreign visitor with a positive genius for vandalism. Tsar Peter the Great, on a fact-finding mission to Europe in 1698, moved in for three months and wrecked the place. His followers tore holes in the lawns, the paths and the bowling-green. Peter himself allegedly did something much more bizarre: he regularly climbed into a wheelbarrow, ordered a servant to push and had himself bowled at high speed through the holly hedges Evelyn had planted fifteen years before.

In all, Evelyn received over £150 in damages. But he never lived in Sayes Court again. Instead, it embarked on a long career as a property to let. In 1759, it became a workhouse. In 1853, it was being used to house an enterprise that made clothes and bedding for emigrants. Along the way, its appearance changed out of all recognition and, by the time the bedmakers got there, the house Evelyn had repaired to his 'great cost' had virtually disappeared. Its next role was that of an almshouse, and this was still in existence in 1930 when it appeared on a London County Council map. In 1949, however, the Ordnance Survey map showed a corresponding gap: the last physical link with the home of Deptford's diarist and gardener had finally vanished. The name of Sayes Court today is attached to a recreation ground, a street and a municipal housing estate.

Among the details noted by Pepys of the coronation of Charles II is an account of the high point of the coronation banquet: the appearance of the King's Champion in armour and on horseback with his weapons carried before him. The diarist's account continues:

> And a Herald proclaims 'That if any dare deny Charles Stewart to be lawful King of England, here was a Champion that would fight with him;' and with these words the Champion flings down his gauntlet, and all this he do three times in his going up towards the King's table. To which when he is come, the King drinks to him, and then sends him the cup which is of gold, and he drinks it off, and then rides back again with the cup in his hand.

The man under the armour in this ceremony was Sir Edward Dymoke, Lord of the Manor of Scrivelsby, hereditary champion of England, and the ninth of his family to be on record as publicly challenging all comers to dispute the monarch's right to the throne.

His successors again performed the family duty as Royal Champion at the coronation of Charles's brother, James II, and at those of William and Mary, Queen Anne and the first four Georges. From all these occasions, a Dymoke carried his gold cup back to Scrivelsby as his fee. He could, by tradition, have claimed the horse as well, although payment in lieu was usually accepted. George III's Champion, however, received both £105 and a more intriguing memento. When the horse he had chosen for the ceremony died—it was allegedly the same charger that had taken George II into the Battle of Dettingen—its neatly labelled tail was added to the Dymoke collection.

Neither banquet nor Champion's challenge took place at the coronations of William IV and Victoria and, by the end of the nineteenth century, it appeared unlikely that the ceremony would ever take place again. But in the twentieth, it was revived in modified form: in 1902 Frank Dymoke officiated at the coronation of Edward VII, carrying the standard of England rather than issuing mailed defiance in Westminster Hall. He was also present at those of George V and VI, while his grandson, John Dymoke, was Queen's Champion and Standard Bearer at the coronation of Elizabeth II in 1953. From all four occasions, the Champions again went back to the home they owned in Lincolnshire, Scrivelsby Court.

As long as the ceremony continues, their successors at Scrivelsby— wherever the Dymokes may have other houses—will sooner or later do

To the Hon.ble Lewis Dymock Esq.t
CHAMPION OF ENGLAND.
This Prospect is humbly Inscrib'd by
his most Obed.t Ser.t Sam Buck

SCRIVELBY HALL, commonly called Scrivelby, the Seat of the Hon.ble
Lewis Dymock Esq.t Champion of England, as Lord of Scrivelby an Antient
Barony which he holds Hereditarily devolved upon his Ancestors from ye
Illustrious & Noble Family of Marmion by that Hon.ble Office & Service
performd on Horse back Armed Cap a pee in Westminster Hall) at the
Coronation of every Soveraign King or Queen of England.

130 The Champion's house at Scrivelsby, engraved by Samuel Buck in the early eighteenth century. Buck's engraving shows Scrivelsby Court as it was before devastated by fire in 1761. The gatehouse, home of the Dymokes today, is in the foreground, deeply shaded

the same. Indeed, they must, since the office of Champion is hereditary only in so far as the property to which it is linked stays within a family. It is the estate of Scrivelsby itself, and not a family line, that confers the role and the courtesy title of 'The Honourable the Queen's (or King's) Champion' on Scrivelsby's owner. (Female owners have had their duty as Champion performed by a male relative.) But the future Champions' house will not be the one to which their predecessors bore back the gold cups, the armour, the weaponry ranging from swords to axes and the old war-horse's tail that were the perquisites of their job.

In was, in fact, fortunate that George III's Champion, an earlier John Dymoke, decided in favour of payment in lieu rather than the horse itself, for he was to need ready cash badly immediately the ceremony was over. While he was trying out his horse and his armour in London (he sensibly practised with both for three-quarters of an hour), his home was devastated by fire. Scrivelsby, some of which dated from the fifteenth century, had been burnt once already, the century before. This time, a principal casualty was the great hall which, according to the sixteenth-century antiquary John Leland, had contained armour for men, armour for horses and the shields of all the English monarchs a Dymoke had represented.

In the early nineteenth century, the main house was rebuilt by John Dymoke's son Lewis, who restored much of the building's prestige. Whether he did much for its appearance, however, is debatable: the new

131 Scrivelsby as rebuilt in 1805, here seen in 1946. The remains of the earlier house, containing kitchens, are shown on the left

132 The nineteenth-century Scrivelsby with, in the background, the gatehouse. Now converted, this contains the demolished building's important collection of stained-glass windows, together with some of its stone-work

Scrivelsby, which retained only the morning-room and kitchens from its damaged predecessor, was Gothic in inspiration and uninspired in execution.. By the end of the century, only the relics of the Champion's office really distinguished it from a thousand other country houses. The gold cups were there—in 1875 they were bequeathed to Queen Victoria, but the Queen presented them back—and so were the weapons and armour, one suit of which was sold for over £1,000. But, wrote Samuel Lodge, the rector of Scrivelsby, in 1893, there was 'nothing remarkable in the interior of the house, the rooms of which are comparatively small . . .. On the whole, we may say that Scrivelsby Court appears to be more suitable to the status of an ordinary country gentleman, than to that of such eminent men as some of the older Champions must undoubtedly have been.'

Scrivelsby Court was demolished, after much thought on the part of its owner, in 1956. It was, he recalls, riddled with dry rot, too large and too awkward to live in, and considerably lacking in architectural merit. (It also lacked mains water and electric light.) But, by the curious turn of circumstance occasionally found elsewhere, its disappearance has meant that today's Dymokes are living in the oldest Scrivelsby building of all: the gatehouse. This, which escaped the fire of 1761, dates back in part to the fourteenth century, the century during which, at the coronation of Richard II, the Champion's challenge on the king's behalf is first known to have been issued to all comers. The Champion was a Dymoke, even then. The armour of Scrivelsby is now in the Tower of London, while the white horse-tail vanished from sight long ago. But the family, the Champion's office and the Lincolnshire estate are still together.

If left to their own devices, some houses can take an astonishing time to die. Their heyday as homes may pass and the tides of social and economic history recede, leaving them vulnerable to all manner of dangers. Demolition squads may remove a wing or so, while the remains are taken over by flora and fauna. And still they go on, survivors to the last ditch.

At Stand, in Bury, a housing estate hides the sites of no fewer than five Stand Halls. Of these, one was short-lived indeed (it burnt down five years after being put up), but the second oldest kept going for over five centuries as, successively, great house, barn and cowshed. It was still there, just, when the bulldozers came to demolish the most junior of its successors, a Victorian house built in the 1850s. The former cowshed, by then reduced to two end walls of brick, vanished at the same time.

This diehard among lost houses is usually remembered as Stand Old Hall. At best, however, the label is a confusing one, since another and newer Stand Old Hall still exists some distance from the site. Nor does the confusion stop there, for the lost Old Hall has also been called Old Stand Hall, Stand Hall Barn, the Old Barn and even Stand 'Chapel' (a name deriving from its mistaken connection with Unitarian meetings). And the muddle becomes still worse when the picture is enlarged to take in the other four Stand Halls built nearby during the past four centuries.

Given such a profusion of lost Stands, the would-be labeller has to walk warily. The best solution is to jettison all local names and stick to numbers: Stand I, Stand II, and so on. This ruthless measure, if unkind to the houses' memories, at least provides some sort of guide through the maze. But, names apart, the only thing that gives any real continuity to the Stand story is the history of Stand Old Hall itself: Stand II.

The origins of the whole collection date back to the site's use in the early Middle Ages as a 'stand' or high point from which the movements of game in the area could be observed. Stand I was a group of buildings of unknown date and appearance, which may have incorporated a hunting lodge erected by a local family called Pilkington. The Pilkingtons, whose origins were Anglo-Saxon, survived the Norman Conquest and rose in the world to the point at which, in about 1400, they were rich and grand enough to build a family home in the area that had once done duty as a huntsman's look-out point. The result, a magnificent timbered building, was Stand II.

133 (*above*) Stand Old Hall in 1954:
the gateposts guard the driveway
to Stand Hall V

134 (*right*) Detail of the interior of
Stand Old Hall in the 1950s. Note
the air-vents in the wall

In layout, Stand II was like a flattened H. At one end of the building was a block probably consisting of the family apartments, balanced at the other by a further block containing kitchen and storerooms. Joining them—the crossbar of the H—was the great hall, over 40ft long, with massive oak pillars and an array of quatrefoil ornamentation on the internal timbering. The northern end was occupied by a dais on which, raised above their household, the owners dined in state.

For almost a century after Stand II went up, the Pilkingtons rode very high indeed. They lent money to Henry V (the royal house took its time about paying them back), and in 1415 they did their feudal duty by sending six lancers and three archers off to Agincourt. At the head of this little train as it rode out from Stand II on its way to Southampton and France were two John de Pilkingtons: Sir John, head of the family, who was made a knight banneret after the battle, and his son, also knighted. Seventy years later, however, another battle changed the family fortunes abruptly. At Bosworth, Sir Thomas Pilkington fought against Henry Tudor and, with the death of Richard III, saw his hopes go down. He was attaindered, the 6,000 acre Pilkington estate was confiscated, and Stand II and the land were both given to a key supporter of the new dynasty, the first Earl of Derby, Lord Stanley.

The Stanleys wasted relatively little time before setting their own mark on the Stand windfall. In the second decade of the sixteenth century, they chose a site 100yd away from the Pilkington family home and built Stand III: a handsome two-storey house with a long gallery and much oak panelling. Meanwhile, Stand II—old-fashioned and surplus to requirements—surrendered its role as a home of the well-born. The tradition is that the Stanleys demolished the two wings, bricked in the ends and straightaway put the building to use as a barn. But, in the view of local historian Derek Pilkington, the brickwork—which survived until 1966—dated from the seventeenth century. He also points to references to 'tenements' at Stand Hall and suggests that Stand II may have done time as a rural slum before ceasing altogether as a human habitation. Either way, the air vents in the brickwork showed that Stand II did become a barn in the end.

In spite of its now humble role, it easily outlasted the house that supplanted it. Stand III continued to be used by the Derbys' agents until the mid-1830s, when it was demolished and a new house was erected on the site. In the usual way, some of the materials from the old building were recycled: the 300-year-old oak timbering from Stand III became the joists of Stand IV. The Derbys' district agent had scarcely settled in,

135 The same interior in about 1880. From Lt Col John Pilkington's *The History of the Pilkington Family of Lancashire*, third edition (1912)

however, when the brand-new dwelling was destroyed by fire. So, after about ten years, up went Stand V: a pleasant looking building with, just by its gateway, an ancient structure that still retained its ornately carved interior.

By World War I, Stand II had experienced another loss of status: it had become a cow-house. And still it survived. The photographs shown here were taken well after World War II. In the summer of 1956, it was declared a listed building, an event which aroused some local interest. As reported in the *Prestwich and Whitefield Guide*, a local councillor commented:

Here we have an 'old chapel' in Whitefield and very few people know anything about it. We should be proud that we are going to preserve it for the future, and I only wish that we could either get the National Trust to buy it or otherwise so plan the building of Whitefield that these old places will be preserved. There is no doubt that we are losing a lot of them in the modern trend of today.

But, that October, the roof of Stand II, already partially stripped of its stone slates, collapsed in a gale. Even so, another ten years were to pass before the very last remnants of the building, along with Stand V, finally came down.

Its history has been such as to give some foundation to the feeling that there is safety in humbleness. Stand II, the building that 'very few people know anything about', can arguably have owed its amazing longevity to the fact that few people did, over the centuries, know or bother. It soon lost its connections with a losing political side; after that, no one viewed it, as they were to view Stand III, with an eye to sweeping and indeed annihilating improvements. It just went on as it was, being quietly useful in a modest capacity. It could be asked how many other Stand IIs exist, still safe in hay-strewn anonymity.

Just south of Stoke-on-Trent is a magnificent, privately run formal garden that has been open to the public for the better part of this century. At its heart is a collection of buildings that includes a clock tower, a colonnaded semi-circular gallery, and St Mary's, parish church of Trentham. These are all that remain of Trentham Hall, one of the seats of the dukes of Sutherland and, in its final guise, the architectural link between Thomas Hope's Deepdene and the Victorian/Italian style of building that found its most famous expression in Queen Victoria's Osborne. In its heyday, Trentham was a monument both to enormous wealth and to the skill of one of the great nineteenth-century architects, Sir Charles Barry. Slightly earlier, it had belonged to a man who, in the blameless cause of Improvement, had caused other people's houses to be laid waste, emptied a countryside and turned the name of a particular breed of sheep into a matter for cursing.

An eighteenth-century Trentham Hall, very plain, with the church tucked in behind it and grounds by Capability Brown, came into the possession of George Granville Leveson-Gower in 1803, when he succeeded to his father's estates and the title of Marquis of Stafford. In fact, Trentham and his other great domain, Lilleshall in Shropshire, were a liability, for they had been badly managed by his parent. However, Stafford now owned more acres than anyone else in Britain—his wife, the Countess of Sutherland in her own right, had brought him a huge area of Scotland—and he had wealth to match. His annual income was in the order of £300,000.

He did not do very much to Trentham itself, apart from creating some new rooms (one a conservatory) and building a mausoleum. His main efforts were directed at putting his English estates to rights, at augmenting the family's superb collection of pictures and at hauling his Scottish territories into the nineteenth century. The last activity involved an operation pivoting on the fact that large farms stocked with Cheviot sheep were much more profitable than small ones based on a mixed arable and cattle system. As happened elsewhere in Scotland, the small farmers on Stafford's lands were driven out of the valley bottoms where they lived and grew their crops, and their houses were destroyed. In Strathnaver, at the instance of Stafford's agent, one house was set on fire with an old bedridden woman still inside it. Though rescued from being burned alive, she died five days later. Stafford's improvements

136 Trentham from the front, dominated by its tower

137 Trentham's new main entrance. The state bedroom is the low block on the left

initiated one of the most infamous of the 'Highland clearances'.

The marquis, who was created the first Duke of Sutherland in the last year of his life, did not want for defenders, who pointed to the material improvements he had brought to the county in the way of roads and bridges. It was stressed that he had lost £60,000 in the operation (he could, of course, afford to), and that, from 1811 to 1833, the Cheviot sheep and the land they grazed over brought him in no rents at all. The implication is, naturally, that this situation was reversed from 1833 onwards —the year in which the duke was succeeded by his son and the year before Barry submitted his estimates for executing an improvement scheme of a different order on the Leveson-Gowers' Staffordshire house. The new duke, and even more so his duchess, wanted something that proclaimed their wealth much more obviously than did the building inherited from the duke's father.

Starting in the 1830s and continuing well into the next decade, Sir Charles Barry remodelled the old house by adding to it in all directions, just as Hope had done in Surrey. The result made his reputation. Trentham acquired a sculpture gallery and clock tower and a state bedroom block with dressing-rooms and its own servants' quarters. Private family quarters were created by building on to an already existing wing at the side of the main building, and the whole was given a point of focus by a tower of the Deepdene type that would reappear at Osborne and in a thousand other houses. A further innovation was a new main entrance: the portico Barry created, surmounted by the Leveson-Gower arms supported by carved life-sized wolves, led into a semi-circular gallery that, on the left, took grand visitors directly to the entrance hall and state bedroom, and, on the right, channelled family and friends to the private ducal apartments. The church was also rebuilt.

The splendour of the building was soon matched by the refinement of the fixtures and fittings. The breakfast-room was decorated with pictures by, among others, Poussin and Gainsborough. The billiard-table was made of wood taken from the lost *Royal George*, celebrated in Cowper's poem. In the conservatory, the marriage of house and garden was performed in the most perfect way possible: the apartment, wrote Jewitt and Hall in their nineteenth-century account of England's stately homes, was

> as elegant in its arrangements and decorations as the most fastidious taste can desire or Art accomplish . . .. The noble ferns and the exotic and other plants are of the choicest kinds, and the arrangement of colour, especially when all are lighted from the number of lamps suspended from the roof, is exquisitely beautiful.

138 George Granville Leveson-Gower, shortly after succeeding to the title of Marquis of Stafford. Portrait by V. Philips

Even the outbuildings had a palatial quality: another book on stately homes, the *Historic Houses of the United Kingdom*, added that the 'poultry-yard—now no longer tenanted—suggests by its size a challenge to rival chanticleers which might have been of times a cause of disturbance even in the most distant bed-rooms of the house'. And the formal gardens overlooked by the Hall were spectacular (it took about fifty gardeners to maintain them).

In spite of all this magnificence, Trentham—unlike many other stately homes—did have a curiously home-like air. This was partly due to the fact that the building contained within itself a real 'home'—the private wing which, Girouard points out in his *Victorian Country House*, in all probability inspired the private wing at Osborne. But the whole building somehow managed to share this atmosphere of near-cosiness: 'it has the aspect of a home which can be inhabited with comfort', the observer of the poultry-yard went on. 'Tho' the state rooms are large, they are not so large as to swallow up a party of moderate size': an additional triumph for the man who had planned them.

The parties of moderate size, and larger, continued to the end of the century and into the next. One, given by the fourth duke and duchess in 1897, found its way into the columns of the *Illustrated London News* and included the Prince and Princess of Wales, one of their daughters, the Marquis and Marchioness of Ormonde and the Earl and Countess of Dartmouth, all of whom attended a bazaar in the nearby Potteries in aid of a church building fund. *Country Life* produced a profile of Trentham Hall in the following year and drew attention to the way that Capability Brown's lake, polluted by Potteries sewage from the Trent, was now fed from other sources. It was only a passing mention but, as things turned out, it was a significant one. The Trent was diverted underground, but the pollution continued and soon proved itself an intolerable and insurmountable flaw in Trentham life.

As at Hamilton, man-made disturbance of the environment led directly to the destruction of a palace. By 1907, Trentham stood empty and, as John Cornforth pointed out in a later *Country Life*, it turned into the most massive of gift horses: no one would buy, no one would even take it as a present. And in 1911, the main building was pulled down.

If the loss of Surrey's Deepdene was akin to having an eye-tooth out, the destruction of another house nearer to London was like an amputation. With Wanstead House there vanished the original pattern from which the great Palladian mansions of Georgian Britain were to develop.

It stood in what is now Wanstead Golf Course, a little way to the east of the large pond called the Basin, and as usual it was not the first building to occupy the site. Its predecessor was a sixteenth-century manor house with royal and aristocratic associations: Mary Tudor had stayed there on her journey to London at the start of her reign; Robert Dudley, Earl of Leicester, had refurbished it and invited his Gloriana on a visit that had lasted five days and featured a *tour de force* of sustained flattery in the form of a masque by Philip Sidney called *The Queen of May*. Later visitors included James I; later owners included the future James II. From this point, however, the property slid down the social scale and, in 1667, ended up in the hands of Josiah Child, a former merchant's apprentice.

Child's origins may have been in trade—his father was a merchant—but Child himself was to become enormously rich and enormously powerful. Ten years after he bought the manor of Wanstead, he became one of the directors of the East India Company. He later rose to be its chairman and ran it as an absolute monarch. In 1678, he was made a baronet. Interestingly, however, he resisted the temptation to proclaim his grandeur through rebuilding the manor house, even though, as Pepys had noticed earlier, it was distinctly old-fashioned. Instead, he turned his attention to the grounds which, inevitably, made an appearance in John Evelyn's *Diary*. 'I went', Evelyn wrote in March 1683, 'to see Sir Josiah Child's prodigious cost in planting walnut-trees about his seat, and making fishponds, many miles in circuit, in Epping Forest, in a barren spot, as oftentimes these suddenly monied men for the most part seat themselves.' The diarist went on to give a very clear indication of just what Child's place in the world now was: his fortune was rumoured to stand at the prodigious figure of £200,000, while he himself had recently confirmed his arrival in the ranks of the mighty by marrying his daughter to the son of the Duke of Beaufort, 'with £50,000 portional present, and various expectations'.

It was left to Josiah's son, Richard, to bring the appearance of the family seat up to the standards of its grounds, with their canals and

139 Wanstead House as it was built, shown here in 1810

avenues of line-trees. To do so, he employed the Scottish architect Colen Campbell, who had recently come to London. In about 1715, the old manor house came down and a new building started to go up in its place. At the same time, Campbell published his designs for the future Wanstead House. Initially, there were two: the first showed a long, three-storey building, topped with a balustrade and fronted with double stairs and a portico. In the second, the number of storeys had dropped to two, except in the centre, and the whole was topped with a prominent cupola. Yet a further design was published later, with the building extended by a pavilion at each end, but it was the second, shorn of its cupola and with slightly different proportions, that had already become translated into Portland stone.

The result—260ft long and 70ft wide—was the prototype of the neo-Palladian mansion: the semi-palace built in the classical style pioneered by the sixteenth-century Italian Andrea Palladio and made famous the following century in England by Inigo Jones. In one form or another, it was to set the pattern for a whole string of noble derivatives. Of these, one of the most important and earliest was Campbell's own Houghton Hall, designed for Sir Robert Walpole and completed (with revisions) by Thomas Ripley. A later example was Thorndon Hall in Essex, designed by James Paine for Lord Petre and started in 1764. Between the two extremes stretched half a century of influence, showing itself in houses as

262

distant from Wanstead as Holkham Hall—in Norfolk, like Houghton—
and Wentworth Woodhouse in Yorkshire.

Meanwhile, the owners of Wanstead were the objects of great admiration and envy. The house they owned was not merely a superior façade;
its accommodation included two dining-rooms (to right and left of the
great entrance hall), two drawing-rooms (also to right and left of the
entrance hall), about fifty other rooms (excluding kitchens), and a ballroom
that stretched the complete depth of the house. The whole was described
by one visitor as 'one of the noblest houses in England'. It was believed
to have cost £100,000.

Visitors came to Wanstead in considerable quantity, genially welcomed
by the family or their representatives. Indeed, the crowds were such that
the Viscount—Richard Child was created Viscount Castlemain in 1718,
and Earl Tylney in 1731—had to tell his servants to restrict opening times
for the gardens to one or two days a week. The future earl had, like his
father, worked hard on the Wanstead grounds and had started on them
well before setting to work on the house itself. Special features, according
to Daniel Defoe, included a heated greenhouse 'fit to entertain a prince'.
Defoe was full of praise for the two Childs' landscaping: from the
Wanstead terrace, he went on, there was a

> most Beautiful Prospect to the River, which is all form'd into Canals and
> Openings, to answer the Views from above, and beyond the River [the
> Roding], the Walks and Wildernesses go on to such a Distance, and in such a
> manner up the Hill, as they before went down, that the Sight is lost in the
> Woods adjoining, and it looks all like one planted Garden as far as the Eye
> can see.

In the heart of this landscape, the house gleamed like a pearl.

> The Building is all of *Portland* Stone in the Front, which makes it look
> extremely Glorious and Magnificent at a distance; it being the particular
> property of that Stone, except in the Streets of *London*, where it is tainted and
> ting'd with the Smoak of the City, to grow Whiter and Whiter the longer it
> stands in the open Air.

A later visitor, Horace Walpole, found his host almost too genial. By
this time—July 1755—Richard Child was dead, and the second Earl
Tylney was one of those people who are embarrassingly open-handed.
Walpole, who did not like the gardens for all their cost of another
£100,000, looked back on his day at Wanstead with mixed feelings:

> The present Earl is the most generous creature in the world: in the first
> chamber I entered he offered me four marble tables that lay in cases about the

room: I compounded, after forty refusals of every thing I commended, to bring away only a haunch of venison: I believe he has not had so cheap a visit a good while. I commend myself as I ought; for, to be sure, there were twenty ebony chairs, and a couch, and a table, and a glass, that would have tried the virtue of a philosopher of double my size!

(Walpole's self-restraint had indeed been heroic in this case: the ebony chairs were of Tudor manufacture and had belonged to Queen Elizabeth I.)

Open-handed hospitality continued to be the hallmark of Wanstead life well after the second earl's death. The property passed sideways in the family to a nephew, then briefly to his son, and then to his underage daughter, who also inherited an annual income of about £75,000. While Katherine Tylney-Long was being besieged by suitors, the house she owned in Essex became something like a Grand Hotel for blue-blooded exiles from France. Residents included Louis XVIII and the Prince de Condé, father of the duke that Sophia Daw probably didn't murder (see page 82).

In 1812, young Miss Tylney-Long finally selected one of her followers out of the ardent mob and, in doing so, sealed the fate of both Wanstead House and of herself. She could hardly have chosen worse. On 14 March, swathed in lace that had cost over £1,000, she was married to the Hon William Pole-Wellesley. Since the Hon William was considerably embarrassed financially, it was all too obvious that he had married Katherine for her money. Now, of course, he had access to enormous wealth, but his response to this change in his fortunes was merely to increase his

View of the West Front of Wansted in Essex, built by Sir Rich. Child Bar.t Hereditary Warden of Waltham Forest &c. and now the Seat of his Descendant John Child Earl of Tylney. F.R.S.

140 Wanstead House: the 'Second Design', with cupola

expenditure. The financial embarrassments returned and, in the end, he found himself in the ignominious position of fleeing down the Thames in a rowing boat, his creditors a few stages behind him.

Ten years and three months after the pair were married, the contents of their magnificent house at Wanstead came under the hammer, ebony chairs and all. The sale, which lasted over a month, produced a mere £41,000—little more than half Katherine's yearly income in happier times. It was not enough; the next stage was to sell the house itself but, tragically, no one wanted to buy it. The Tudor house at Wanstead had looked old-fashioned to Pepys; the Child mansion now also looked chillingly out-of-date to a public that, like Thomas Hope at Deepdene, worshipped at the shrines of nature and Rousseau. It was all too white an elephant, and the solution was, as in the case of so many other lost houses, only too evident. Campbell's superb creation came down, the materials were sold off, the creditors of Mr Pole-Tylney-Long-Wellesley (he had added his wife's names to his own at the time of their marriage) were left to make what they could of the proceeds. In 1825, the wretched Katherine died—by tradition, of a broken heart.

On 13 August 1868—in the same issue that favourably reviewed *Alice's Adventures in Wonderland*—*The Times* printed a call for some systematic picture record to be kept of the buildings that were being carelessly erased from London's landscape. The occasion was the demolition of the eighteenth-century front of Burlington House in Piccadilly. 'So far,' *The Times* said,

> The country has a pictorial record of this old building to refer to, but many such places have been destroyed during the last 20 years to make way for London improvements, without even a photograph being taken of the demolished structures . . .. The Record-office preserves documents, but not views of places, and imitators of Stow and Strype, if such writers exist, have nothing but their memories and chance collections of pictures to work upon.

In the century since this plea was published, much has happened on the twin fronts of record-keeping and preservation. In 1877, for example, the Society for the Protection of Ancient Buildings, oldest of the preservation societies, was founded. In 1895, the National Trust was set up. In 1900 the first volume of the magnificent *Survey of London* appeared: an event which must have pleased *The Times*. In 1908, Royal Commissions for England, Wales and Scotland were created to make inventories of ancient and historical monuments and to identify those which seemed 'most worthy of preservation'. And, in 1941, the National Buildings Record was established to amass material on buildings damaged or threatened by bombing.

This record covered the whole country until the 1960s, when it was divided into English, Scottish and Welsh sections; it also changed its name to the National Monuments Record. The archives of the English NMR, which is attached to the Royal Commission on Historical Monuments (England), now contain more than 2 million items—plans, photographs, maps and documents. Among them are those secured when the

141 (*opposite above*) Saved: the gates from Devonshire House, now sited on Green Park's Piccadilly frontage

142 (*opposite below*) Saved: Barlaston Hall, Staffordshire, bought in 1981 for £1 by SAVE Britain's Heritage, the independent charity formed in 1975 to publicise threatened buildings of historical or architectural importance. Barlaston, a Grade I listed building, had stood empty since 1952 and was, SAVE commented at the time of its purchase, in a 'serious state of delapidation'. The house was designed by Sir Robert Taylor in 1756

Commission records a listed building for which permission to demolish has been granted. Although the written records, when taken, concentrate on a building's architectural rather than social history, there are exceptions: a country house with important owners would, for example, attract more documentation.

However, it is only since 1968 that the law has insisted that the Commission be notified of pending demolitions of listed buildings (the 'listed' heading, in fact, covers all manner of constructions, residential and otherwise). Again, the English Commission alone receives news of an annual average of 2,000 applications for consent to demolish or part-demolish. Many fail but even so the Commission points out that it has to be 'extremely selective in its recordings'. And, although the process of listing buildings of importance is a continuing one (as is that of up-grading those already listed), there are still the ones that have got away: the buildings that have slipped through the listing net, and through that of the record-keepers as well. As the English Commission commented in its interim report in 1976: 'In those cases where there is no obligation on the owner to inform the Commission of his intention to pull his house down, we are dependent for such information on the Press and on private sources, and, for permission to record the building, on the goodwill of the owner himself.'

Just as there are gaps in the country's pictorial record of its invisible heritage, so there are gaps in the historical one: a fact that holds true even of houses that vanished recently. And, in the case of all the houses that vanished a long while ago, the gaps can yawn wide indeed. In one sense, of course, the task of filling them can be seen as a pleasant, leisurely one compared with, say, setting up the photography of a building in the minimum grace of one month allowed to the Royal Commission by law. Family records, for instance, will not run away, not yet will such invaluable sources as the transactions of local history societies. Or will they?

One house studied by the writer yielded to inquiry with spectacular ease. The main source was a local branch library's enormous collection of works relating to the area, all available to the inquirer with time to work through their indexes. On a checking expedition four months later, the writer found that most of that magnificent array—twentieth-century, Victorian and earlier—had been shifted away to the cellar; still available,

143 (*opposite*) Saved: Two details of the Hercules ceiling from Emral Hall, now in the Hercules Hall at Portmeirion

144 Lost: Northumberland House, recorded in the final weeks of its existence

certainly, but only readily useful to someone with an idea of what titles to look for. Furthermore, family records get out of order, go missing or are destroyed by later generations who deplore some aspect of their contents. And obviously the inquirer first has to find the family, which is not always an easy task outside the peerage. There are still Spekes at Jordans and Dymokes at Scrivelsby, but this, where a lost house is concerned, is pure luck—as is the rarity of the names involved. The last long-term occupant of Didlington Hall was, alas, called Smith.

Smith of Didlington died in 1948, and this is another obvious difficulty —people move away, people die and the people who knew them die. The threads of information become twisted and broken; time nibbles at them constantly, just as woodworm nibbles at the physical fabric of a house. Marcus Binney pointed out in his article in *Country Life* of November 1974 that the only surviving pictorial record of many lost houses was a lone photograph from someone's family album. The same is true of material relating to the houses' histories: a fragment here, a snippet there, a misremembered account somewhere else. And information differs from pictures in one very important respect. When the picture researcher has, for instance, discovered photographs showing four sides of a building at a certain date, he knows he has a good grasp of the truth. Where information is concerned, you do not know what you have missed until you have found it. A building is, by its very nature, a finite structure; facts are, for all practical purposes, infinite in their number and variety.

Despite the ravages of time, however, large quantities of facts continue to survive. Many are recorded, for instance, in the celebrated *Victoria County Histories*. Many can be found 'raw' in record offices and record collections, in standard contemporary works such as the Lysons or Thorne *Environs of London*, or *Country Life*, in biographies, letters, diaries and, above all, in the domains ruled by local history societies and local history librarians. This book owes much of its contents to the help of the latter: to their reference systems, their newspaper files, their lists of contacts (with addresses) and their enormous enthusiasm. Just as the National Monuments Record guards the nation's records of how a lost house looked, so do the country's local libraries have custody of an extraordinary wealth of detail on how a lost house developed, was used and felt to live in. The fullest possible use should be made of what they have to offer.

The holocaust that swept over Britain's great houses in, particularly, the 1950s has happily become a thing of the past. The total demolition of a Grade I or Grade II* listed building is now extremely rare, although the problem of 'latent dereliction' (the situation in which a house bids fair to fall apart of its own accord) is still a pressing one. Here again, though, there are signs of hope. In a 1981 publication, *Silent Mansions*, SAVE have pointed out that over two-thirds of the houses listed as at risk in their *Tomorrow's Ruins?*, published three years earlier, had in one way or another received a new lease of life. (Many *Ruins* entries presented a frightening picture of deserted buildings, tottering walls and general neglect.)

So the tide does seem to be turning. And, given this, it is not totally inconceivable to imagine that a time could arrive when energy and money become available at a national level for recording the gigantic backlog: the backlog of distinguished houses that vanished a long while ago, or whose passing went unnoticed at the time, or whose merits were dwarfed by those of more important or more pressing cases. If this should happen, this writer feels that it would be a pity if records and references on past life in all the houses concerned were not added to those outlining their architectural development. The information needed is, to a welcome extent, ready and waiting. But it should be noted that local history collections and their guardians are themselves subject to time's nibbling effect. Photographs disappear, the specialist in the Jacobean period moves on, the man who knew all about the Big House retires. Advances in technology may preserve the written word in forms that can be stored easily; there is no way of preserving all the words that are never written. The task of recreating the life of Britain's lost houses, large or small, may not seem aggressively urgent. But there is never much time to lose.

Sources

Main sources are arranged alphabetically by house. To avoid repetition, the following frequently used works are abbreviated:

Colvin, Howard and Harris, John(eds). *The Country Seat: Studies in the History of the British Country House Presented to Sir John Summerson* (Allen Lane, The Penguin Press, 1970)

Defoe, Daniel. *A Tour Thro' the Whole Island of Great Britain*, with introduction by G. D. H. Cole (Peter Davies, 1927)

Evelyn, John. *Diary and Correspondence*, ed by William Bray (Henry Colburn, 1850)

Girouard, Mark. *Life in the English Country House* (Yale University Press, 1978)

Girouard, Mark. *The Victorian Country House* (Yale University Press, 1979)

Lloyd, Nathaniel. *A History of the English House* (Architectural Press, 1931, reprinted, 1949)

Murray's Handbook for Scotland (*1894*), published as *Handbook for Travellers in Scotland* (reprinted, David & Charles, 1971)

Stephen, Leslie, and Lee, Sidney (Ed) *Dictionary of National Biography* (Smith, Elder, 1885-1900)

Strong, Roy; Binney, Marcus; Harris, John; and others. *The Destruction of the Country House 1875-1975* (Thames and Hudson, 1974)

Thorne, James. *Handbook to the Environs of London* (1876, reprinted Adams & Dart, 1970)

INTRODUCTION
I General

Binney, Marcus. 'How Many Country Houses Have Gone ?', *Country Life*, 21 November 1974

Colvin and Harris, *The Country Seat*

Girouard. *Life*

Girouard, *Victorian Country House*

Kilvert, Francis. *Kilvert's Diary: Selections from the diary of the Rev. Francis Kilvert* (see Llanthomas)

Lloyd. *English House*

Murray's Handbook

Royal Commission on Historical Monuments (England)

SAVE Britain's Heritage

Strong. *Destruction*

Thorne. *Environs*

Williams, Neville. *The Royal Residences of Great Britain* (Barrie & Rockliff, 1960)

Individual Houses
Beaudesert

Staffordshire County Council (Library Service)

Tipping, H. Avray. 'Beaudesert', *Country Life*, 22 and 29 November 1919

Cassiobury

Evelyn. *Diary*

Hertfordshire County Council (Library Service)

Stephen and Lee, *Dictionary of National Biography*

Thorne. *Environs*

Coleshill House

Berkshire, Royal County of (Library Service)

Girouard. *Life*

Lloyd. *English House*

Strong. *Destruction*

Tipping, H. Avray. 'Coleshill House', *Country Life*, 26 July and 2 August 1919

Dawpool

Cheshire County Council (Libraries and Museums Department)

Girouard. *Victorian Country House*

L. W. 'Dawpool', *Country Life*, 18 February 1911

Didlington Hall

Eastern Daily Press, 19 April 1950, 'Two-day Sale at Didlington Hall'

Eastern Daily Press, 4 October 1956, 'Fall of the Tower of Didlington'

Norfolk County Council (Library Service)

Norfolk Daily Standard, 26 October 1895, 'Didlington'

Powe, Miss Helen, and other local residents

Dupplin Castle

Defoe. *Tour Thro' the Whole Island*

Millar, A. H. *The Historical Castles and Mansions of Scotland: Perthshire and Forfarshire* (1890)

Perth & Kinross District Council (Library Service)

Eaton Hall

Cheshire County Council (Libraries and Museums Department)

Country Life, 20 April 1901, 'Eaton Hall'

Girouard. *Victorian Country House*

Tipping, H. Avray. 'Eaton Hall', *Country Life*, 29 May 1920

Edderachalda (also 'Calda') House

Highland Regional Council (Department of Leisure and Recreation/Library Service

Murray's Handbook

The Fonthills

Lees-Milne, James. *William Beckford* (Compton Russell, 1976)

Pevsner, Nikolaus. *Wiltshire* (Penguin, 1963)

Wiltshire County Council (Library and Museum Service)

Glencoe
Fairweather, Miss B., and other local residents
Highland Regional Council (Department of Leisure and Recreation/Library Service)
Macdonald, Donald J. *Slaughter under Trust: Glencoe—1692* (Robert Hale, 1965)
National Trust for Scotland, *Glencoe and Dalness* (1972)
Prebble, John. *Glencoe* (Secker & Warburg, 1966; Penguin, 1968)

Grove House, Chiswick
Wisdom, James, and Bott, Valerie. *The Grove Park Estate, Chiswick* (The Grove Park Group, 1980)

Penicuik House
Midlothian District Council (Library Service)

Silverton Park
Colvin and Harris, *Country Seat*
Devon County Council (Library Service news cuttings, including material from the *Devon & Exeter Gazette, Western Morning News* and *Express and Echo*)

Weald Hall
Bolton, Arthur T. 'Weald Hall', *Country Life*, 3 October 1914
Broughton, Edith. 'Country Homes: Weald Hall'; *Country Life*, 20 November 1897
Essex County Council (Record Office)

MAIN ENTRIES

Alloa House
I would like to thank the Right Honourable The Earl of Mar and Kellie for his very kind help with the closing passage of this section. Other sources are:
Archibald, James. *Alloa Sixty Years Ago* (Buchan, 1911)
Burton, J. H. *The History of Scotland* (William Blackwood, undated)
Clackmannan District Council (District Library)
Defoe. *A Tour Thro' the Whole Island*
Drummond, A. I. R. *Old Clackmannanshire* (Robert Cunningham, 1953)
Gordon, T. Crouther. *A Short History of Alloa* (John B. Rae, 1937)
Lothian, James. *Alloa and its Environs* (The Alloa Advertiser, 1861)
Marshall, Rosalind K. *The Days of Duchess Anne* (Collins, 1973)
Murray's Handbook
Stephen and Lee. *Dictionary of National Biography*

Arundel House
My grateful thanks are due to Jeanne Lambert of Old Hall who most kindly allowed me to inspect the Arundel House site. Other sources are
Aubrey, John. *Aubrey's Brief Lives*, ed and introduced by Oliver Lawson Dick (Secker & Warburg, 1958)
Camden, London Borough of (Libraries and Arts Department)
Haringey, London Borough of (Civic Amenities Department)
The Letters and the Life of Francis Bacon, with commentary by James Spedding (Longmans, Green, Reader and Dyer, 1874)
Lloyd, John H. *The History, Topography and Antiquities of Highgate* (1888)
Lovell, Percy W. and Marcham, William McB. *Survey of London, vol 17: the village of Highgate (St Pancras, part I)*, issued by the Joint Publishing Committee representing the London County Council and the London Survey Committee (LCC, 1936)
Thorne. *Environs*

Aston Clinton House
Battersea, Baroness (Constance Flower, *née* de Rothschild). *Reminiscences* (Macmillan, 1922)
Buckinghamshire County Council (Library Service)
Camp, John. *Portrait of Buckinghamshire* (Robert Hale, 1972)
Roth, Cecil. *The Magnificent Rothschilds* (Robert Hale, 1939)
Sheahan, J. J. *History and Topography of Buckinghamshire* (Longman, 1852)
Thomas, E. P. Director of Training, Green Park Youth and Community Service Training Centre

Bachegraig
Boswell, James. *Boswell's Life of Johnson* (which contains Johnson's *Journey into North Wales in the Year 1774*, ed by George Birkbeck Hill, revised and enlarged edition by L. F. Powell (Oxford, 1950)
Clwyd County Council (Library Service and Record Office)
Colvin and Harris. *The Country Seat*
Grose, Francis. *The Antiquities of England and Wales* (1797)
Gwyndaf, Robin. 'Richard Clough of Denbigh', *Denbighshire Historical Society Transactions,* 1973
Hyde, Mary. *The Thrales of Streatham Park* (Harvard University Press, 1977)

Berkeley House and Devonshire House
Barrow, Andrew. *Gossip* (Hamish Hamilton, 1978)
City of Westminster (Archives Department)
Clinch, George. *Mayfair and Belgravia* (Truslove & Shirley, 1892)

Colby, Reginald. *Mayfair—A Town within London* (Country Life, 1966)

Evelyn. *Diary*

Foster, Elizabeth. *Children of the Mist* (Hutchinson, 1960)

Girouard. *Life*

Hobhouse, Hermione. *Lost London* (Macmillan, 1971)

Knight, Charles (ed). *London* (Charles Knight, 1841)

Leach, Henry. *The Duke of Devonshire* (Methuen, 1904)

Thornbury, G. W., and Walford, Edward. *Old and New London* (Cassell Petter & Galpin, undated)

Turner, E. S. *Amazing Grace* (Michael Joseph, 1975)

Blyth Hall

Bramley, J. 'Hodsock Priory', *Transactions of the Thoroton Society of Nottinghamshire 1938*

Cossons, Arthur. 'The Villagers Remember', *Transactions of the Thoroton Society of Nottinghamshire 1962*

Firth, J. B. *Highways and Byways in Nottinghamshire* (Macmillan, 1916)

Laird, Mr *A Topographical and Historical Description of the County of Nottingham* (Sherwood & Jones, 1820)

Lowe, A. E. Lawson (ed). *Black's Guide to Nottinghamshire* (Adam & Charles Black, 1876)

Morning Telegraph (Sheffield), 12 August 1972 ('Showpiece Parkland is Put up for Sale' by Keith Bishop)

Morning Telegraph (Sheffield), 16 August 1972 ('Historic Building Plots Snapped up' by Keith Bishop)

Nottinghamshire Councy Council (Leisure Services Department)

Royal Commission on the Ancient and Historical Monuments and Constructions of England, *Monuments Threatened or Destroyed (1963-74)* (HMSO, 1976)

Boleyn Castle

I am very much in the debt of the London Borough of Newham, who supplied me with invaluable information on the building, and to the Society for the Protection of Ancient Buildings, who most generously allowed me access to all their material on Boleyn Castle. Other sources are:

Chapman, Hester W. *Anne Boleyn* (Jonathan Cape, 1974)

Daily Telegraph, 27 October 1951

Evening Standard, 29 April, 1953

Godfrey, Walter H. *A History of Architecture in London* (Batsford, 1911)

Pugh, R. B. (ed), *Victoria History of the Counties of England: Essex* (University of London Institute of Historical Research, 1973)

Royal Commission on Historical Monuments (England), *An Inventory of the Historical Monuments in Essex* (HMSO, 1921)

Walford, Edward. *Greater London* (Cassell, 1898)

Brandenburgh House

Dodington, George Bubb. *The Diary of the Late George Bubb Dodington* ed H. P. Wyndham (E. Easton, 1784)

Faulkner, Thomas. *An Historical and Topographical Account of Fulham* (T. Egerton and others, 1813)

Faulkner, Thomas. *The History and Antiquities of the Parish of Hammersmith* (Nichols & Son and others, 1839)

Fèret, Charles James. *Fulham Old and New* (Leadenhall Press and others, 1900)

Hammersmith and Fulham, London Borough of (Leisure and Recreation Department/Libraries)

Huish, Robert. *Memoirs of Caroline, Queen Consort of England* (Thomas Kelly, 1821)

Lysons, Daniel. *The Environs of London* (T. Cadell and W. Davies, 1795)

Parry, Edward. *Queen Caroline* (Benn, 1930)

Pope, Alexander. *The Poems of Alexander Pope*, (Twickenham edition), ed John Butt (Methuen, 1963)

Richards, Denis, and Hunt, J. W. *Modern Britain* (Longmans, 1950)

Sanders, Lloyd. *Patron and Place-Hunter: a Study of George Bubb Dodington Lord Melcombe* (John Lane, The Bodley Head, 1919)

Stephen and Lee. *Dictionary of National Biography*

Thorne. *Environs*

Brooke House

I am deeply indebted to the Society for the Protection of Ancient Buildings for access to their files on Brooke House. Other sources are:

Aubrey, John. *Aubrey's Brief Lives*, ed and introduced by Oliver Lawson Dick (Secker & Warburg, 1958)

Daily Telegraph, 12 February 1954

Defoe. *Tour Thro' the Whole Island*

Evelyn. *Diary*

Evening Standard, 25 March 1954

Godfrey, Walter H. *A History of Architecture in London* (Batsford, 1911)

Hackney Gazette, 22 February 1954

Hackney, London Borough of (Library Services)

Sheppard, F. H. W. (ed). *Survey of London (vol 28)*: *Brooke House* (published for the London County Council by the Athlone Press, University of London, 1960)

Star, 20 March 1954

Stephen and Lee, *Dictionary of National Biography*

The Times, 29 January 1954

Bure Cottage and Bure Homage

Davey, Simon, Curator, Red House Museum, Christchurch (Hampshire County Museum Service)

England, R. E. *The History of Mudeford* (unpublished). The late Mr England's collection of notes on the Mudeford area was deposited for student use at Christchurch Library in 1961. I am much obliged to the Dorset and Hampshire County Library Service for supplying the notes, and I am grateful to the Dorset Library Service for allowing me to quote the baron's verdict on Sophia

Hampshire County Council (Library Service)

Hare, Augustus J. C. *The Story of Two Noble Lives, Being Memorials of Charlotte, Countess Canning, and Louisa, Marchioness of Waterford* (George Allen, 1893)

Royal Commission on Historical Monuments (England), *Monuments Threatened or Destroyed—a Select List 1956-1962* (HMSO, 1963)

Stephen and Lee, *Dictionary of National Biography*

Strong. *Destruction*

The Times, 17 January, 1843

The Times, 8 July, 1843

Canons

The chief source here is the invaluable *Life and Circumstances of James Brydges, First Duke of Chandos* by C. H. Collins Baker and Muriel I. Baker (OUP, 1949). Other sources are:

Barnet, London Borough of (Educational Services/Libraries)

Defoe. *Tour Thro' the Whole Island*

Flower, Newman, *George Frideric Handel* (Cassell, new revised edition 1947)

Friedman, Terry and Linstrum, Derek. 'Country Houses through Georgian Eyes', *Country Life*, 1 February 1973

Harrow, London Borough of (Education Department/Library Service)

Hobhouse, Hermione. *Lost London* (Macmillan, 1971)

Pope, Alexander, *The Poems of Alexander Pope*, (Twickenham edition), ed John Butt (Methuen, 1963)

Stephen and Lee. *Dictionary of National Biography*

Thorne. *Environs*

Turner, E. S. *Amazing Grace* (Michael Joseph, 1975)

Walford, Edward. *Greater London* (Cassell, 1898)

Weaver, Lawrence. 'Canons Park', *Country Life*, 28 October 1916

Clarendon House

City of Westminster (Archives Department)

Clinch, George. *Mayfair and Belgravia* (Truslove & Shirley, 1892)

Colby, Reginald, *Mayfair—a Town within London* (Country Life, 1966)

Evelyn. *Diary*

Girouard. *Life*

Kenyon, J. P. *Stuart England.* (Penguin, 1978)

Knight, Charles (ed). *London* (Charles Knight, 1841)

Pepys, Samuel. *Memoirs of Samuel Pepys . . . comprising his diary,* edited by Richard, Lord Braybrooke (Henry Colburn, 1828)

Thornbury, G. W., and Walford, Edward. *Old and New London* (Cassell Petter & Galpin, undated)

Tipping, H. Avray. 'Coleshill House', *Country Life*, 26 July and 2 August 1919

Clumber House

Country Life, 12 September and 19 September 1908 ('Clumber' by 'T')

Jacks, Leonard. *The Great Houses of Nottinghamshire* (W. and A. S. Bradshaw, 1881)

Jewitt, Llewellynn, and Hall, S. C. *The Stately Homes of England* (J. S. Virtue, undated)

Nottingham Evening News, 16 October 1937

Nottingham Guardian, 23 October 1937

Nottingham Guardian, 25 May 1938

Nottingham Journal, 25 May 1938

Nottinghamshire County Council (Leisure Services Department/Libraries)

Redfern, Roger A. *The Dukeries of Nottinghamshire* (Dalesman Books, 1974)

Stephen and Lee. *Dictionary of National Biography*

Turner, E. S. *Amazing Grace* (Michael Joseph, 1975)

Deepdene

Cullen, Tom. *Maundy Gregory: Purveyor of Honours* (Bodley Head, 1974)

Dennis, John. *A Hand-book of Dorking* (1855, reprinted Kohler & Coombes, 1974)

Dorking Advertiser, 15 January 1965

Dorking Advertiser, 2 June 1972

Evelyn. *Diary*

Girouard. *Life*

Girouard. *Victorian Country House*

Lees-Milne, James. *William Beckford* (Compton Russell, 1976)

Mercer, Doris. 'The Deepdene, Dorking—Rise and Decline through Six Centuries', Surrey Archaeological Society *Collections*, vol 71, 1977

Nairn, Ian and Pevsner, Nikolaus. *Surrey*, revised by Bridget Cherry (Penguin, 1971)

Pike, W. T. (ed). *Surrey at the Opening of the Twentieth Century* (Pike, 1906)

Prosser, G. F. *Select Illustrations of the County of Surrey* (C. & J. Rivington, 1828)

Surrey County Council (Education Department/Libraries)

Thorne, *Environs*

Denbies

Builder, 14 April and 29 December 1855

Dennis, John. *A Hand-book of Dorking* (1855, reprinted Kohler & Coombes, 1974)

Dorking Advertiser, 17 April 1953

Evening News, 28 April 1953

Hobhouse, Hermione. *Thomas Cubitt, Master Builder* (Macmillan, 1971)

Malden, H. E. (ed). *Victoria History of the County of Surrey* (Constable, 1911)

Prosser, G. F. *Select Illustrations of the County of Surrey* (C. & J. Rivington, 1828)

Rose, Charles. *Recollections of Old Dorking* (1878, republished as part of *Memories of Old Dorking,* ed Margaret K. Kohler, Kohler & Coombes, 1977)

Stephen and Lee. *Dictionary of National Biography*

Surrey County Council (Education Department)

Surrey Magazine, November 1980

Derwentwater House and Panmure House

Angus District Council (Libraries and Museums Department) ('Panmure House—famous mansion which outlived its era', report of an account given by Mr Ferguson of Panmure's history)

Arbroath Guide, 8 February 1958

Arbroath Herald, 23 January 1890

Baker, W. King. *Acton, Middlesex (Acton & Chiswick Gazette/Acton & Chiswick Express,* 1912)

Ealing, London Borough of (Library Service)

Local sources (Angus)

Lysons, Daniel. *The Environs of London* (T. Cadell and W. Davies, 1795)

Murray's Handbook

Skeet, F. J. A. *The Life of the Right Honourable James Radcliffe, Third Earl of Derwentwater* (Hutchinson, 1929)

The Scotsman, 8 March 1955

Thomson, James. *Forfarshire Illustrated* (Cumming, 1848)

Walford, Edward. *Greater London* (Cassell, 1898)

Dr Dee's House

Anderson, J. *History of Mortlake* (Thomas Laurie, 1886)

Aubrey, John. *Aubrey's Brief Lives,* edited and introduced by Oliver Lawson Dick (Secker and Warburg, 1958)

Casaubon, Meric (ed). *A True and Faithful Relation of What Passed for Many Years between Dr John Dee and Some Spirits,* printed by D. Maxwell for T. Garthwait, 1659

Dee, John. *The Private Diary of Dr John Dee,* ed James Orchard Halliwell (Camden Society, 1842)

'Hippocrates Junior'. *The Predicted Plague; Value of the Prediction* (Simpkin, Marshall, Hamilton, Kent 1900)

Richmond upon Thames, London Borough of (Libraries Department)

Society for Psychical Research

Smith, Charlotte Fell. *John Dee (1527-1608)* (Constable, 1909)

Thorne, *Environs*

Walford, Edward. *Greater London* (Cassell, 1898)

Easton Lodge

Blunden, Margaret. *The Countess of Warwick* (Cassell, 1967)

Essex County Council (Record Office)

Glyn, Elinor. *Romantic Adventure* (Ivor Nicholson and Watson, 1936)

Mee, Arthur. *Essex,* revised and edited by E. T. Long (Hodder & Stoughton, 1966)

The Times, 27 July 1938

Tipping, H. Avray. 'Easton Lodge, Essex', *Country Life,* 23 November 1907

Warwick, Frances, Countess of. *Life's Ebb and Flow* (Hutchinson, 1929)

Webb, Beatrice. *Beatrice Webb's Diaries 1924-1932,* edited and with an introduction by Margaret Cole (Longmans, Green, 1956)

Elsyng Hall

I am greatly endebted to the London Borough of Enfield, who supplied a most comprehensive paper on Elsyng Hall prepared by the borough's local history and museums officer, David Pam. Other sources are:

Chamberlin, Frederick. *The Private Character of Queen Elizabeth* (John Lane, The Bodley Head, 1922)

Lysons, Daniel. *The Environs of London,* printed for T. Cadell and W. Davies, 1795

Pam, D. O. 'Elizabethan Enfield 1572', *Edmonton Hundred Historical Society, Occasional Paper New Series* No 30, 1975

Stephen and Lee. *Dictionary of National Biography*

Thorne. *Environs*

Emral Hall

Clwyd County Council (Library Service; County Planning Office; County Record Office)

Country Life, 4 December 1897 ('A State of Ruin')

Country Life, 19 February 1910 ('Emral Hall, Flintshire' by 'T')

Edwards, J. M. *Flintshire* (Cambridge University Press, 1914)

Fraser, Maxwell. *Wales* (Robert Hale, 1952)

Gwynedd County Council (Meirionnydd Area Library)

McDermot, Mrs Irene, Portmeirion.

Mitford, Nancy (ed) *Noblesse oblige* (Hamish Hamilton, 1956; Penguin, 1959)

Puleston, T. H. G. *The Story of a Quiet Country Parish* (Roxburghe Press, undated)

Royal Commission on the Ancient and Historical Monuments and Constructions in Wales and Monmouthshire, *An Inventory of the Ancient Monuments in Wales and Monmouthshire—County of Flint* (HMSO, 1912)

Gordon Castle

Burton, J. H. *The History of Scotland* (William Blackwood, undated)

Carruthers, R. *The Highland Note-book* (Adam & Charles Black, 1843)

Defoe. *Tour Thro' the Whole Island*

Graham, Cuthbert. *Grampian: the Castle Country* (Department of Leisure, Recreation and Tourism, Grampian Regional Council, 1977)

Mitchell, Joseph. *Recollections of my Life in the Highlands* (1883, reprinted David & Charles, 1971)

Moray District Council (Department of Libraries)

Murray's Handbook

North East of Scotland Library Service

Stephen and Lee. *Dictionary of National Biography*

Turner, E. S. *Amazing Grace* (Michael Joseph, 1975)

Gowrie House

Burton, J. H. *The History of Scotland* (William Blackwood, 1897)

Cromerty [Cromarty], George, Earl of. *An Historical Account of the Conspiracies by the Earls of Gowry* (James Watson, 1713)

Lang, Andrew. *James VI and the Gowrie Mystery* (Longmans, 1902)

Murray's Handbook

Perth & Kinross District Council (Library Service)

Roughead, William. *The Riddle of the Ruthvens* (W. Green, 1919)

Thomson, George Malcolm. *A Kind of Justice: Two Studies in Treason* (Hutchinson, 1970)

Willson, D. Harris. *King James VI and I* (Cape, 1956)

Gunnergate Hall and Marton Hall

There are two important debts to acknowledge. The first is to the Cleveland County Council library authorities, who not only sent me material on the two houses but also supplied an invaluable digest of key events at each. The second is to Ron Gott, whose *Henry Bolckow, Founder of Teesside* (published by Mr Gott, 1968) is essential reading on the careers of the two ironmasters. As far as this writer is aware, it is the only biography of Bolckow in existence. The account of the Bolckow-Thomas negotiations, in particular, is entirely derived from it. Other sources are:

Briggs, Asa. *Victorian Cities* (Odhams Press 1963; Penguin, 1968)

Evening Gazette, 30 August 1870

Gale, W. K. V. *Iron and Steel* (Longmans, 1969)

Girouard. *Victorian Country House*

Hill, C. P. *British Economic and Social History 1700-1964* (Edward Arnold, 1970)

Illustrated London News, 15 August 1868

Page, William (ed). *Victoria History of the Counties of England: Yorkshire North Riding* (St Catherine Press, 1923)

Stephen and Lee. *Dictionary of National Biography*

Hamilton Palace

Boswell, James. *The Journal of a Tour to the Hebrides with Samuel Johnson, LL. D.* (Charles Dilly, 1785)

Brown, John. *Brown's Directory and Hand-book of Hamilton (1859-60)* (Naismith, 1860)

Defoe. *Tour Thro' the Whole Island*

Guide to Hamilton Palace (R. W. Dick, undated, but between 1901 and 1910)

Hamilton District Council (Libraries and Museum Department)

Lees-Milne, James. *William Beckford* (Compton Russell, 1976)

Marshall, Rosalind K. *The Days of Duchess Anne* (Collins, 1973). Essential reading; also the perfect book about past life in a great house, whether lost or still existing

Naismith, William. *Hamilton Directory, 1878-79* (Naismith, 1879)

Strathclyde Regional Council (Leisure and Recreation Department; especially their booklet 'Strathclyde Park—Hamilton Mausoleum')

Tipping, H. Avray. 'Hamilton Palace', *Country Life*, 7, 14 and 21 June 1919

Walker, G. *Hamilton Palace, a Photographic Record*, ed C. Smith (Hamilton District Libraries and Museum Department)

Wordsworth, Dorothy. *Recollections of a Tour Made in Scotland A.D. 1803*, ed J. G. Shairp (Edmonston and Douglas, 1874)

Hope End

I have received invaluable help from Mr John Hegarty, owner of the Hope End Country House Hotel. Other sources are:

Browning, E. B. *The Poetical Works of Elizabeth Barrett Browning*, ed Frederic G. Kenyon (Smith, Elder & Co, 1897)

Browning, E. B. *The Barretts at Hope End: the Early Diary of Elizabeth Barrett Browning*, edited with an introduction by Elizabeth Berridge (John Murray, 1974). Both diary text and introduction are essential reading.

Hereford & Worcester County Council (Libraries Department)

Taplin, Gardner B. *The Life of Elizabeth Barrett Browning* (John Murray, 1957)

Transactions of the Woolhope Naturalists' Field Club, 1911 ('Fourth Field Meeting, August 29'), 1923

('Colwall and the Neighbourhood' by Allan Bright), and 1925 ('Elizabeth Barrett and Hope End' by Alfred Watkins), published by the Club; and the club secretary, F. M. Kendrick

Horton Hall and Horton Old Hall
Bradford Pictorial, August 1966
City of Bradford Metropolitan Council (Directorate of Educational Services/Libraries)
Cudworth, William. *Rambles Round Horton* (Thos Brear & Co, 1886)
Royal Commission on Historical Monuments (England), *Monuments Threatened or Destroyed; a Select List: 1956-1962* (HMSO, 1963)
Yorkshire Post, 13 August 1963

Jordans
I am most grateful to Mrs Joan Speke of Jordans for her very kind help in connection with the last stage of the house's existence. Other sources are:
Burke's Landed Gentry (Burke's Peerage, 1972)
Maitland, Alexander. *Speke and the Discovery of the Source of the Nile* (Constable, 1971)
Pevsner, Nikolaus. *South and West Somerset* (Penguin, 1958)
Royal Commission on Historical Monuments (England), *Monuments Threatened or Destroyed—a Select List: 1956-1962* (HMSO, 1963)
Somerset County Council (Library Service)
Stephen and Lee. *Dictionary of National Biography*
Toulson, Shirley, of Wells (to whom I am most indebted for her patient search for references to Jordans in Somerset guidebooks)

Kendal House
Bate, G. E. *And So Make a City Here* (Thomasons, 1948)
Coxe, William. *Memoirs of the Life and Administration of Sir Robert Walpole, Earl of Orford* (Longman, 1816)
Hounslow, London Borough of (Department of Arts and Recreation/Library Services)
Newall, Venetia. *Discovering the Folklore of Birds and Beasts* (Shire Publications, 1971)
Stephen and Lee. *Dictionary of National Biography*
Thorne, *Environs*
Walford, Edward. *Greater London* (Cassell, 1898)
Walpole, Horace. *Letters,* ed Peter Cunningham (Richard Bentley, 1891)

Kenyon Peel Hall
I owe great thanks to local historian Frank Mullineux of Worsley for his help with this section. Other sources are:
City of Salford (Cultural Services Department/ Libraries; Technical Services Department)
Manchester Evening News (16 January 1930-9; exact date unknown)

Manchester Faces and Places, vol 3, 1892
Royal Commission on Historical Monuments (England), *Monuments Threatened or Destroyed—a Select List: 1956-1962* (HMSO, 1963)
Strong. *Destruction*
Taylor, Henry. *Old Halls in Lancashire & Cheshire* (J. E. Cornish, 1884)
Victoria County History of Lancashire, edited by William Farrer and J. Brownbill; University of London Institute of Historical Research, 1911; reprinted Dawsons, 1966)

Llanthomas
I owe a deep debt of gratitude to the Honorary Secretary of the Kilvert Society, Mr E. J. C. West of Ross-on-Wye, for his unstinting help with this section. Other sources are:
Jones, S. R. *The Houses of Breconshire, Brycheiniog,* vol 10, 1964 (Brecknock Society)
Kilvert, Francis. *Kilvert's Diary: selections from the diary of the Rev Francis Kilvert,* chosen, edited and introduced by William Plomer (Jonathan Cape, 1938-40; one-volume selection, 1944; Penguin Books, 1977)
Le Quesne, A. L. *After Kilvert* (Oxford University Press, 1978)
Local sources
Powys County Council (Library Service)

Merton Place
Merton, London Borough of (Library Service, to whose 'Notes on Local History (9)—Nelson and Merton' I am much indebted)
Nelson, Horatio. *The Dispatches and Letters of Vice Admiral Lord Viscount Nelson,* with notes by Sir Nicholas Harris Nicolas (Henry Colburn, 1845)
Oman, Carola. *Nelson* (Hodder & Stoughton, 1947)
Pettigrew, T. J. *Memoirs of the Life of Vice-Admiral Lord Viscount Nelson* (T. and W. Boone, 1849)
Rathbone, Philip. *Paradise Merton: the Story of Nelson and the Hamiltons at Merton Place* (Philip Rathbone, 1973)
Russell, Jack. *Nelson and the Hamiltons* (Anthony Blond, 1969)
Warner, Oliver. *Nelson* (Weidenfeld & Nicolson, 1975)

Mirefleur
National Maritime Museum
Richardson, H. S. *Greenwich* (Simpkin & Marshall and H. Richardson, 1834)
Thorne. *Environs*
Webster, A. D. *Greenwich Park* (Henry Richardson and Simpkin, Marshall, Hamilton, Kent, 1902)
Williams, Neville. *Elizabeth: Queen of England* (Weidenfeld & Nicolson, 1967)
Williams, Neville. *The Royal Residences of Great Britain* (Barrie & Rockliff, 1960)

Montagu House

British Museum

Dunlop, Ian. 'First Home of the British Museum', *Country Life*, 14 September 1951

Evelyn. *Diary*

Stephen and Lee. *Dictionary of National Biography*

Thornbury, G. W., and Walford, Edward. *Old and New London* (Cassell Petter & Galpin, undated)

Turner, E. S. *Amazing Grace* (Michael Joseph, 1975)

Walpole, Horace. *Letters*, edited by Peter Cunningham (Richard Bentley, 1891)

Nonsuch Palace

For this chapter, I owe a very great debt of gratitude to John Dent's *The Quest for Nonsuch* (Hutchinson, 1962), which deals with the palace's history and reappearance in the most comprehensive detail. (*Quest* was published in paperback in 1981 by the London Borough of Sutton Libraries and Arts Services.) Other sources are:

Devereux, Walter Bourchier. *Lives and Letters of the Devereux, Earls of Essex* (John Murray, 1853)

Evelyn. *Diary*

Pepys, Samuel. *Memoirs of Samuel Pepys . . . comprising his diary*, edited by Richard, Lord Braybrooke (Henry Colburn, 1828)

Stephen and Lee. *Dictionary of National Biography*

Surrey County Council (Education Department Libraries/Parks Department)

Thorne. *Environs*

Williams, Neville. *Elizabeth: Queen of England* (Weidenfeld & Nicolson, 1967)

Williams, Neville. *The Royal Residences of Great Britain* (Barrie & Rockliff, 1960)

Northumberland House

City of Westminster (Archives Department)

Evelyn. *Diary*

Hobhouse, Hermione. *Lost London* (Macmillan, 1971)

Hunt, Leigh. *The Town* (1848, republished Oxford University Press, 1907)

Knight, Charles (ed). *London* (Charles Knight, 1842)

Pollard, Michael. *Discovering English Folksong* (Shire Publications, 1982)

Turner, E. S. *Amazing Grace* (Michael Joseph, 1975)

Thornbury, G. W., and Walford, Edward. *Old and New London* (Cassell, 1890)

Old Somerset House

City of Westminster (Archives Department)

Colvin, H. M. (ed). *The History of the King's Works* (HMSO, 1976)

Hunt, Leigh. *The Town* (1848, republished Oxford University Press, 1907)

Kenyon, J. P. *Stuart England* (Penguin, 1978)

Knight, Charles (ed). *London* (Charles Knight, 1842)

Needham, Raymond, and Webster, Alexander. *Somerset House Past and Present* (T. Fisher Unwin, 1905)

Thornbury, G. W., and Walford, Edward. *Old and New London* (Cassell, 1890)

Williams, Neville. *The Royal Residences of Great Britain* (Barrie & Rockliff, 1960)

Osborne House

Girouard. *Victorian Country House*

Groves, Dr. 'Osborne, Isle of Wight, and the families who have held it', *Hampshire Field Club Proceedings* (1893)

Hobhouse, Hermione. *Thomas Cubitt, Master Builder* (Macmillan, 1971)

Illustrated London News, 16 March 1844

Isle of Wight County Council (Cultural Services)

Longford, Elizabeth. *Victoria R. I.* (Weidenfeld & Nicolson, 1964)

Matson, John. *Dear Osborne* (Hamish Hamilton, 1978)

Peterborough House

Faulkner, T. *An Historical and Topographical Account of Fulham* (T. Egerton and others, 1813)

Flower, Newman. *George Frideric Handel* (Cassell, revised edition, 1947)

Hammersmith and Fulham, London Borough of (Leisure and Recreation/Library Service)

Lysons, Daniel. *The Environs of London* (T. Cadell and W. Davies, 1795)

Stephen and Lee. *Dictionary of National Biography*

Swift, Jonathan. *Works*, arranged by Thomas Sheridan; new edition, corrected and revised by John Nichols (J. Johnson and others, 1803)

Swift, Jonathan. *Works*, with notes by Sir Walter Scott (Archibald Constable and Hurst, Robinson & Co, 1824)

Thorne. *Environs*

Sayes Court

I am extremely grateful to the library staff of the London Borough of Lewisham for the very full account they have given me of the various stages in Sayes Court's career. Other sources are:

Evelyn. *Diary*

Evelyn, John. *Memoirs*, Bray Edition (Henry Colburn, 1827)

Pepys, Samuel. *Memoirs of Samuel Pepys . . . comprising his diary*, edited by Richard, Lord Braybrooke (Henry Colburn, 1828)

Ponsonby, Arthur. *John Evelyn* (Heinemann, 1933)

Thorne. *Environs*

Wheatley, H. B. *Life of John Evelyn* (Bickers, 1906)

Scrivelsby Court
I am greatly indebted to Lt Col John Dymoke M.B.E., of Scrivelsby Court, for his most generous help and advice with this section. Other sources are:
Burke's Landed Gentry, edited by Peter Townend (Burke's Peerage, 1965)
Lincolnshire County Council (Library Service)
Lodge, Samuel. *Scrivelsby, the Home of the Champions* (Elliot Stock, 1893)
Martineau, H. D. 'The Champion of England', *Lincolnshire Life Magazine*, vol 10, December 1970
Pepys, Samuel. *Memoirs of Samuel Pepys . . . comprising his diary*, edited by Richard, Lord Braybrooke (Henry Colburn, 1828)
Royal Commission on Historical Monuments (England), *Monuments Threatened or Destroyed—a Select List: 1956-1962* (HMSO, 1963)
Stephen and Lee. *Dictionary of National Biography*

Stand Old Hall
This section would not have been written without the very generous help of Derek Pilkington, of Helmshore, Lancashire, who guided me through the Stand maze and provided the numbering system used here. Other sources are:
Bury, Metropolitan Borough of (Library Service)
Bury Times, 7 September 1973
Pilkington, Lt Col John. *History of the Pilkington Family of Lancashire*, (privately printed for the author, Liverpool, 1912)
Prestwich and Whitefield Guide, 7 September 1956
Prestwich and Whitefield Guide, 11 January 1974
Royal Commission on Historical Monuments (England), *Monuments Threatened or Destroyed—a Select List: 1956-1962* (HMSO, 1963)
Victoria History of the Counties of England—Lancashire edited by William Farrer and John Brownbill (Constable, for the University of London, 1911)

Trentham Hall
Cornforth, John. 'Trentham, Staffordshire', *Country Life*, 25 January, 1 and 8 February 1968
Girouard. *Victorian Country House* (especially in connection with Deepdene-Trentham-Osborne links)
Historic Houses of the United Kingdom, 'Trentham Hall' by the Reverend Professor Bonney, (Cassell, 1892)
Illustrated London News, 9 January 1897
Jewitt, Llewellynn, and Hall, S. C. *The Stately Homes of England* (J. S. Virtue, undated)
Leyland, John. 'Trentham, Staffordshire', *Country Life*, 5 and 12 March 1898

Prebble, John. *The Highland Clearances* (Secker & Warburg, 1963; Penguin, 1969)
Staffordshire County Council (Library Service)
Stephen and Lee. *Dictionary of National Biography*
Turner, E. S. *Amazing Grace* (Michael Joseph, 1975)
Youngson, A. J. *After the Forty-five* (Edinburgh University Press, 1973)

Wanstead House
Andrews, William (ed). *Bygone Essex* (1892, republished S. R. Publishers, 1969)
Cornish, C. J. 'The Lake Sanctuary at Wanstead Park', *Country Life*, 26 May 1900
Defoe. *Tour Thro' the Whole Island*
Evelyn. *Diary*
Girouard. *Life*
Kimball, Fiske. 'Wanstead House, Essex', *Country Life*, 2 December 1933
Lloyd. *English House*
Redbridge, London Borough of (Libraries Department)
Stephen and Lee. *Dictionary of National Biography*
Stutchbury, Howard E. *The Architecture of Colen Campbell* (Manchester University Press, 1967) (especially with reference to Wanstead's architectural influence)
Thorne, *Environs*
Walford, Edward. *Greater London* (Cassell, 1898)
Walpole, Horace. *Letters*, edited by Peter Cunningham (John Grant, 1906)

CONCLUSION

Ancient Monuments Society
Binney, Marcus. 'How Many Country Houses Have Gone?' *Country Life*, 21 November 1974
Daily Telegraph, 13 January 1982
Department of the Environment
National Monuments Record (England)
Royal Commission on the Ancient and Historical Monuments and Constructions of England, *Monuments Threatened or Destroyed (1963-74): Interim Report* (HMSO, 1976)
Royal Commission on Historical Monuments (England)
SAVE Britain's Heritage (and, in particular, their publications *Tomorrow's Ruins?* by Sophie Andreae and Marcus Binney, and *Silent Mansions*, by Sophie Andreae, Marcus Binney and Catherine Griffiths)
Strong. *Destruction*
The Times, 13 August 1868

✤ Acknowledgements

A great many people and organisations have helped me to write this book, and I am deeply grateful to all of them for their assistance. The majority of sources that have most kindly given me advice, information and references are listed in the acknowledgements and bibliographical notes on each chapter. However, I also owe a debt of gratitude to the library services of the following areas for their help in the initial research stages: Argyll and Bute, Avon, Bedfordshire, Borders, Clydesdale, Cumbria, Dorset, Dumfries and Galloway, Dunfermline, Gwynedd, Havering, Kent, Kilmarnock and Loudoun, Lambeth, Lancashire, Leicestershire, Northamptonshire, Shropshire, Suffolk and Wigan.

In addition, I have received invaluable help at different stages of writing from the Ancient Monuments Society, the Georgian Group, SAVE Britain's Heritage and the Society for the Protection of Ancient Buildings; my warmest thanks to them, to the Caithness Field Club and the National Trust (East Anglia) and to the staff of the National Monuments Record.

I am most grateful to the Society for the Protection of Ancient Buildings for their kind permission to use and quote from information in their files on Boleyn Castle and Brooke House. My thanks are also due to the following for their kind permission to reproduce extracts:

Mrs J. Dent: *The Quest for Nonsuch* by John Dent, Hutchinson, 1962; courtesy of the *Dorking Advertiser*: *Dorking Advertiser*, 15 January 1965; the Evening Standard Co Ltd: *Evening Standard*, 25 March 1954; William Heinemann Ltd: *A Tour Thro' the Whole Island of Great Britain* by Daniel Defoe, introduced by G. D. H. Cole, Peter Davies, 1927; Mrs. Sheila Hooper and Jonathan Cape Ltd: *Kilvert's Diary: Selections from the Diary of the Rev. Francis Kilvert* by Francis Kilvert, edited by William Plomer, 1938-40; IPC Magazines Ltd/*Country Life*: *Country Life*, 4 December 1897, 12 September 1908, 7 June 1919; the London School of Economics and Political Science (University of London): *Beatrice Webb's Diaries* 1924-32 by Beatrice Webb, edited by Margaret Cole, Longmans, Green, 1956 (© the London School of Economics and Political Science); Macmillan, London and Basingstoke: *Reminiscences* by Baroness Battersea, 1922, and *Thomas Cubitt, Master Builder* by Hermione Hobhouse, 1971; Methuen & Co Ltd: *The Duke of Devonshire* by Henry Leach, 1904, and *The Poems of Alexander Pope* (Twickenham edition) by Alexander Pope, edited by John Butt, 1963; John Murray (Publishers) Ltd: *The Barretts at Hope End: the*

Early Diary of Elizabeth Barrett Browning edited with an introduction by Elizabeth Berridge, 1974; Oxford University Press: *The Life and Circumstances of James Brydges, First Duke of Chados* by C. H. Collins Baker and Muriel I. Baker, Oxford at the Clarendon Press (in co-operation with the Huntington Library), 1949, and *Boswell's Life of Johnson* by James Boswell, edited by George Birkbeck Hill, revised and enlarged edition by L. F. Powell, Oxford at the Clarendon Press, 1950; *The Prestwich and Whitefield Guide: Prestwich and Whitefield Guide,* 7 September 1956; and Martin Secker & Warburg Ltd: *Aubrey's Brief Lives* by John Aubrey, edited and introduced by Oliver Lawson Dick, 1958.

I owe a further debt to the authors of a group of books and other publications which have, overall, played key roles in the writing of this one. Of these, the most important is the collection of essays by Roy Strong, Marcus Binney, John Harris and others titled *The Destruction of the Country House* 1875-1975 (Thames and Hudson, 1974); this is essential reading for any student of houses lost within comparatively recent years. Two others—particularly important on the relationship between architecture and social history—are Mark Girouard's *Life in the English Country House* and *The Victorian Country House,* revised and enlarged edition (both Yale University Press, 1978 and 1979). Much help has also been given by the reports and other publications of the Royal Commission on the Ancient and Historical Monuments and Constructions of England. Going back to the nineteenth century, there is James Thorne's *Handbook to the Environs of London* (1876, republished by Adams & Dart, 1970) and *Murray's Handbook for Scotland (1894)* (republished by David & Charles, 1971); *Environs* is especially helpful in that it contains much material from Daniel Lysons' *Environs of London* of the 1790s, which is now very hard to obtain. And further back still there are Daniel Defoe's *Tour Thro' the Whole Island of Great Britain* and John Evelyn's matchless *Diary.* The *Dictionary of National Biography* and (for checking names, dates and relationships) the *Encyclopaedia Britannica* have provided their usual invaluable assistance, while the country house 'profiles' of *Country Life* are in a class of their own.

Finally, some deeply felt thanks to two more libraries and to two individuals: to the London Library, for the richness stored on its shelves; to Swaffham Branch Library, for the unfailing help given by its staff; to my mother, who provided material on Bathford and Foots Cray and pointed me in the direction of Hope End; and to my husband, whose encouragement and map-reading skills have been outstanding.

ACKNOWLEDGEMENTS

Photographs are reproduced by kind permission of the following: Berkshire County Library 7; Metropolitan Bradford Library 88, 89; the British Library 45, 127; courtesy of the Trustees of the British Museum 16, 23, 104, 107; Arthur Cannings and the Bathford Local History Society 8; Clackmannan District Libraries 13; Cleveland County Council 77, 78, 79; Clwyd Library Service 68; Clwyd Record Office 21; Country Life 3, 4, 12, 69, 82, 83, 136, 137; *The Courier & Advertiser*, Dundee 62; Lt Col John Dymoke MBE 130, 131, 132; Essex Record Office 65, 66; the Francis Frith Collection 18; the London Borough of Hackney Library Services 40, 41, 42; Hamilton District Libraries and Museum 81; Hammersmith and Fulham Public Libraries 37, 38, 123; the Hampshire County Museum Service 43; John Hegarty 85; Hounslow Library Services 93; Isle of Wight County Library 120, 122; the Kilvert Society 95, 96, 97, 98; Anthony J. Lambert 5, 51, 141; City of Manchester Cultural Services: Local History Library 133, 134; Mansell Collection 20, 64; the National Maritime Museum, London 100, 101, 103; National Monuments Record 55, 58, 94; National Portrait Gallery, London 14, 17, 19, 22, 26, 27, 32, 33, 34, 35, 36, 39, 44, 46, 47, 48, 50, 56, 59, 60, 63, 67, 73, 86, 91, 92, 99, 102, 105, 106, 109, 110, 111, 113, 118, 119, 121, 124, 125, 126, 128, 129, 138; London Borough of Newham Library Service—Local Studies Collection 29, 30, 31; Norfolk County Library 1, 2; Local Studies Library, Nottinghamshire County Library 28, 52, 53; Perth Museum & Art Gallery 75, 76; Derek Pilkington 135; Redbridge Public Libraries 139, 140; Royal Commission on Ancient Monuments, Scotland 61, 80; SAVE Britain's Heritage 142; copyright, Walter Scott Bradford 87; Scottish National Portrait Gallery 15, 71, 72, 74, 84; Scottish Record Office 70; Somerset Archaeological and Natural History Society 90; Anna Sproule 143; Sara Sproule 6, 9, 10, 11; Surrey County Library 54, 57; Crown copright, Victoria & Albert Museum 108; Westminster City Libraries Archives Department 24, 25, 49, 112, 114, 115, 116, 117, 144. Two photographs, 143, were taken specially for the author by Nigel Hughes of Porthmadog and are reproduced by courtesy of Lady Annabel Williams-Ellis.

Every effort has been made to trace the owners of copyright in both text and pictures; if any have been overlooked, it is by accident, and they should contact the publishers.

Index

Page numbers in *italics* indicate illustrations